TO MAKE A VILLAGE SOVIET

MCGILL-QUEEN'S STUDIES IN THE HISTORY OF RELIGION

Volumes in this series have been supported by the Jackman Foundation of Toronto.

SERIES ONE: G.A. RAWLYK, EDITOR

1 Small Differences
Irish Catholics and Irish Protestants, 1815–1922
An International Perspective
Donald Harman Akenson

2 Two Worlds
The Protestant Culture of Nineteenth-Century Ontario
William Westfall

3 An Evangelical Mind
Nathaneal Burwash and the Methodist Tradition in Canada, 1839–1918
Marguerite Van Die

4 The Dévotes
Women and Church in Seventeenth-Century France
Elizabeth Rapley

5 The Evangelical Century
College and Creed in English Canada from the Great Revival to the Great Depression
Michael Gauvreau

6 The German Peasants' War and Anabaptist Community of Goods
James M. Stayer

7 A World Mission
Canadian Protestantism and the Quest for a New International Order, 1918–1939
Robert Wright

8 Serving the Present Age
Revivalism, Progressivism, and the Methodist Tradition in Canada
Phyllis D. Airhart

9 A Sensitive Independence
Canadian Methodist Women Missionaries in Canada and the Orient, 1881–1925
Rosemary R. Gagan

10 God's Peoples
Covenant and Land in South Africa, Israel, and Ulster
Donald Harman Akenson

11 Creed and Culture
The Place of English-Speaking Catholics in Canadian Society, 1750–1930
Edited by Terrence Murphy and Gerald Stortz

12 Piety and Nationalism
Lay Voluntary Associations and the Creation of an Irish-Catholic Com-munity in Toronto, 1850–1895
Brian P. Clarke

13 Amazing Grace
Studies in Evangelicalism in Australia, Britain, Canada, and the United States
Edited by George Rawlyk and Mark A. Noll

14 Children of Peace
W. John McIntyre

15 A Solitary Pillar
Montreal's Anglican Church and the Quiet Revolution
Joan Marshall

16 Padres in No Man's Land
Canadian Chaplains and the Great War
Duff Crerar

17 Christian Ethics and Political Economy in North America
A Critical Analysis
P. Travis Kroeker

18 Pilgrims in Lotus Land
Conservative Protestantism in British Columbia, 1917–1981
Robert K. Burkinshaw

19 Through Sunshine and Shadow
The Woman's Christian Temperance Union, Evangelicalism, and Reform in Ontario, 1874–1930
Sharon Cook

20 Church, College, and Clergy
A History of Theological Education at Knox College, Toronto, 1844–1994
Brian J. Fraser

21 The Lord's Dominion
The History of Canadian Methodism
Neil Semple

22 A Full-Orbed Christianity
The Protestant Churches and Social Welfare in Canada, 1900–1940
Nancy Christie and Michael Gauvreau

23 Evangelism and Apostasy
The Evolution and Impact of Evangelicals in Modern Mexico
Kurt Bowen

24 The Chignecto Covenanters
A Regional History of Reformed Presbyterianism in New Brunswick and Nova Scotia, 1827– 1905
Eldon Hay

25 Methodists and Women's Education in Ontario, 1836–1925
Johanne Selles

26 Puritanism and Historical Controversy
William Lamont

SERIES TWO IN MEMORY OF GEORGE RAWLYK
DONALD HARMAN AKENSON, EDITOR

1 Marguerite Bourgeoys and Montreal, 1640–1665
Patricia Simpson

2 Aspects of the Canadian E vangelical Experience
Edited by G.A. Rawlyk

3 Infinity, Faith, and Time
Christian Humanism and Renaissance Literature
John Spencer Hill

4 The Contribution of Presbyterianism to the Maritime Provinces of Canada
Edited by Charles H.H. Scobie and G.A. Rawlyk

5 Labour, Love, and Prayer
Female Piety in Ulster Religious Literature, 1850–1914
Andrea Ebel Brozyna

6 The Waning of the Green
Catholics, the Irish, and Identity in Toronto, 1887–1922
Mark G. McGowan

7 Religion and Nationality in Western Ukraine
The Greek Catholic Church and the Ruthenian National Movement in Galicia, 1867–1900
John-Paul Himka

8 Good Citizens
British Missionaries and Imperial States, 1870–1918
James G. Greenlee and Charles M. Johnston

9 The Theology of the Oral Torah
Revealing the Justice of God
Jacob Neusner

10 Gentle Eminence
A Life of Cardinal Flahiff
P. Wallace Platt

11 Culture, Religion, and Demographic Behaviour
Catholics and Lutherans in Alsace, 1750–1870
Kevin McQuillan

12 Between Damnation and Starvation
Priests and Merchants in Newfoundland Politics, 1745–1855
John P. Greene

13 Martin Luther, German Saviour
German Evangelical Theological Factions and the Interpretation of Luther, 1917–1933
James M. Stayer

14 Modernity and the Dilemma of North American Anglican Identities, 1880–1950
William H. Katerberg

15 The Methodist Church on the Prairies, 1896–1914
George Emery

16 Christian Attitudes towards the State of Israel
Paul Charles Merkley

17 A Social History of the Cloister
Daily Life in the Teaching Monasteries of the Old Regime
Elizabeth Rapley

18 Households of Faith
Family, Gender, and Community in Canada, 1760–1969
Edited by Nancy Christie

19 Blood Ground
Colonialism, Missions, and the Contest for Christianity in the Cape Colony and Britain, 1799–1853
Elizabeth Elbourne

20 A History of Canadian Catholics
Gallicanism, Romanism, and Canadianism
Terence J. Fay

21 The View from Rome
Archbishop Stagni's 1915 Reports on the Ontario Bilingual Schools Question
Edited and translated by John Zucchi

22 The Founding Moment
Church, Society, and the Construction of Trinity College
William Westfall

23 The Holocaust, Israel, and Canadian Protestant Churches
Haim Genizi

24 Governing Charities
Church and State in Toronto's Catholic Archdiocese, 1850–1950
Paula Maurutto

25 Anglicans and the Atlantic World
High Churchmen, Evangelicals, and the Quebec Connection
Richard W. Vaudry

26 Evangelicals and the Continental Divide
The Conservative Protestant Subculture in Canada and the United States
Sam Reimer

27 Christians in a Secular World
The Canadian Experience
Kurt Bowen

28 Anatomy of a Seance
A History of Spirit Communication in Central Canada
Stan McMullin

29 With Skilful Hand
The Story of King David
David T. Barnard

30 Faithful Intellect
Samuel S. Nelles and Victoria University
Neil Semple

31 W. Stanford Reid
An Evangelical Calvinist in the Academy
Donald MacLeod

32 A Long Eclipse
The Liberal Protestant Establishment and the Canadian University, 1920–1970
Catherine Gidney

33 Forkhill Protestants and Forkhill Catholics, 1787–1858
Kyla Madden

34 For Canada's Sake
Public Religion, Centennial Celebrations, and the Re-making of Canada in the 1960s
Gary R. Miedema

35 Revival in the City
The Impact of American Evangelists in Canada, 1884–1914
Eric R. Crouse

36 The Lord for the Body
Religion, Medicine, and Protestant Faith Healing in Canada, 1880–1930
James Opp

37 Six Hundred Years of Reform
Bishops and the French Church, 1190–1789
J. Michael Hayden and Malcolm *R. Greenshields*

38 The Missionary Oblate Sisters
Vision and Mission
Rosa Bruno-Jofré

39 Religion, Family, and Community in Victorian Canada
The Colbys of Carrollcroft
Marguerite Van Die

40 Michael Power
The Struggle to Build the Catholic Church on the Canadian Frontier
Mark G. McGowan

41 The Catholic Origins of Quebec's Quiet Revolution, 1931–1970
Michael Gauvreau

42 Marguerite Bourgeoys and the Congregation of Notre Dame, 1665–1700
Patricia Simpson

43 To Heal a Fractured World
The Ethics of Responsibility
Jonathan Sacks

44 Revivalists
Marketing the Gospel in English Canada, 1884–1957
Kevin Kee

45 The Churches and Social Order in Nineteenth- and Twentieth-Century Canada
Edited by Michael Gauvreau and Ollivier Hubert

46 Political Ecumenism
Catholics, Jews, and Protestants in De Gaulle's Free France, 1940–1945
Geoffrey Adams

47 From Quaker to Upper Canadian
Faith and Community among Yonge Street Friends, 1801–1850
Robynne Rogers Healey

48 The Congrégation de Notre-Dame, Superiors, and the Paradox of Power, 1693–1796
Colleen Gray

49 Canadian Pentecostalism
Transition and Transformation
Edited by Michael Wilkinson

50 A War with a Silver Lining
Canadian Protestant Churches and the South African War, 1899–1902
Gordon L. Heath

51 In the Aftermath of Catastrophe
Founding Judaism, 70 to 640
Jacob Neusner

52 Imagining Holiness
Classic Hasidic Tales in Modern Times
Justin Jaron Lewis

53 Shouting, Embracing, and Dancing with Ecstasy
The Growth of Methodism in Newfoundland, 1774–1874
Calvin Hollett

54 Into Deep Waters
Evangelical Spirituality and Maritime Calvinist Baptist Ministers, 1790–1855
Daniel C. Goodwin

55 Vanguard of the New Age
The Toronto Theosophical Society, 1891–1945
Gillian McCann

56 A Commerce of Taste
Church Architecture in Canada, 1867–1914
Barry Magrill

57 The Big Picture
The Antigonish Movement of Eastern Nova Scotia
Santo Dodaro and Leonard Pluta

58 My Heart's Best Wishes for You
A Biography of Archbishop John Walsh
John P. Comiskey

59 The Covenanters in Canada
Reformed Presbyterianism from 1820 to 2012
Eldon Hay

60 The Guardianship of Best Interests
Institutional Care for the Children of the Poor in Halifax, 1850–1960
Renée N. Lafferty

61 In Defence of the Faith
Joaquim Marques de Araújo, a Comissário in the Age of Inquisitional Decline
James E. Wadsworth

62 Contesting the Moral High Ground
Popular Moralists in Mid-Twentieth-Century Britain
Paul T. Phillips

63 The Catholicisms of Coutances
Varieties of Religion in Early Modern France, 1350–1789
J. Michael Hayden

64 After Evangelicalism
The Sixties and the United Church of Canada
Kevin N. Flatt

65 The Return of Ancestral Gods
Modern Ukrainian Paganism as an Alternative Vision for a Nation
Mariya Lesiv

66 Transatlantic Methodists
British Wesleyanism and the Formation of an Evangelical Culture in Nineteenth-Century Ontario and Quebec
Todd Webb

67 A Church with the Soul of a Nation
Making and Remaking the United Church of Canada
Phyllis D. Airhart

68 Fighting over God
A Legal and Political History of Religious Freedom in Canada
Janet Epp Buckingham

69 From India to Israel
Identity, Immigration, and the Struggle for Religious Equality
Joseph Hodes

70 Becoming Holy in Early Canada
Timothy Pearson

71 The Cistercian Arts
From the 12th to the 21st Century
Edited by Terryl N. Kinder and Roberto Cassanelli

72 The Canny Scot
Archbishop James Morrison of Antigonish
Peter Ludlow

73 Religion and Greater Ireland
Christianity and Irish Global Networks, 1750–1950
Edited by Colin Barr and Hilary M. Carey

74 The Invisible Irish
Finding Protestants in the Nineteenth-Century Migrations to America
Rankin Sherling

75 Beating against the Wind
Popular Opposition to Bishop Feild and Tractarianism in Newfoundland and Labrador, 1844–1876
Calvin Hollett

76 The Body or the Soul?
Religion and Culture in a Quebec Parish, 1736–1901
Frank A. Abbott

77 Saving Germany
North American Protestants and Christian Mission to West Germany, 1945–1974
James C. Enns

78 The Imperial Irish
Canada's Irish Catholics Fight the Great War, 1914–1918
Mark G. McGowan

79 Into Silence and Servitude
How American Girls Became Nuns, 1945–1965
Brian Titley

80 Boundless Dominion
Providence, Politics, and the Early Canadian Presbyterian Worldview
Denis McKim

81 Faithful Encounters
Authorities and American Missionaries in the Ottoman Empire
Emrah Şahin

82 Beyond the Noise of Solemn Assemblies
The Protestant Ethic and the Quest for Social Justice in Canada
Richard Allen

83 Not Quite Us
Anti-Catholic Thought in English Canada since 1900
Kevin P. Anderson

84 Scandal in the Parish
Priests and Parishioners Behaving Badly in Eighteenth-Century France
Karen E. Carter

85 Ordinary Saints
Women, Work, and Faith in Newfoundland
Bonnie Morgan

86 Patriot and Priest
Jean-Baptiste Volfius and the Constitutional Church in the Côte-d'Or
Annette Chapman-Adisho

87 A.B. Simpson and the Making of Modern Evangelicalism
Daryn Henry

88 The Uncomfortable Pew
Christianity and the New Left in Toronto
Bruce Douville

89 Berruyer's Bible
Public Opinion and the Politics of Enlightenment Catholicism in France
Daniel J. Watkins

90 Communities of the Soul
A Short History of Religion in Puerto Rico
José E. Igartua

91 Callings and Consequences
The Making of Catholic Vocational Culture in Early Modern France
Christopher J. Lane

92 Religion, Ethnonationalism, and Antisemitism in the Era of the Two World Wars
Edited by Kevin P. Spicer and Rebecca Carter-Chand

93 Water from Dragon's Well
The History of a Korean-Canadian Church Relationship
David Kim-Cragg

94 Protestant Liberty
Religion and the Making of Canadian Liberalism, 1828–78
James M. Forbes

95 To Make a Village Soviet
Jehovah's Witnesses and the Transformation of a Postwar Ukrainian Borderland
Emily B. Baran

TO MAKE A VILLAGE SOVIET

Jehovah's Witnesses and the Transformation of a Postwar Ukrainian Borderland

EMILY B. BARAN

McGill-Queen's University Press
Montreal & Kingston · London · Chicago

ISBN 978-0-2280-1054-8 (cloth)
ISBN 978-0-2280-1055-5 (paper)
ISBN 978-0-2280-1246-7 (ePDF)
ISBN 978-0-2280-1247-4 (ePUB)

Legal deposit third quarter 2022
Bibliothèque nationale du Québec

Library and Archives Canada Cataloguing in Publication

Title: To make a village Soviet : Jehovah's Witnesses and the transformation of a postwar Ukrainian borderland / Emily B. Baran.
Names: Baran, Emily B., author.
Series: McGill-Queen's studies in the history of religion. Series two ; 95.
Description: Series statement: McGill-Queen's studies in the history of religion. Series two ; 95 | Includes bibliographical references and index.
Identifiers: Canadiana (print) 20220180555 | Canadiana (ebook) 20220180636 | ISBN 9780228010548 (cloth) | ISBN 9780228010555 (paper) | ISBN 9780228012467 (ePDF) | ISBN 9780228012474 (ePUB)
Subjects: LCSH: Jehovah's Witnesses—Persecutions—Ukraine—Bila TSerkva—History—20th century. | LCSH: Jehovah's Witnesses—Ukraine—Bila TSerkva—History—20th century. | LCSH: Jehovah's Witnesses—Soviet Union—History—20th century. | LCSH: Government, Resistance to—Ukraine—Bila TSerkva—History—20th century. | LCSH: Bila TSerkva (Ukraine)—Church history—20th century.
Classification: LCC BX8525.8.R9 B37 2022 | DDC 289.9/2094779—dc23

This book was typeset by True to Type in 10.5/13 Sabon

For Mike

Contents

Acknowledgments

This book began as an offshoot of my first monograph on Soviet Jehovah's Witnesses, and it has benefited enormously from all the scholars and archivists who assisted me in that earlier endeavour. Donald Raleigh has been a source of support and feedback since that time. Mayhill Fowler was an invaluable resource when I needed some sage advice on Ukrainian history. Jeff Jones and Jared McBride read the entire manuscript and helped me place this microhistory in its broader historical context. Kathryn David offered practical library assistance and early access to her dissertation on Greek Catholicism in Ukraine. Students and scholars at the University of Tennessee, Knoxville; Vanderbilt University; the University of Michigan, Ann Arbor; and the University of North Carolina at Chapel Hill offered feedback on draft chapters. Jessica Pisano assisted me in navigating Ukrainian regional archives in Uzhhorod and Berehove. Many other scholars have offered feedback over the years, for which I am grateful.

The branch office of Jehovah's Witnesses in Ukraine assisted in locating the families of survivors and setting up interviews. Ivan Bokoch's family graciously served as my host in Bila Tserkva, and Ivan himself drove me around to various spots in the village and helped arrange the interviews. He and other Jehovah's Witnesses in Bila Tserkva shared their stories and their homes with me. Staff members of the Office of Public Information at the World Headquarters of Jehovah's Witnesses assisted with various research questions. I have depended throughout my work on the pioneering scholarship on Jehovah's Witnesses by Zoe Knox and George Chryssides. Tatiana Vagramenko's research into newly declassified state-security files in Ukraine gave me an invaluable glimpse into materials I had not had access to during my own earlier research trips. Lindsey Martin and Valeriu Turea transcribed portions of interviews. Archivists in the state regional archives of Uzhhorod and Berehove helped me to locate files, and the archivists at the regional office of the Ministry of State Security (SBU) generously allowed me to photograph the entire case file, making this project possible in the first place.

My colleagues in the History Department at Middle Tennessee State University have been wonderfully supportive of my research. Portions of the research were supported by funds from a Faculty Research and Creative Activity Grant from Middle Tennessee State University. Earlier research was funded in part by a Fulbright-Hays Doctoral Dissertation Research Fellowship Abroad and a Social Science Research Council–American Council of Learned Societies (SSRC-ACLS) International Dissertation Research Fellowship. The two anonymous readers for McGill-Queen's University Press provided feedback that strengthened the book. The press and especially my editor Richard Ratzlaff have been patient as this book slowly inched toward completion. Paul Robert Magocsi generously allowed me to reprint several maps from his invaluable work, *Carpathian Rus': A Historical Atlas*; John Beadle edited the maps to fit the contents of this book.

Michael Paulauskas assisted with the recording of interviews in Bila Tserkva. He also did not complain when some of these interviews were scheduled on our first wedding anniversary. Hannah and Eleanor kept me entertained and busy, and I have no regrets about letting them distract me from my book for long periods at a time. Any errors in the final version are entirely my own.

Cast of Characters

THE DEFENDANTS

Dmitry Bokoch (b. 1905)
Vasily Bokoch (b. 1913)
Nutsu Guzo (b. 1905)
Dmitry Marinchan (b. 1913)
Vasily Marinchan (b. 1911)
Ivan Nan (b. 1911)
Ivan Ona (b. 1905)

THE AGITATORS

Ivan Dan (b. 1923)
Irina Danilash (b. 1930)
Mikhail Grin (b. 1923)
Yury Kogut (b. 1925)
Mikhail Ona (b. 1907)
Mikhail T. Popsha (b. 1901)
Vasily Stan (b. 1908 or 1909)
Nutsu Tsiple (b. 1924)

OTHER INFORMANTS

Anna Porchan (b. 1923): wife of Peter Porchan
Todora Moish (b. 1926): sister of Anna Porchan

THE LOCAL LEADERS

Ivan Baider (b. 1905): district-level Communist Party official
Maria Chuban (b. 1923): deputy chair of village soviet (council)
Yury Fonduriak (b. 1923): chair of village soviet in neighbouring Serednie Vodiane
Maria Lumei (b. 1931): Komsomol secretary
Todor Moish (b. 1905): former New Life collective farm director
Yury Moish (birthdate not indicated): chair of village soviet
Alexander Pelladi (b. 1914): School principal
Yury Pop (b. 1926): schoolteacher
Mikhail D. Popsha (b. 1891): Zhdanov collective farm chair in neighbouring Serednie Vodiane
Peter Porchan (b. 1919): New Life collective farm director and member of village soviet
Yury Tsiple (b. 1926): schoolteacher

Map 1 Romanian Communities in Transcarpathia, c. 1930. Paul Robert Magocsi, *Carpathian Rus': A Historical Atlas* (Toronto: University of Toronto Press, 2017), 55. Modified by John Beadle and used with permission.

SUBCARPATHIAN RUS'/CARPATHO-UKRAINE, 1938-1939

Map 2 Interwar Transcarpathia, 1938–39. Paul Robert Magocsi, *Carpathian Rus': A Historical Atlas* (Toronto: University of Toronto Press, 2017), 57. Modified by John Beadle and used with permission.

Map 3 Postwar Eastern Europe, 1945–89. Paul Robert Magocsi, *Carpathian Rus': A Historical Atlas* (Toronto: University of Toronto Press, 2017), 65. Modified by John Beadle and used with permission.

CARPATHIAN RUS' TODAY

Map 4 Post-Soviet Transcarpathia, 1991 to the present. Paul Robert Magocsi, *Carpathian Rus': A Historical Atlas* (Toronto: University of Toronto Press, 2017), 69. Modified by John Beadle and used with permission.

TO MAKE A VILLAGE SOVIET

Introduction

In June 1949 the state arrested seven men from the village of Bila Tserkva. They were not known outside their Romanian-speaking community. All were simple farmers. None was wealthy or powerful. Few people had ever heard of their small, isolated village on the southwestern border of Soviet Ukraine. Nevertheless, the state decided that these men were dangerous subversives: They belonged to an underground network of criminals bent on destroying the Soviet Union. If allowed to continue, they would undermine the Soviet state and threaten public order.

Escorted from their homes after dark, the men were transported to Uzhhorod, the regional capital. It was farther than most of the men had ever travelled in their lives. Uzhhorod was a bustling multicultural river town, yet of it the men only experienced the inside of a prison cell. Weeks of interrogation followed. The men had only their own words with which to defend themselves. They had neither legal counsel until trial, nor right to review the materials against them. Satisfied that the state had nabbed the right men, a regional court sentenced them to twenty-five years of imprisonment. Prison convoys transported them throughout the notoriously inhumane Gulag, a sprawling network of prison camps that stretched across the Soviet Union. They had little reason to believe that they would survive their sentences or see their families again.

This book explores why a powerful state singled out these individuals for removal from society. The Bila Tserkva investigation has a lot to tell us about what it meant to make a village and its residents "Soviet" in postwar Ukraine. This book is aimed primarily at students who may be less familiar with the region and its history. Students benefit when historians look into the neglected corners of the history of Europe, Russia, and the Soviet Union by incorporating peripheral regions and marginalized communities. Moreover, state-security records are an open window into all the challenges, frustrations, and excitement that historians experience when working with primary sources.

This book follows the fate of the seven men but, more important, it examines what this investigation reveals about the relationship between a state and its citizens. All modern states seek some level of control over their citizens, even liberal-democratic states. They establish laws that regulate acceptable behaviour, and they police those boundaries. They also establish a set of expectations for citizens and encourage citizens to meet these expectations through secular holidays, rituals, and other shared experiences. All states and their rulers "have attempted to create pure communities, or remake subjects or citizens in some preconceived vision of a perfect, or at least a better, society." By the twentieth century, states possessed increased power, and their ambitions to remake society became ever greater.[1] Thus, the Soviet Union is not unique in wanting to make its citizens "Soviet." Yet what happened in Bila Tserkva is notable because of the sheer ambition of state plans for "Sovietization" of communities. The state aimed to utterly transform life for every man, woman, and child, and to integrate them into the Soviet body politic. The stakes for non-compliance were extraordinarily high; failure to conform could cost individuals their freedom or lives. To a great extent, the state achieved the goals that it set for itself. By the 1950s the village had a collective farm. Its residents voted in elections at nearly universal levels. Its children received state-approved instruction at the local school. Every citizen carried official Soviet documents with them at all times. Bila Tserkva had become a Soviet space in which Soviet laws and institutions reigned supreme.

At the same time, Sovietization was as much an aspiration as a reality. All seven men belonged to the Jehovah's Witnesses, a religious faith that challenged the state's attempts to force the village into becoming one with a secular, socialist society. They had joined this faith before Soviet power arrived, as had many of their family members and neighbours. After the state removed the men from the village, other Witnesses remained in Bila Tserkva in numbers larger than when the state first opened its investigation in 1949. Some joined the farm, but others found ways to survive without it. Few voted in elections. Their children attended school but skipped lessons that contradicted their beliefs. They carried passports and even registered for the military draft, but they refused to complete mandatory military service. In short, an alternative community emerged and sustained itself alongside Soviet society. The power and scope of the state dwarfed this alternative society, but it did not destroy it.

The story of Bila Tserkva reveals how the local population played a critical role in defining who belonged in the new socialist society and who did not. It took time for the Soviet state to get to know its new citizens, and it had little immediate help from the Communist Party, which barely existed in the remote village. Since it did not yet have the infrastructure to gather information from an established and loyal bureaucracy, the state could only find out what was going on by asking local residents. The state investigation of Bila Tserkva is impossible to imagine without their participation.

Moreover, the villagers had every reason to look for someone to blame. The investigation happened at a time of heightened repression following World War II. The Soviet state had lost control over much of its territory and citizenry during the war, and it moved quickly to remedy that. For many Soviet citizens who had found themselves on occupied soil during the conflict, their loyalty came under immediate suspicion. From 1945 until the death of Soviet leader Joseph Stalin in 1953, more Soviet citizens than ever before found themselves arrested and thrown into labour camps and prisons. Most had done little more than survive a war, but that was enough to label them as traitors.[2] For the villagers of Bila Tserkva, the Soviet police state was a new experience, and the late 1940s offered obvious challenges as they struggled to figure out the system and how to navigate it. Even in such remote locations, far from the metropoles of Moscow or Kyiv, newly minted citizens learned how to avoid personal danger and advance their own interests.

In this environment, the Witnesses represented the ideal scapegoat for many reasons. Postwar propaganda denounced religious belief as a holdover from the capitalist past. Villagers knew that claims of subversive religious activity would attract the state's attention. More important, however, they knew their Witness neighbours enough to recognize that they held strong critical views about Soviet institutions. Indeed, some residents likely shared these sentiments about the lacklustre collective farm and school. It was in their best interest for the state to focus on a religious minority community rather than probe the loyalties of everyone in the village. With this in mind, villagers offered the state a compelling portrait of local opposition to Soviet power that was, if not the whole truth, true enough for investigators. Villagers did not have to lie so much as obscure the bigger picture. They could rightly claim that their Witness neighbours opposed Sovietization, even as they avoided scrutiny of their own complex, often ambivalent views about Soviet power. All this suggests that local communities had significant agency in the early years of Soviet power.

The state investigation into Bila Tserkva left behind a rich paper trail. The Ministry of State Security for Soviet Ukraine, which conducted the investigation, generated hundreds of pages of documentation. Nearly all of it is in Russian, though the trial record itself and some of the post-investigation materials are in Ukrainian. None of it is written in Romanian, the language of the defendants, not even their appeal letters. Most of the file is handwritten in careful script by the one individual who conducted nearly the entire investigation: a Lieutenant Patsula, senior investigator for the investigative office of the regional Ukrainian Ministry of State Security. He conducted the interrogations and interviews with informants, and his signature appears on these records throughout the file. Only a small number of documents are typed; this includes nearly all the post-conviction materials. In 1949, however, it is clear that the state-security apparatus still relied heavily on pen and paper to conduct its official business.

All the case material was neatly organized, bound into hefty volumes, and deposited within the regional state-security office in Uzhhorod. Over the years, it collected additional pages as some of the men appealed their sentences, seeking mercy from the court. Later, the file added brief notes indicating the men's release from prison. Just days before the collapse of the Soviet Union in 1991, the file received one final addition. As part of its review of Soviet-era convictions for state crimes, the regional prosecutor's office returned to the case and overturned the verdict. The men were officially declared innocent, and their families notified.

These materials were never intended for public review. During the Soviet period, the only individuals with access to the file were state investigators. With the collapse of the Soviet Union, however, much that was secret became known. This included some (but not all) of the vast holdings of the Soviet security ministries. In Ukraine victims of state repression could request access to their files (or those of their family members). Many did so. Historians could also access such materials, though finding them required some legwork. Not all cases stayed on their original shelves; some travelled quite a bit. The central security offices in Kyiv requested files for their growing archive. Regions shared files among one another, especially when citizens had been prosecuted in more than one locale. In at least a few cases, files travelled to Moscow, which meant that gaining access to Ukrainian records became an international affair.

In the case of Bila Tserkva, the file remained in Uzhhorod, collecting dust in the archives of the regional security service.[3] After Ukrainian independence in 1991, the pale pink building just steps from the centre of town changed hands. Its new owner, the Ukrainian State Security Service, retained much of its predecessor's responsibilities, including the maintenance of files. Well into the first decade of the twenty-first century, the process for requesting these materials was difficult, to say the least. To request a record there, as at many other regional offices, one would have had to know already that such an investigation had happened. There were no public finding aids to guide the researcher, who was expected to supply the names of victims, their dates of birth, times of arrest, and other relevant information. If the state had not rehabilitated the men years earlier, the case file would have remained on the shelf, inaccessible to outsiders. That the case file still exists at all marks a bit of good luck. Some records have gone missing, perhaps purged or even discarded after decades of storage. Yet there is reason for optimism among historians and the public. The momentous events in Ukraine in 2014, in which popular demonstrations ultimately led to a new government in Kyiv, changed this situation significantly and made it far easier to access security files. The challenging and often fruitless search for documents that defined this book's research may itself be a relic of a now-bygone past.

Using materials produced by a repressive state intent on the destruction of dissenting voices raises both methodological and ethical questions. In this case and others like it, the file begins with the arrest warrant detailing the major allegations against the individuals. It includes a list of informants who supplied this information. In this case, however, the list is only partial. How exactly these men and women came to inform on their neighbours is not indicated. Did state officials ask, or did neighbours come to the state of their own accord? It is possible that some of the informants were chosen because they had at least a rudimentary knowledge of Russian. The records suggest that only one informant, an illiterate housewife, had the formal assistance of a translator.[4] Some informants claimed they did not need a translator as they had sufficient command of Russian. Given that almost none of the villagers had any formal education in the Russian language and would have had no reason to encounter it before the war, it is unlikely that their language skills were advanced. We cannot know how much was lost in translation.

No piece of evidence is more fraught with challenges than the tidy descriptions of interrogations prepared by the investigator. While an interpreter was present and signed his name to the forms, there would have been a significant communicative gulf between a trained agent of the Soviet state and a minimally educated Romanian-speaking peasant. Nor do we have any information with which to assess the skill of the translator, who may have been less than fluent in one or both of these languages. The arrested men themselves generally refused to sign the forms on religious grounds, considering their signature on a government record a form of apostasy. Even if they had signed, this would not have proved consent. In the separate case against Vasily Dan, another Bila Tserkva resident tried a few years later, the state pressured him to consent to interrogation without an interpreter present. Later, at his trial, the state admitted it would need an interpreter due to Dan's weak understanding of the Russian language. This was after the state claimed the man had waived his right to an interpreter, citing his fluency in the language. Not surprising, Dan's appeal letter notes that he barely understood what was said to him during the investigation.[5]

The interrogation records are full of lacunae on many aspects of life in the village. Diana Dumitru, who uses postwar Soviet investigations to examine the Holocaust, writes that there are certain common "silences" across these sorts of records: emotions are scant, men are overrepresented, and social ties between accused and accuser are rarely acknowledged.[6] The case in Bila Tserkva has all these limitations and others as well. The file reveals nothing about the religious sensibilities of the Witnesses' neighbours. Supporting documentation makes clear that the village had been largely Greek Catholic until the war. Yet the church is otherwise absent from state records. The Witnesses also obscure much in their testimony. They speak rather openly about their own actions but say little about a larger network of believers and almost nothing about contacts with Witnesses beyond their village. Likewise, statements by other villagers leave out information about how they interacted with their Witness neighbours before the war. Personal relationships and conflicts that might have shaped their opinions or suggested bias are not acknowledged in their accusations. We should also be careful to remember that these records can only tell us what informants said. As Wendy Goldman notes in her study of Communist Party meetings in which members denounced their fellow citizens, such documents "do not tell us what individuals thought or felt in their hearts. They do, however, show us how people acted, and these actions, no matter what they believed or how they felt, had powerful consequences."[7]

Moreover, interrogations are not verbatim records. Everything said was not recorded. The start and end times listed on the document tell us that most interrogations lasted an hour, sometimes two, and only occasionally more. In this regard, the case is unusual.[8] It was a common tactic for Soviet interrogations to stretch for several hours, sometimes overnight, to break down an individual. This method was used in other postwar cases against Witnesses. In at least one instance, a Witness elder (a responsible male member of the congregation appointed by the Watch Tower Bible and Tract Society) died under such brutal interrogation.[9] Yet even though the Bila Tserkva Witnesses endured unusually short interrogations, far more was said in these encounters than was included in the interrogator's transcripts. We cannot know what this missing dialogue contained.

Written in the interrogator's hand and filtered through the state's worldview, the transcripts infuse Soviet language into the men's answers to questions. The men repeatedly refer to themselves as "Jehovists" in the records. The term "Jehovist" is a Soviet slang term for Witnesses. It was never used by Witnesses themselves, who considered it offensive, and was certainly never uttered by the men. For their part, Bila Tserkva's local informants parrot Soviet language as they describe the treasonous actions of their neighbours. Even so, the deployment of "Sovietisms" does not necessarily mean that the underlying message was penned entirely by the state. Take this example from an interrogation transcript of a Jehovah's Witness a few years after the Bila Tserkva case:

> I do not deny that I, along with all members of the anti-Soviet Jehovist underground, studied anti-Soviet literature and explained these so-called "teachings" of Jehovism to the population. All this anti-Soviet Jehovist propaganda is geared toward explaining the Jehovist "teaching" that believers will allegedly live forever. At the same time, to scare the uneducated portion of the population, the Jehovist underground determined that unbelievers of the so-called "Jehovah God" would allegedly be destroyed during the so-called "war of Armageddon," which I explained to the population. All this was done so that a person would hear this message and think about the necessity of joining the Jehovist underground.[10]

On the surface, the statement is contrite. It is also framed entirely within Soviet terminology, with repeated use of "so-called" and "anti-Soviet" to make clear that the man's faith is illegitimate and opposed to Soviet power. At the same time, the man making this statement claimed immediately beforehand that he had never "recruited" anyone into his faith, and he repeated this declaration afterward. One assumption we could make is that the passage above was entirely fabricated and therefore bears no relation to the individual at all. But this premise would be problematic for two reasons. First, if the state produced this record on its own, it would have no reason to include contradictory statements: a long acknowledgment that the man had talked about his faith with others, sandwiched between disavowals of having recruited anyone. Second, this particular interrogation was focused almost entirely on forcing the man to name names and admit his connections to other Witnesses. A long monologue about Armageddon does not fit this goal.

Read more closely, this statement could be seen as a testimonial of faith, with awkward insertions of Soviet jargon, likely by the interrogator. Consider this modified version of the man's statement, in which the Sovietisms have been removed:

> I, along with my fellow Jehovah's Witnesses, studied religious literature and explained these teachings of our faith to our neighbors. All this literature is geared toward explaining our faith so that believers will live forever. Our faith organization teaches that unbelievers in Jehovah God will be destroyed during the war of Armageddon, which I explained to my neighbors. All this was

> done so that the person would hear this message and think about the necessity of joining our faith.

While we cannot know with certainty what was originally voiced in the interrogation, the above version may more closely resemble the original responses of the man than the "Sovietized" version that appeared in the formal record. Imagine if we compare it with a modern-day testimonial from another Witness, a relative of the arrested men from the same village:

> Already from a young age, I began to understand after I started studying the Bible at fifteen years old. Until fifteen, you do not understand anything. You go to school, then here, then there. My parents firmly instilled in my sister and I that you must believe because many were saying that Armageddon would come soon. Do you know what Armageddon is? The end of the world. And word spread that it was already nearing the end of the world. They [my parents] thought that if we were worldly, we would not serve [God], and then we would die. If we would serve God, then we would live ... And that choice was ours. We could have chosen to serve God or not to serve God. We chose to serve.[11]

Like the arrested men, the villager speaks about the need to be converted to be saved from destruction in Armageddon, and about the role of religious literature in this decision. From this vantage point, it is possible to hear the voices of both Soviet interrogator and Jehovah's Witnesses in the interrogation records. The interrogator who transcribed the original man's remarks saw them as anti-Soviet and as an admission of guilt. This view infuses the official version of the transcript. In contrast, the man saw his words as offering an explanation of his religious motivations; they bolster his claim to the innocence of anti-Soviet activity. A nuanced reading acknowledges that interrogation records have layered meanings and cannot be either simply accepted as wholly true or discarded as entirely false.

The transcripts also record a worldview and language that is at times utterly un-Soviet. For example, when one of the men, Ivan Nan, seeks to recant some of his previous statements, he tells the interrogator, "I was not in control of myself; I was under the power of the devil." Similarly, when the state asks Vasily Bokoch to reveal who baptized him, it obviously seeks a concrete individual whom it can interview (and possibly arrest). Instead, Vasily responds that "Jehovah God baptized me."[12] This recorded answer does nothing to bolster the state's case, nor does it provide a useful lead on other individuals for the state to target in subsequent investigations. Overall, it would be a mistake to see the case as amplifying a single, unified Soviet voice. Rather, it presents a messy, entangled web of voices, each with its own competing interpretation of events.

Many of these voices come from local villagers who acted as informants for the investigation. Interrogators interviewed schoolteachers, collective farm members, agitators, the village soviet (or council) chair, housewives, and others. Their information formed the backbone of the state's case against their neighbours. It is worth noting that interrogations featured an element that made such denunciations strikingly personal. Once both informant and defendant had been interviewed, the investigator brought the two individuals together in the same room for a confrontation. The informant then repeated his or her accusations, and the defendant had a chance to offer a rebuttal. Such face-to-face sessions pitted neighbour against neighbour. In short, denunciations were not anonymous; the men knew exactly who had voiced complaints against them.

While Soviet interrogations have a deserved reputation for producing false confessions, this case shows scant evidence of this fact. There are no fantastical assertions of international espionage, conspiracy, or attempted murder. None of the men confessed to crimes that extend beyond the normal, expected responsibilities of an active member of the Witnesses. Nor is it plausible that the men were not Witnesses or religious at all. Although none of them survived long enough to be interviewed for this book, I interviewed several of their children and spoke with the Ukrainian branch office of the Witnesses, all of whom confirmed that these men were Witnesses and that they participated in the postwar religious activities for which they were convicted. For them, the injustice of the case was not that the men had been innocent according to Soviet laws at the time, but that they were prosecuted for actions that amounted to little more than the ordinary practice of their faith.

The availability of outside information from regional archives and Witnesses themselves helps avoid the danger of putting too much trust in the file alone. In his 2012 monograph, *Conscience on Trial*, Hiroaki Kuromiya carefully shows the pitfalls of such an approach by dissecting what might seem like a similar case. In 1952 fourteen alleged Adventists were brought to trial in the city of Bila Tserkva, near Kyiv. Other than sharing a name, however, this case is quite different. First, the men and women arrested in 1952 had lived under Soviet rule for decades, interrupted only by Nazi occupation in World War II. They spoke the same language as their interrogators and had more experience with Soviet law and justice. Second, many of the informants were family members and relatives, rather than neighbours and agitators (though there were some of those as well). Third, the defendants offered a more conflicted narrative under interrogation, at trial and on appeal. From this evidence, Kuromiya concludes that much of the case was "faked." The defendants had no interest in disrupting the state and no particular animus to Soviet power. Moreover, there was little proof that they even belonged to the splinter denomination of Reformed Adventists.[13]

In contrast, the 1949 investigation explored in this book tells us a great deal about not only the wider community in the village but also the conflict between an admittedly oppressive state and a faith community. The file offers much information on this point, but so do a wealth of documents from state archives and the recollections of family members. Without their testimony, we might conclude that, as in 1952, men and women had not actually opposed military service, met in secret, or shared their faith with others. With this evidence on hand, however, it is impossible to draw these conclusions.

In this regard, the case against the Bila Tserkva Witnesses is perhaps best compared with the postwar trials of alleged collaborators and war criminals in Ukraine. The "crimes" are obviously wholly different, but they offer a model for sorting through the state inventions and lived reality embedded in postwar investigations. Historians who work with these case files convincingly argue that we cannot simply dismiss them because they were produced by an authoritarian state with a history of coerced false confessions. To do so would be to miss these sources' unique insights into both wartime survival and local participation in the Holocaust.[14] Tanja Penter, who studies these postwar trials, writes that unlike in the 1930s, "postwar trials often concluded with the conviction of real war criminals." Sometimes these records are the only surviving information on wartime atrocities.[15] Another historian calls them an "indispensable resource" on wartime occupation. The job of the researcher is to "deduce from the case files where politics intervene and end."[16] In this instance, the case file offers invaluable information on both postwar Jehovah's Witness communities in Ukraine and the arrival of Soviet power in the western borderlands.

In Bila Tserkva, the state accused seven men of crimes that they almost certainly committed. These "crimes," moreover, were arguably more dangerous to the Soviet state because, unlike the often-mythical conspiracies of the Stalinist Terror, they did happen. The men did preach their faith to others. They did tell their children about God. They did gather as a community. And they did reject a Soviet order that denied God. Each of these actions directly threatened a major pillar of Sovietization. For the Witnesses, these so-called crimes were the duties of true Christians. For the state, these were the illegal operations of an underground, anti-Soviet organization. Both worldviews are embedded in the state records.

While this book is based on the investigation records, it also draws on supporting materials to give a richer picture of postwar life in Bila Tserkva. Regional archival materials reveal much of the state's broader plans for Sovietization. Files of the local collective farm, New Life, shed light on the state's collectivization of private farms. The regional government office in charge of monitoring religious life, the Council for Religious Cult Affairs, makes clear what the state knew about Witnesses in the initial postwar period. Local newspapers broadcast the state's goals for the region and its frustrations when plans fall short.

An additional case file in the state-security archive is of particular assistance in establishing context. A few years after the men's conviction, a wider investigation across Ukraine resulted in the arrest of dozens of Jehovah's Witnesses. Months of interrogation in Kyiv followed. Ultimately, the men, and a few women, were brought before military tribunals and sentenced to lengthy prison terms. This later investigation is valuable for several reasons. Many of the arrested individuals allegedly occupied leadership roles in the underground religious community, smuggling not only literature but also printing equipment abroad to and from Poland and Romania. This period also saw security operations that infiltrated the Witnesses and gave the state much more intimate knowledge of the underground religious community, its organizational structure, and its activities in western Ukraine.[17] While much of this information tells us little about the lived experience of citizens during Sovietization, the testimonials of the arrested individuals do shed light on some important matters. First, they affirm that the Bila Tserkva men were part of a broader community that shared a worldview at odds with Soviet power. Second, they confirm information conveyed in other sources about early Witness activity in this region.

Perhaps most important, one of the captured men was Vasily Dan, a Bila Tserkva resident who had been on the state's radar for years.[18] While he was not the first person to convert to the faith in the village, he was one of the first to come to the state's attention. Early attempts to arrest him failed after he repeatedly hid from state officials. Both the arrest warrants and denunciations of Dan by fellow residents appear in this file. Some of the same villagers who testified against the seven men in 1949 reprised their role as informants for this later case. Dan's answers under interrogation provide an additional window into developments in the village both before and after the 1949 investigation.

Last, I conducted several interviews in the village, which offer what government records cannot: a window on how the families grappled with persecution and loss. None of the seven men was alive when I began this project. Yet I was able to locate most of the families, who largely remained in Bila Tserkva. I interviewed children and relatives of five of the seven men, all still members of the Jehovah's Witness community.

***

A few words on names. Bila Tserkva is a borderland community, and each change in ownership altered the spelling of names and places. In this book the village and other geographic locations are always referred to by their current Ukrainian names. Thus, Bila Tserkva is always Bila Tserkva in this book, and never Belaia Tserkov (Russian), Biserica Albă (Romanian) or Tiszafejéregyház (Hungarian), though all three names mean essentially the same thing: "White Church." The issue of personal names is trickier. There is, simply put, no way to know for certain how villagers would have referred to themselves in the 1940s based on the official records available from the state.

This may seem like a problem common to borderland villages, but it is arguably a universal truth. Almost everyone adopts more than one name over the course of their lives. To offer a fictious example, a person may be Michael Penden on a birth certificate. When he is born, his parents take one look at him and start calling him Mish-Mish. They never drop this silly name even as he gets older. When he starts school, his teachers settle on "Mike." His friends nickname him Bo for reasons that are forgotten over time. As he enters adulthood, he decides to go with a variation of his middle name, "Victor" and call himself Vick. The shift reflects both his desire to distance himself from his childhood and that he likes how it sounds. When he dies, most people who know him never knew anyone other than Vick Penden.

In writing a person's history, a historian always has to reckon with such variations. Bila Tserkva's names reflect multiple national identities that go beyond personal preference and family dynamics. Yet even these factors will not be so foreign to Western readers. Many, even most, American names are at least partly the product of the twin processes that formed this country: immigration and enslavement. Enslaved Americans were deprived of the right to choose their names. Decisions made about their names by others were passed on through generations.[19] Many former enslaved persons and their descendants later chose new names for themselves as part of what one scholar has called "mental decolonization."[20] After individuals immigrated to America, they or their children sometimes altered the spelling of their names, often dramatically, to versions that sounded less "foreign" in their new homeland; some families adopted wholly new names.[21] This story is so ubiquitous in American culture that oftentimes people assume it happened, even when it did not.[22] Indeed, it is an urban legend among Americans that officials at Ellis Island changed the names of immigrants as they arrived at this major point of entry.[23] In short, few individuals ever have one name, given at birth, which remains their sole identifier until death. Names reflect choices made by individuals over their lifetimes and decisions made for them. They also tell us a great deal about how the broader society viewed them, and this, too, often changed over time.

The men and women of Bila Tserkva were Romanians who lived most of their adult lives in the Ukrainian republic of the Soviet Union. Their parents would have named them during the rule of the Austro-Hungarian Empire. Most of the men, but not all, have first names that are common across more than one of the regional languages. However, the case file almost always uses Russianized versions of their names. Hence, the village men are always Mikhail, and never

Mihai (Romanian) or Mykhailo (Ukrainian). This issue is made more complicated by the fact that the men did not have passports or any other Soviet identity papers at the time of arrest. The chief investigator made notes in the file as he sorted through the different possible spellings of the men's names. Thus, the state arrested one man under the name Vasily Fedorovich Bokach, but after using a few different versions of the name in its files, ultimately tried and convicted him as Vasily Todorovich Bokoch. The same situation arose for his brother when he was arrested.[24]

Naming gets even more complicated when it comes to the many Ivans of Bila Tserkva. The name John, and derivations of it, are common throughout much of the world. The popularity of the name reflects the spread of Christianity, as multiple Johns appear prominently in Christian scripture. In Romania, John is Ioan or Ion. In Russia and Ukraine, John is Ivan. In Bila Tserkva, however, John could be neither. Multiple men in the village, including one of the arrested men, are referred to by the first name "Nutsu" (Nuţu), which is typically an informal version of John in Romanian. At the same time, other men in the village are referred to as "Ivan." It is possible that all three arrested men referred to in the case file as "Ivan" or "Nutsu" went by "Ion" at home and among friends. Yet there is substantial evidence that "Nutsu" was a formal first name used by some men in this particular region, and not just as an informal nickname.[25] We simply do not have documentary evidence to establish for certain when a man is an Ivan, Ion, or Nutsu, and in what context.

Overall, there is no "right" version of villagers' names but rather multiple iterations based on identifiers assigned by the villagers themselves and others. A man may have been Ion or Nutsu at birth, but he would have increasingly answered to "Ivan" after Soviet power arrived in his village and official records listed his name in Ukrainian or Russian. One of the men's relatives introduced himself as both George (Romanian) and Yury (Russian) in the same conversation with me.[26] Moreover, it is worth noting that Jehovah's Witnesses regard national identity with minimal interest and consider it meaningless compared with membership in their faith community. As such, while this question vexes historians (and frustrated Soviet officials), it would have had little value for the men themselves.

Ultimately, this book uses the case file versions (and therefore Russianized forms) of first and last names for those individuals who appear within it. It is the only consistent source for names across all individuals who appear in the record. Rather than view these names as a reflection of personal identity, we should see them for what they are: a site of Soviet power. This book is about how Soviet power arrived in one village, and the names are one small piece of this larger story. Just as Bila Tserkva became Soviet, so, too, did the villagers' identities as rendered in official records. To help English-language readers, I have used common English spellings for first names when they exist (Vasily, Alexander, Dmitry, Peter), and transliterated names when not. In rendering Slavic words into English, I have dropped the standard apostrophes used to indicate Russian and Ukrainian soft signs from the main text but preserved them in the endnotes and bibliography. Readers should note that the villagers of Bila Tserkva share a small number of last names. Just as there are many, many Ivans in this story, so, too, are there multiple Bokochs and Moishs. Two individuals may share a last name, but that does not necessarily indicate that they have any close familial relation to each other. To help readers keep track of individuals across chapters, I have included a cast of characters at the start of this book.

1

The Village

Bila Tserkva is not a village of great historical significance. It first appears sporadically in historical records during the late Middle Ages. The name, which means "White Church," derives from a monastery on its eastern outskirts. The monastery had long since fallen into ruin by the time the seven defendants were born, but the name remained.[1] Bila Tserkva can easily be confused with the far larger town of the same name that sits an hour south of the Ukrainian capital of Kyiv.[2] The village of Bila Tserkva, in contrast, lies in the southern region of Transcarpathia.[3] The closest administrative centre is Rakhiv, the district seat. Uzhhorod, where the men were imprisoned, is roughly three hours west by car along rural roads and highways.

Transcarpathia's location endowed the region with a diverse ethnic makeup. To the west, it borders Polish and Slovak lands. To the south, the Tysa River forms a natural boundary with modern-day Hungary and Romania.[4] Ethnic minorities dominate in many villages and towns, and Ukrainian is often spoken only as a second language. Much of the remaining population in the region considers itself Rusyn, a Slavic national minority with its own distinctive dialect.[5] The population of Bila Tserkva is neither mostly Ukrainian nor mostly Rusyn. Instead, it belongs to a cluster of Romanian-speaking villages near the Romanian border. Even today the vast majority of villagers communicate in Romanian.[6]

The region is known primarily as a destination for Ukrainian hikers and campers. While few tourists have ever ventured to Bila Tserkva, the neighbouring town of Solotvyno has transformed its salt-mining roots into a health resort industry that caters to travellers. Much of the region is mountainous and covered in forests. The wooded scenery gave birth to a steady timber industry, but farming sustained most residents who continued to eke out an existence from the land. The seven arrested men and their families were no different. Their parents farmed, and they worked alongside them in their formative years. Few other alternatives would have entered their minds.

One option that did increasingly appeal to Transcarpathians in the late nineteenth century was emigration. George Liber refers to the region in this period as "the most illiterate, the most impoverished, and the most isolated area within the entire [Austro-Hungarian] empire."[7] Beginning in the late nineteenth century, many men and women in Transcarpathia fled the region, seeking opportunity elsewhere and an escape from the crushing rural poverty that surrounded them. Nearly half a million migrated to western Europe and the United States.[8] The seven men and their families stayed behind.

Paul R. Magocsi calls Transcarpathia "a borderland par excellence."[9] Before World War I, Transcarpathia belonged to the Austro-Hungarian Empire but then changed hands repeatedly in the decades that followed. The villagers of Bila Tserkva learned that living on a border meant repeatedly adjusting to life under new ownership. Each state brought with it a new set of rules that the villagers had to navigate as best they could. In the Austro-Hungarian period, Hungarian identity dominated the region and was promoted in the schools and local bureaucracy.[10] When World War I began, the seven men were too young to be called to fight in a conflict that ultimately destroyed the empire, fracturing it into a fragile hodgepodge of nation-states. Instead, they watched from the sidelines. When the conflict was over, their parents' farms laid within the borders of the newly created state of Czechoslovakia.

The dissolution of Austria-Hungary left many nation-states and national communities dissatisfied with new borders that did not correspond to the elaborate patchwork of nations across the former empire. Rusyns in Transcarpathia rallied around an independent state of their own. Meanwhile, a now-independent Hungary voiced bitter resentment over its territorial losses. These "lost" lands included Transcarpathia, which now sat on the far eastern border of Czechoslovakia. In the ensuing two decades, global economic depression and resurgent nationalism undermined the fledging governments of Eastern Europe, which slowly dissolved into dictatorship. Czechoslovakia and its nascent democratic system proved more resilient. It is hard to know how much of the political wrangling in the distant capital city of Prague would have reached the village. The men most likely spent their early adulthood on the periphery of this new state both in a literal and figurative sense. The daily difficulties of farm life along the new border loomed much larger than distant political realities.

By the time the men had married and established farms and families of their own, the region changed ownership again. This time, war had much more profound consequences for their lives. Hungary found a powerful ally for its territorial claims in Nazi Germany.[11] When German troops entered Czech lands in 1939, Transcarpathia declared its independence. On its first day, the newly formed government settled on a national flag and national anthem. The government did not have time to do much else, as it did not survive to see a second day. Instead, Hungarian troops entered Transcarpathia, and the incipient state was no match for this organized invasion. In the months that followed, Hungarian troops gradually overran more distant districts, including that which contained Bila Tserkva. The villagers likely never knew that they had enjoyed a brief moment of independence at all.[12]

The initial period of Hungarian annexation did little to disturb the patterns of life in the village. Elsewhere in Europe, however, war had begun. The German invasion of western Poland sparked a second world war that quickly led to a succession of German military victories. In June 1941 Germany launched an invasion of the Soviet Union. This was a massive undertaking that required additional soldiers from Germany's allies. In particular, Germany demanded troops from Hungary, which, in turn, looked to its expanded territories to provide soldiers for the front.

Bila Tserkva villagers found themselves conscripted to fight in the lacklustre Hungarian army on the eastern front. Some Witnesses ran afoul of the new authorities and were imprisoned. Mikhail Chuban, a local resident, had been one of the earliest converts in the village. After spending years in a concentration camp, he returned home permanently disabled after the war. None of the seven arrested men experienced this situation, but they would have known about what happened to members of their community who were not so lucky.[13]

Still, the region experienced comparatively little military action. Wartime deprivations paled in comparison to the utter horror of Nazi occupation in Ukraine directly to the north. The local situation deteriorated, however, by spring 1944. Frustrated with the Hungarian government, Germany took greater control of Hungarian territories. This had devastating consequences for the country's Jewish population, which had largely avoided the Final Solution well underway elsewhere in occupied Europe. Shortly after German occupation, the Hungarian government began rounding up Jewish residents for deportations to the killing centre of Auschwitz-Birkenau in Poland. Over four hundred thousand Hungarian Jews were deported. Nearly all were murdered immediately upon arrival, the "Nazi's last victims."[14]

In Transcarpathia, however, the roughly seventy-eight thousand Jewish residents were vulnerable even before the German occupation of Hungary. Bila Tserkva itself lay within a district with one of the largest concentrations of Jews in the region, most of whom were Orthodox and spoke Yiddish. The Hungarian state had labelled many of these Jews "aliens," which gave them less protection than those considered "Hungarians." The earliest ghettos in Hungary appeared in this region, forcing Jews to leave behind their homes and possessions and endure squalid, overcrowded living conditions in a handful of towns and cities. Ultimately, however, their fate was the same as that of "Hungarian" Jews. Hungary deported nearly all the Transcarpathian Jews to their deaths by the end of the war. This included the Jews of Bila Tserkva.[15]

By the time Soviet power arrived in Transcarpathia that fall, therefore, the village had seen significant loss of life during the war, even if most of its inhabitants had not perished in war. As the German army retreated back on to its own territory, the Red Army marched westward toward Berlin and victory in World War II. Red Army troops entered Bila Tserkva on 16 October 1944.[16] The war would not end for several more months, but already Soviet victory was a foregone conclusion. By this point the Soviet Union had absorbed much of the other western territories along its border. The Baltic States, eastern Poland, and parts of eastern Romania were once again in Soviet hands, and the state moved to make these acquisitions permanent.

Transcarpathia was different. It had no historic ties to Russia, a reality that the Soviet Union acknowledged only with regret. Soviet publications glossed over the multi-ethnic character of the region. Instead, they portrayed Transcarpathia as Ukrainian territory and its residents as largely Ukrainian.[17] They lamented that the region had been so long separated from its allegedly historic homeland in Soviet Ukraine. In this regard, Transcarpathia is most similar to the German region of Königsberg, annexed to the Soviet Union after World War II. Like Transcarpathia, Königsberg had not been Soviet before the war, nor part of the Russian Empire before that. In both cases, the Soviet Union resorted to mythmaking and invention to suggest that the two lands had common historic roots. In Königsberg, Stalin and other Soviet leaders spoke of it as "ancient Slavic soil," an absurd claim that required citizens to view the previous seven hundred years of history as an aberrant time of German subjugation.[18]

Likewise, Transcarpathia as historic Slavic land required a leap of the imagination. Soviet historians had to go back nearly a millennium to claim a shared past between Russia and Transcarpathia.[19] Nikita Khrushchev mused in his memoirs, "Ukrainians used to say among themselves: 'Well, for the time being the Transcarpathian Ukrainians aren't part of our Ukrainian state. But the hour will come when they will join us.' And that's exactly what happened after the war."[20] At least, that is how Khrushchev claimed that Ukrainians felt about the matter. For the Soviet Union, the annexation was framed as the long overdue unification of Ukrainians and Russians unjustly kept apart for centuries.[21] This view was hardly shared by the Rusyn population, who saw themselves as distinct from Ukrainians. And it certainly did not describe the feelings of the national minority communities scattered across Transcarpathia. The residents of Bila Tserkva, with almost no Ukrainians or Rusyns among them, would have felt no strong call to join an imagined motherland.

But, of course, Soviet expansion did not depend on popular opinion. Soviet annexation was no more popular in the Baltic States, Poland, Romania, or Königsberg, but it happened nonetheless. As in these territories, the Soviet Union moved quickly to formalize its seizure of Transcarpathia. Czechoslovakia, only just re-established, acquiesced to the demand, though it had little choice to do otherwise.[22] Transcarpathia was now Soviet territory. Its lands were formally integrated into the republic of Soviet Ukraine.

The Soviet Union was the fourth state to demand the loyalty of Bila Tserkva residents since the turn of the century. The arrested men were born in an empire, grew up in an independent state, and lived through wartime occupation and Soviet annexation. Amazingly enough, many villagers, including a few of the arrested men, survived to see yet another state assert its authority over their lands. In December 1991, the Soviet Union collapsed, and they became citizens of an independent Ukraine.

Bila Tserkva's position as a border community defined life for its residents in the twentieth century. This is evident in the changing demands made by each successive government that claimed Bila Tserkva as its own. The border allowed residents to see themselves as members of different communities and to understand the fluidity and multiplicity of modern identity. While we have grown accustomed to the militarization of borderlands in modern states, including those of the United States, border regions are also sites of blurred lines and cross-cultural contact. This is certainly the case in Bila Tserkva. The villagers had not always lived on this side of the Soviet border, even though most had never moved their whole lives. Rather, Soviet power came to them, just as other powers had done in decades prior.

Today both Ukrainians and Romanians swim in the same shallow waters of the Tysa River that divides the two countries. A bored soldier sits along the banks to ensure that no one crosses the invisible halfway point between the shores. A visitor might reasonably fail to notice that a border exists at all. Upon closer inspection, however, evidence of what was once a much more controlled border still exists only a short distance from the waterfront. Weathered posts dot the terrain along the upper riverbanks, the remnants of the old border fence. Soviet authorities had constructed it in the postwar era as part of the state's effort to demarcate its newly acquired lands. In this regard, making Bila Tserkva "Soviet" was of particular importance because of its location on the very edge of Soviet territory. What happened in Bila Tserkva could never be just a local issue because Bila Tserkva and the Tysa River were national security concerns.

Even so, the village itself was not a particularly prized possession for Soviet authorities in 1945. The Soviet state devoted more energy to an unsuccessful attempt at annexing the larger, wealthier city of Sighet across the river in Romania.[23] After the war, Sighet (now Sighetu Marmației, in Romania) became notorious as a prison site for political prisoners, including Greek Catholic clergy. Today it hosts a museum dedicated to the history of this terror, as well as a public memorial to its murdered Jewish community, deported to Auschwitz-Birkenau. Nobel Prize–winner and Holocaust survivor Elie Wiesel was deported from Sighet to Auschwitz-Birkenau in 1944.[24] In contrast, Bila Tserkva, the smallest village in its district, had little significance and less to offer the Soviet state. It had minimal industry or natural resources, and no communists. It did not even have any native Russian speakers. The Romanian identity of the village made it rather insular and removed from interwar or wartime politics.

Interwar Czechoslovakia had done little to bring the wonders of modern life to its easternmost territory. The village had one road that cut through the centre of town. The modest homes of villagers had no electricity or indoor plumbing. Still, there was reason to assume that Soviet control would set a more ambitious agenda for rural development. After the October Revolution that brought the Communist Party to power in Russia in 1917, revolutionary leader Vladimir Lenin made infrastructure a central part of his plan for Soviet power. At the Eighth Congress of Soviets in 1920, he declared that "Communism equals Soviet power plus electrification of the entire country." Communism could not happen without this critical component of modern society. Early Soviet propaganda posters equated electricity with worldwide victory over capitalism. The Soviet Union invested significant resources into bringing light and power to all its citizens in the two decades before the war.[25]

Now in the immediate postwar period, the state worked to extend the power grid into its newly acquired regions. Even so, Bila Tserkva was at the bottom of the list. The village was rural and had no industry to justify any special treatment. Nearby villages got electricity. Bila Tserkva waited and waited. A few months after the men were arrested, and a full four years into Soviet control, the village collective farm began work on its first power station.[26] This brought power to the farm itself but not to individual homes. The men and their families continued to make do without it or running water.

Without power, communication with the outside world was haphazard. The government building in the centre of town did not have a phone.[27] The Soviet postal system took time to establish. Homes, scattered around the village, received a rather random numerical system to identify them. Mail arrived sporadically and at the mercy of new postmen who could not always be bothered to show up at their jobs.[28] By 1949 Bila Tserkva made regional news when equipment was installed to allow radio signals to reach the village. Officials hoped to supply the major institutions of Soviet life with radios: the school, the collective farm, the club, and the government building.[29] Information could now reach the village, but this was a one-way form of communication. Moreover, these radio broadcasts were made almost certainly in Russian or Ukrainian, which few in the village spoke or understood.

If there was one factor that made the village stand out to Soviet officials in this early period, it was its religious makeup. Most of the roughly 1,500 residents were at least nominally Greek Catholic.[30] Of the Jewish survivors of the Holocaust from Bila Tserkva, only a handful still lived in the village after the war.[31] Yet the village had an unusually large community of Jehovah's Witnesses who first appeared in the region in the interwar period. They arrived in the form of missionaries, carrying with them literature from the Watch Tower Bible and Tract Society, a religious organization then based in Brooklyn, New York. Founded in the late nineteenth century in the northeastern United States, the Society produced a steady stream of publications, which its readership distributed both at home and abroad. The Society's regular magazine, the *Watchtower*, advised readers of the signs of a coming Armageddon, to be followed by the establishment of a millennial kingdom on earth.[32] Man would no longer suffer from want or injustice, and humans and animals would live together in harmony. A select few would ascend to heaven itself to join Jehovah. Until then, the faithful forswore involvement in secular society and government, which they viewed as irrevocably corrupted by Satan. The Society strongly rebuked Christian churches for what it saw as the abandonment of the form and substance of early Christianity. Yet beyond this basic apocalyptic message, it was a rather loose organization similar to other millenarian faiths of the late nineteenth century. In the early period, those who joined the Society were known simply as Bible Students.[33]

The first Bible Students to travel to interwar Czechoslovakia were not particularly impressed by what they encountered. A 1927 report on missionary activity in the region concluded by expressing the desire for "better results in another year."[34] Three years later, this hope had yet to bear fruit. Missionaries blamed their slow progress on widespread illiteracy and the fact that the local population was, it noted, "especially ignorant with reference to the Bible." This situation was itself blamed on "the domination of the Roman priests."[35] Difficulties with establishing local offices were likewise pinned on opposition from local clergymen.[36]

Yet despite this largely pessimistic outlook, Transcarpathia appeared to offer an opportunity for missionary growth. Already in the mid-1920s, the region produced enough converts to warrant individual mention in the pages of the *Watchtower*. An annual report printed in the magazine identified the village of "Beli-Ceakva." In 1925, it noted, forty-three residents attended the annual memorial service to mark Christ's death.[37] In neighbouring Solotvyno, nearly five hundred people attended a Bible Students convention in 1932.[38] The convention was a chance to meet other likeminded individuals and belong to something bigger than their fledgling congregation. Given the remote, rural location, at least some of these people would likely have come from Bila Tserkva.

The convention was also a space to warn converts that they had just joined a rather unpopular religious minority and should be prepared for opposition. Visiting German and Hungarian elders offered a rather ominous vision for the crowd. Local elder Mikhail Tylniak recalled that "with tears in their eyes, they encouraged us to remain faithful under the coming trials."[39] The message might seem rather dour, but it reflected the speakers' views of the secular world as irrevocably corrupt and destined for destruction. This was both what attracted some to the Society and what repelled others. Moreover, this vision happened to be rather accurate in this instance. Just a few months before the postwar arrests in Bila Tserkva, Mikhail and his brother, Vasily, were detained in Solotvnyo. Both received ten-year sentences.[40]

In the interwar period, the positive reception by some locals may have encouraged the Society to invest more heavily in outreach to Transcarpathia. A regional office opened in the town of Berehove, and a literature depot in Uzhhorod. The German branch office dispatched a full-time missionary specifically for Rakhiv, the district that contained Bila Tserkva.[41] When Prague hosted a national convention for all Czechoslovak members, the Society rented an entire train to pick up delegates. It departed from Solotvyno.[42]

The interwar period was a time of transformation for Bible Students worldwide. Under the leadership of Joseph Franklin Rutherford, the Society increasingly resembled a formal church, though it did not use this term. The organization established clear guidelines for congregations and exercised direct control in appointing individuals to positions of responsibility. It also selected a new name, Jehovah's Witnesses, to reflect this shift. The name was drawn from the initial words of Isaiah 43:10: "'You are my witnesses,' declares Jehovah, 'Yes, my servant whom I have chosen, so that you may know and have faith in me and understand that I am the same One.'"[43] The new name symbolized two important tenets of the faith. First, adherents must acknowledge the name of God, Jehovah, which they believe has been ignored by other Christians. Second, adherents must demonstrate their commitment by "witnessing," or sharing their faith with others. The call to missionary activity was instrumental in sending Bible Students (now Witnesses) around the world, including to Transcarpathia. Some Bible Students balked at the more centralized authority of the Society. More than a few drifted back to other denominations or formed splinter groups of their own. By the mid-1930s, however, the Society had formed a centralized religious organization set apart from mainline Christianity.[44]

In Bila Tserkva and elsewhere in Romanian-speaking territories, Bible Students formally became Jehovah's Witnesses, but they were rarely called by this name in casual conversation. Instead, most villagers would have referred to one of their Witness neighbours as a *pocăit*, or "penitent." The colloquial term, derived from Romanian, was widely used in Romanian-speaking regions and remains in circulation today. "Penitent" did not always mean Witness, even if it did carry this association in Bila Tserkva. Romanians applied the label to all manner of Christian religious minorities but particularly those associated with neo-Protestant movements. "Penitent," though seemingly a neutral term, carried a negative connotation for Romanians and marked the Witnesses as different from their neighbours.[45]

Vasily Dan's story illustrates how some Transcarpathian villagers first encountered the Witnesses during this period. Dan, a Romanian, was born in the nearby village of Serednie Vodiane. A child of farmers, his formal education consisted of three short years spent at the local schoolhouse. It was enough to teach him how to read and write. He eventually moved down the road to Bila Tserkva, where he married and started a family. Until the war, he belonged to the Greek Catholic Church. Like most converts, Dan found out about the faith not from a foreign missionary but from another resident who "witnessed" to him. Based on these conversations, Dan became convinced that there was a fundamental disconnect between his life and his faith. The Greek Catholic Church, the centre of religious life in the village, no longer satisfied him. He decided that how he had been taught to worship as a child was not consistent with his new understanding of God's commandments.

This was a common refrain among those who joined the Jehovah's Witnesses. For them, conversion required the abandonment of one religious tradition as much as it did the adoption of another. A letter to the *Watchtower* from a Polish convert during this period is instructive in this regard:

I send you my deep gratitude for your honorable toil. I was brought up by religious Catholic parents, and started out to discover God's righteous way, and soon I found myself among sects of all kinds of names. One of them urged me to observe the sabbath day; another one would persuade me that it is necessary to speak in unknown tongues, and then a loud proclamation of "purgatory," and with these I was not satisfied, because it was difficult to harmonize them with the everlasting love of God.

Being wearied with the confusion of all kinds of interpretation, and with continued thirst for knowledge of the truth, I decided to apply to God in prayer and ask Him for help, and soon I was visited by one of the brethren from Lodz, which was the first falling upon me of the rays of light amidst the darkness around me. He placed with me some literature and also gave me the address from which I began to receive *The Watchtower* (in the Russian language).

The second year elapsed from that time as the gladsome "Herald of Christ's Presence" continued to visit me alone. I truly acknowledge that at every meeting with your explanation of the truth our God raised me upward out of the confusion that wearied me in past time under man's traditions. Very often I reflect upon the words of our Teacher Christ Jesus, "Ye shall know the truth, and the truth shall make you free."-John 8: 32.

Your brother in Christ by his grace, ANTONI PLESZAR, Poland.[46]

For converts such as Antoni Pleszar and Vasily Dan, joining the Society represented a fundamental break with their previous lives and with other forms of Christianity. While Dan's life story comes from an interrogation record, his brother, Mikhail, related a strikingly similar conversion experience nearly sixty years later for a Society publication.[47]

Unfortunately for Dan, he came to this revelation in 1943, in the middle of the global conflict that had engulfed his village. Shortly after his conversion, the occupying authorities detained him and accused him of espousing communism. After torturing him to admit his communist sympathies, they released him back into the community. This disturbing incident did not deter Dan from what was clearly a dangerous affiliation in wartime. Reflecting on this period, he later wrote, "I began a new life to glorify God and serve mankind, recognizing the authority of Jehovah and Jesus Christ. I was ready to serve Him always, knowing that my duty to Jehovah and Jesus Christ means eternal death." His brother also joined the faith, and other family members may have followed suit.[48]

The wartime environment contributed significantly to the growth in converts.[49] The Witnesses' dire warnings of an impending Armageddon seemed less far-fetched in a climate of uncertainty and mass violence. By late 1945, the community counted 150 baptized adult members. That year, a mass baptism in the Tysa River welcomed over fifty Bila Tserkva residents into the faith.[50] In fact, the number of people involved was significantly higher, as villagers often waited years before baptism. Among Witnesses, baptism was a sign of mature commitment to the faith and therefore a ritual conducted only after considerable study and preparation. Most Witness families also had several children who typically were not baptized until late youth or even early adulthood.[51] Taking this into account, the total number of people in the faith community was easily at least two to three times this size.[52] In a sign of the altered religious landscape of the postwar period, the empty home of a Jewish neighbour became a convenient meeting spot for these new Witnesses.[53]

Overall, the Witnesses' rapid growth in the Romanian villages of Transcarpathia reflects a confluence of factors. Some converts were disillusioned with the dominant Greek Catholic Church and wanted an alternative form of Christianity. Some were drawn to the promise of an earthly paradise in the immediate future and to the condemnation of secular governments. Both aspects of the Witnesses' belief system would have been particularly appealing in the midst of a brutal war in which allegiance to neither church nor state offered much protection from violence and death. Beyond these local factors, many converted for the same reasons that others did and continue to do so worldwide: someone they knew and trusted had already done so, and invited them to join them. In this regard, conversions built on one another, and made others more likely to consider the faith. The presence of fellow believers in the village made Witnesses feel less isolated and part of a broader community.

The Witnesses' apocalyptic message ultimately won over the seven men later arrested in Bila Tserkva and brought them into conflict with the newly arrived Soviet state. In all other respects, the men differed little from their neighbours. They were Romanians and, like most middle-aged men there, married. The group included two sets of brothers – Dmitry and Vasily Marinchan, and Dmitry and Vasily Bokoch – as well as three others: Ivan Ona, Nutsu Guzo, and Ivan

Nan. Having grown up on modest farms, they had received only a few years of education before their parents' need for help in the fields kept them out of the schoolhouse. Dmitry Marinchan had tried his hand in the timber industry, but even he, like the rest of the men, had eventually acquired land and begun to farm in adulthood. Nutsu Guzo, though a member of the Bila Tserkva community of Witnesses, resided outside the village. His modest farm was in the neighbouring village of Serednie Vodiane.

We do not know exactly what the men looked like because the case file does not contain any photographs of them.[54] We are left, therefore, with only the tersest descriptions of the men's physical features, sketched out on the intake forms. These forms included lists of common descriptors for the intake officer, who had only to underline the appropriate option for each category. For weight: "obese, overweight, average, slender, thin." For eyes: "blue, grey, green, hazel, brown, black." And so on for noses, mouths, lips, chins, ears, and foreheads, among other physical features. The end result is both detailed and entirely useless in creating a visual portrait of the men. It cannot possibly have assisted anyone in tracking down suspects. Adding to the vagueness of whole affair, almost none of the men had the sorts of unusual attributes that would have caught a person's attention. One also suspects that the intake officer conducted only a cursory outward study of each man. On the form for Dmitry Marinchan, a wounded war veteran with a badly damaged right leg, the officer wrote: "no special features."

Still, this scant information provides at least a blurry snapshot of the seven men. Both Vasily Marinchan (b. 1911) and his younger brother, Dmitry (b. 1913), were married. Their father was deceased, and they had one other sibling, Yury. Each of the arrested brothers had three young children. The intake form allowed officers to select a height range, and so we know that Vasily was on the tall side for men in the Soviet Union. He was of average build, with black hair and grey eyes. His brother Dmitry was shorter, and with lighter hair.

Likewise, Dmitry Bokoch (b. 1905) was married, with two boys at home. Mikhail, the elder son, was sixteen years old; Yury was thirteen. Dmitry's younger brother, Vasily (b. 1913), was also married, with a five-year-old son. His wife was pregnant at the time of arrest, a fact he noted during the trial in asking for mercy from the court. There were three other siblings in the Bokoch family. As with the Marinchans, the patriarch of the Bokoch family had died sometime before the arrest. The two brothers may have shared some similar looks, but Vasily was taller, with darker hair, and grey eyes as opposed to Dmitry's hazel ones.

The description of Nutsu Guzo (b. 1905), the lone non-resident of Bila Tserkva, paints a similar portrait: both his parents were deceased, and he had three brothers. Nutsu was married with four children, three boys and one girl. Unlike the rest of the men, the intake officer apparently noticed something of interest in Guzo. He had a birthmark under his left eye and another on his right cheek. Otherwise, his description could apply to many men in the village. He was neither tall nor short, a bit on the slim side, and had grey eyes, a big nose, and big ears.

Although Ivan Ona (b. 1905) was one of the two oldest men arrested in the investigation, he also had the smallest household. While he had grown up in a family of six children and was married by the time of his arrest, he and his wife had no children of their own. His parents did not survive to witness his arrest, and one of his siblings lived across the river in the Romanian town of Sighet. The rest of his family remained in Bila Tserkva. Ona himself was of average height and build, with grey eyes, an oval face, big nose, and thick lips.

While the last of the men, Ivan Nan (b. 1911), was among the youngest, he also had the heaviest burden of family responsibility. Although only in his late thirties, his blond hair had begun to grey, perhaps from stress as much as from age. Having married early in life, he already had seven children to care for at home. Still, this would not have seemed entirely out of the ordinary to him or his relatives. Nan himself was one of six siblings. Indeed, all the men had brothers or sisters, a normal pattern given the farming life of the community. Children provided much needed labour around the household and in the fields. Birth control and information on modern family planning would also not have been widely available.

Exactly how these seven men came to be Witnesses remains vague, and the men's own accounts under interrogation are contradictory. Some credited their conversion solely to reading the Bible, a far-fetched explanation but one almost certainly intended to avoid implicating others. Others recalled encounters with local believers who sold them religious literature. Most likely, some version of the latter explanation is correct. While the Society eventually abandoned the practice of seeking payment for its magazines and books, selling religious literature was a common evangelizing strategy for Witnesses in the interwar period. By this time, the Society had invested heavily in translation work, which meant that at least some of this literature would have been in Romanian, making it relatively accessible to local residents.[55] The men's education, though modest, would have been sufficient to allow them to read basic texts, perhaps with some assistance. Moreover, Society reports make clear that there were at least a few dozen Witnesses in this village already in 1925.[56] Any one of these individuals could have sold them the literature. What the men did not mention, but which certainly occurred, is that they began to attend Bible studies to formally learn the faith and gathered for worship in private homes.

This faith journey likely began after the interwar period, which nearly all the men spent on their family farms. We know this because four of them completed obligatory military service in the Czechoslovak army, an act that would have been forbidden to them as baptized Witnesses. A fifth man, Dmitry Bokoch, was ruled medically ineligible due to poor hearing.[57] A few years later, these same men had a different response to a second round of drafts, this time by the Hungarian army during its occupation of Transcarpathia in World War II. Only the Marinchan brothers enlisted, suggesting their commitment to the faith came somewhat later than for the other men. Vasily was quickly discharged for health reasons and never fought in the war.[58] His brother Dmitry was sent to reinforce the Axis position on the eastern front. By mid-1943, the Hungarian Second Army had been largely destroyed on the urban battlefield of Stalingrad, which began to turn the larger tide of war in favour of the Allies.[59]

By the war's end or shortly thereafter, the men, including Dmitry, had made a lifetime commitment to the faith. After he returned home, Dmitry told his children that the war had changed his attitude toward religion. He was disillusioned by how the clergy had participated in the war effort and how they seemed to sanction the bloodshed. Now back in the village, he connected with the Witnesses and became more open to their message.[60] If Dmitry and the others had joined the faith in the United States, their entry into full membership in the community would have been rather different. They might have been baptized at a large convention in full view of their peers. It would have been a public celebration. Pictures might have been taken, and speeches given to mark the occasion. In Transcarpathia, the men had to settle for the cold waters of the Tysa River.

It is unlikely that the men were surprised when they ran into trouble with the Soviet state. They had just joined a faith that believed secular institutions target true Christians for persecution. It is impossible to know exactly which of the Society's publications these men read among the hundreds of magazines, tracts, and books produced in this period. Certain themes, however, were ubiquitous, and persecution by secular authorities was one of them. Society publications repeatedly covered the persecution of Witnesses for standing up for their beliefs elsewhere in the world. Moreover, Society rhetoric became increasingly hostile toward secular authorities and Christians outside their community, which only furthered such tensions.[61] In the United States and Great Britain, Witnesses faced angry crowds when they held signs in public that read, "Religion is a Snare and a Racket." An American man was arrested for evangelizing in public after he called a city marshal a "damned fascist" and "God damned racketeer."[62]

Far more worrying was the situation in Germany. After Hitler's rise to power, thousands of German Witnesses were arrested, and many were imprisoned in concentration camps. German authorities saw Witnesses and their provocative beliefs and practices as a threat to their authority, and Witnesses in turn refused to obey or acknowledge the new government to avoid punishment. Their enormous suffering filled pages of the Society's publications. By the war's end, over a thousand German Witnesses had perished as a result of their religious affiliation.[63] To this day, the persecution of German Witnesses in Nazi Germany remains the most well-known example of state hostility to this religion. The Society itself regularly refers to this history in its publications, including through interviews with survivors.[64]

Closer to home, the Soviet state had already begun arrests of Witnesses in Transcarpathia. Mikhail Tylniak, an elder in the small congregation next door in the neighbouring town of Solotvyno, had been on the state's radar for some time. As noted, he and his brother were arrested in early 1949. After a brief investigation, both received ten-year sentences. Mikhail Dan, a resident of Bila Tserkva, was arrested in late 1948 and earned an identical sentence.[65] These arrests signalled to the community that everyone was in immediate danger. Most vulnerable were men who hosted religious services or occupied some responsible position in their congregations. Some of these men went into hiding, anticipating that it would be only a matter of time before they also received a knock at their door. This included the brothers of two of the men.[66] It makes sense, then, that the men arrested in 1949 were not necessarily the most senior individuals in the congregation. Although the Witnesses had a presence in the village for at least twenty-five years, these men had joined within the last decade. The arrests and flight of others would have left gaps in the leadership that someone in the village had to fill. The men likely had taken on greater responsibility in the wake of this persecution.[67]

That all the individuals in the investigation were men is no coincidence. Jehovah's Witnesses do not have a formal clergy, but all positions of responsibility are restricted to men. This is true of individuals who serve not only at various branch offices and the worldwide headquarters but at all levels, including in local congregations.[68] Even so, women sometimes took on duties that had no formal status but were necessary to maintain their congregations in postwar Soviet Ukraine. Some women acted as couriers of information or handled the reproduction and duplication of illegal religious literature, and still others sheltered fellow believers in their homes after they were wanted by authorities. When caught, women faced arrest and imprisonment along with the men.[69] Still, the vast majority of arrests targeted men, a fact that reflected both the real power dynamics of congregations and the assumptions of Soviet authorities that men posed a greater threat to the social order.[70]

Of the seven men, Dmitry Bokoch was surely the least caught off guard by the arrest. When the state issued the warrant for his arrest, he was already in jail, having just been sentenced to five years for not carrying a passport. Given this brush with the law, his brother might have expected to find himself the subject of an investigation as well. Why did the men not flee before their arrest? It is worth remembering that nearly all of them were the primary breadwinners for families with young children. Moreover, where would they have gone? Most had spent nearly their entire lives in this village and would have had few connections outside the immediate area. Disappearance may not have been a viable option.

Thus, the men largely remained at home until authorities came for them. Vasily Marinchan was so accustomed to the knocks at the door from the local authorities that he had already taken to sleeping away from home some nights.[71] Some of the men's children were old enough to remember the arrests of their fathers. As was typical in the Stalin era, the police sometimes arrived late at night at their homes. They were heavily armed; resistance would have been impossible. The police did not always wait for someone to answer the knock. They let themselves in to the home of Dmitry Marinchan, awakening his frightened children along with Dmitry and his wife.[72] They also went next door for Vasily, whose son was still in his bed. The boy was certain that they were going to kill him. His mother sent him to warn other nearby Witnesses, but it was too late.[73] Ivan Nan's daughter, however, recalled that the officers arrived in daytime and took her father down to the village soviet, where he was then transported to Uzhhorod.[74]

Once arrested, the men's fate was a foregone conclusion. They were interrogated for weeks, and then tried, sentenced, and shipped to prison camps. Their families struggled to survive in the absence of husbands and fathers for this long, painful stretch of time. Even after the men eventually made their way home years later, they carried the stigma of dangerous criminality against the state. This remained the situation until the end of the Soviet Union in 1991, when the men's cases were finally re-examined and their convictions overturned.

2

The Passport

When the Red Army arrived in Bila Tserkva in fall 1944, there was no fence and no border. Even after the land across the river became foreign territory, villagers easily crossed over the water to Romania, which was only a stone's throw away. When the water level was low enough, local men and women walked along rock paths to the other shore. When the river was higher, they carefully stripped off their clothes, swam across, then re-dressed. Some of the men owned farmland across the river. They travelled back and forth to tend to it.[1]

Jehovah's Witnesses also made quick trips back and forth as part of their preaching work. Religious literature crossed over on some of these jaunts across the border. A statewide investigation into the Witnesses in the early 1950s centred on these illegal journeys and on alleged communications between Soviet and Romanian Witnesses. Under interrogation, Alexander Bara, one of the arrested Witnesses, told investigators that the river had made such contacts possible. Local residents could swim from bank to bank, exchanging information with their brethren across the border.[2]

For the Soviet state, an open border was a major security concern. A porous border allowed both goods and people to travel back and forth across the river without state scrutiny. If the Soviet state intended to control Transcarpathia, it needed to be able to decide who and what entered and exited the territory. On an even more basic level, this meant establishing exactly who had the right to live and work in Transcarpathia. Even though Soviet power now extended across the region, residents did not always see the situation in black and white. Their farms spanned across the river, as did their trading partners and sometimes their family members. In theory, annexation meant that the Romanian-speaking villagers had become Soviet citizens, but it took time to make that a concrete reality. The villagers had no voice in the matter, no ability to refuse this designation. Short of resettling their homesteads on the other side of the border, they were now under the rule of the Soviet Union.

On a practical level, all these newly minted citizens needed documents to establish their new identities. In the United States, the state provides all citizens with a social security card, but most Americans use their driver's licences for identification purposes. In the Soviet Union, the nearest equivalent was the "internal passport." This piece of paper allowed citizens to establish identity, obtain employment, and relocate to new regions.[3] Although called a passport, it did not allow citizens to travel abroad. And unlike in the United States, the internal passport was mandatory for all citizens sixteen years of age or older (regardless of whether they worked or not).[4]

The Soviet state had first initiated what it called "passportization" in the early 1930s. Genrikh Iagoda, then head of the NKVD, the Soviet secret police, praised the new passports as a way to protect society from dangerous persons: "The passport is the first and chief line of social defense against criminals and socially harmful elements." Soviet officials used identity papers to cleanse their cities of undesirable populations. Hooligans, the homeless, grifters, prostitutes, Roma, the infirm, and the elderly, among others, all found themselves targets of arbitrary passport enforcement by local police. Failure to provide a passport could result in imprisonment and deportation to distant regions in the Soviet interior.[5] Over time, the passport became one of the Soviet system's primary means of enforcing social control and keeping tabs on its citizens.[6]

Other state-issued documents further allowed authorities to restrict who could live where. Local officials had the power to register citizens as legal residents of a given town or city. By denying registration, officials could force individuals to move elsewhere, or face prosecution. Historian David Shearer notes, "Through passport and residency laws, officials could (or so they thought) systematically categorize, quantify, and locate or relocate, with reliable exactness, loyal and potentially dangerous populations."[7] Witnesses often found themselves on the wrong end of this law. Few lived in major urban areas, where registration was more difficult to come by, opting instead for marginal territories that already had established Witness communities. This helps to explain how in 1975, Soviet statistics recorded no Witnesses in either the Ukrainian capital of Kyiv or the Soviet capital of Moscow, and none in the regions surrounding both cities. At the same time, officials recorded nearly four thousand Witnesses in Transcarpathia.[8] Some of this disparity is a result of the early presence of Witnesses in rural communities such as Transcarpathia, but at least some of it is due to discriminatory registration practices.

The Soviet passport system also kept collective farm workers tied to their rural communities. The state did not issue them passports at all until the 1970s, which meant that rural citizens had limited ability to travel or resettle outside their farms.[9] In the border zones, however, the need to carefully monitor and control all residents outweighed the desire to restrict out-migration from rural regions. Thus, the state required all border residents to obtain both a state passport and a residential permit for permission to live within this zone.[10] This requirement now extended to Bila Tserkva.

Passportization in Transcarpathia began in earnest in summer 1946. Regional authorities recruited bilingual staff to coordinate the efforts in places where residents did not speak Russian. The presence of Ukrainian-speaking officials would have been of little help in Bila Tserkva, where everyone spoke Romanian.[11] Residents were to immediately obtain a passport, and then local authorities would issue a residency permit on the basis of this document. No passport meant no permit and therefore no legal right to continue to reside in the district. In theory, no one was legally allowed to remain in Rakhiv district without both documents.[12]

This, of course, was how it was supposed to work. Yet passportization did not reach everyone immediately. For nearly a decade, regional authorities complained that many local residents had either a temporary passport or no passport at all. In the frantic atmosphere of postwar reconstruction, work sites needed manpower badly enough that they hired workers with no documents at all. The pressure to meet labour demands trumped state calls for greater border security.[13] Some village authorities in Rakhiv district took the extraordinary step of issuing their own papers to residents in lieu of state-sanctioned documents.[14] This allowed authorities to continue to meet work norms and to staff their farms, but it also greatly concerned the regional Communist Party leadership.

The problem of undocumented residents was especially acute in Bila Tserkva.[15] The village now sat within a 2-km security zone that extended out from the river. It was a border zone within a borderland,

and authorities wanted assurance that it was under control. It was not just Jehovah's Witnesses who violated the new regime in order to preach and tend their lands. Bila Tserkva residents routinely ignored the new regulations in favour of doing things as they had done for years. They swam in the river and brought their livestock down to the riverbanks. With the border fence apparently still under construction, the state instituted fines and official warnings to deter villagers from such actions.[16]

The state chalked up much of these violations to a lack of awareness by villagers. In the absence of Romanian-speaking officials, the state struggled to convey the new rules to residents. At the same time, residents may also have found the language barrier a useful justification for feigning ignorance. The river offered a valuable opportunity to smuggle foreign goods, which could be resold on the black market back in the Soviet Union. The potential profit from speculation was significant and encouraged locals to turn a blind eye to these activities. Local drivers, including those who operated state-owned vehicles, sometimes ferried strangers after dark through the border zone. In response, district officials attempted to mandate regular searches of local transport. They even banned residents from having unregistered guests in their homes overnight.[17] Beyond the trade income, however, the river was a steady source of water for a village that lacked the modern conveniences of indoor plumbing and irrigation. Villagers needed a watering hole for their livestock. They needed a place to do laundry. In the absence of sufficient militarization, villagers had strong incentive to find ways to maintain access to the river and its southern shore.

Passportization also faltered because some residents stalwartly refused to obtain the required documents. Some of these were undocumented workers who may not have been local residents or who had other compelling reasons for wanting to remain off the state's radar. In Bila Tserkva, many, if not most, of these violators were Jehovah's Witnesses.[18] The village's Witness population lived a largely undocumented existence, an increasingly untenable position for a location within sight of an international border. In fact, the lack of documents led to the first arrest among the men. Dmitry Bokoch, like much of the rest of his congregation, had no documents at all. Months before the arrest of the others, local authorities issued a citation to Dmitry for violating the newly established passport system. Dmitry was ordered to pay the fine and obtain papers immediately. He did neither.

Dmitry's decision carried serious consequences. Authorities came to his home and arrested him shortly thereafter. His case went to trial in the district court that June. Given his day in court, Dmitry seized the opportunity to justify his actions, even if the closed proceeding meant that only a few Soviet officials would hear his words. In his statement before the presiding judge, Dmitry explained that he did not obtain papers because he did not recognize Soviet laws as equal to the laws of God. The court transcript conveys both Dmitry's attempt to situate his objections within his religious worldview and the Soviet judiciary's struggle to make sense of this explanation:

> At the court hearing the defendant spoke about how Jehovah God bestowed laws on Mount Sinai. These laws allowed Moses to lead an army of 600,000 against the civilian population who lived in the lands of Canaan (now Israel). The civilian population, including children, was utterly destroyed. The invaders ordered the seizure of all of the population's personal property and lands. The defendant stated that Jehovah God has not yet issued similar orders today.[19]

This brief and convoluted retelling of Moses, the Ten Commandments, and the Israelites' entrance into Canaan is not a full transcript of Dmitry's original remarks. It leaves many unanswered questions: Did the state understand Dmitry's attempted explanation of how his beliefs stood in conflict with Soviet law? This particular biblical story is hardly obscure, but even the brief summary suggests that Dmitry went into a fair amount of detail about events in the Old Testament. Did the court willfully misread Dmitry's statement so as to make him seem more dangerous? The document certainly reframes Dmitry's words as threatening. In its version, Dmitry recounts the murder of "peaceful" civilians, even children, and frames the story as akin to a modern military invasion. He even comments that God has not "yet" told him to carry out similar orders on Soviet soil. It seems likely that Dmitry made a statement about Moses and the Israelites in Canaan, and it is equally probable that he did not use precisely these words to explain himself. We cannot know the mind of the court, but we can conclude that Dmitry's religious beliefs were seen as incompatible with the new Soviet order. What Dmitry meant as a theological explanation was refracted through politics. Whether this was due to ignorance, intentional misinterpretation, or both, is not known. What we do know is that on the basis of this testimonial, the court labelled Dmitry a "socially dangerous theologian." He was convicted and received a five-year sentence.[20]

Dmitry's quick trip through the Soviet criminal justice system suggests the charges against him were not all that uncommon in the region at the time. It did not warrant a lengthy investigation or transfer to the regional capital of Uzhhorod, which handled cases involving state crimes. Local officials had sufficient authority to work the case and were confident enough not to involve outsiders in the process. Before Dmitry could begin serving out his time, however, more serious charges against him appeared.

This was the investigation that resulted in the arrest of the six other men. Dmitry, still in custody, was now transferred to Uzhhorod for additional interrogation. His wife and children were not immediately informed of either the original court decision or the new charges. The refusal to carry documents became one piece in a larger investigation of the Bila Tserkva Witnesses. The other six men shared with Dmitry a refusal to accept documents issued by the Soviet state. Under interrogation, investigators demanded to know if the men's wives also refused passports. Although they must have known the answer, the men feigned ignorance of their wives' affairs.[21] Vasily Marinchan's interrogation is representative:

> Q: Does your wife have a passport?
> A: I don't know.
> Q: Why do you refuse to provide the investigation with any information?
> A: I am a Jehovist and will not provide information on anyone else.[22]

The exact wording here is almost certainly not an accurate reflection of how Vasily described his actions, but the overall point is clear. The interrogator wanted information on others; Vasily refused. An informant, a young homemaker and collective farm member who lived next door to a family of Witnesses, filled in some of the missing information on passports. She recalled talking a few years earlier to the wife in the household, who told her that neither she nor her husband had obtained passports because passports were "forbidden" by Jehovah God.[23]

Interestingly, of all the aspects of Soviet power, the question of documents was the most mutable of conflicts between the state and Witnesses. Jehovah's Witnesses worldwide do not require or even encourage their members to abstain from signing official forms or acquiring identity papers. A Witness in the United States is just as likely to have a driver's licence as his non-Witness neighbour. The Bila Tserkva community in the 1940s were too isolated to know that. Passportization was a new phenomenon to them. Whatever pre-war religious literature had made its way into the village, it had not addressed this particular question. The local community only knew the information filtered across a border that was increasingly difficult to traverse. Faced with an unclear situation and no immediate answers, Witnesses resolved to abstain from Soviet documents rather than risk violating their faith. Ironically, then, it was the border itself that exacerbated this conflict. With more ready access to the international Society, this particular clash with Soviet authorities could likely have been avoided entirely.

The question of documents created another problem for interrogators due to the nature of Soviet interrogation methods. Interrogations could last for hours. If interrogators had transcribed these conversations, each interrogation could easily have spanned several dozen typed pages of text. The resultant case file would be far, far longer than the one preserved in the archive. Interrogators did not do this, however. Instead, they prepared formal summaries of each interrogation in a question-and-answer format. For each question posed, there is a response from the accused. And there is always a response, even if only a terse denial. Interrogation records do not record silences. In this sanitized version of events, the interrogator never threatens physical harm. Once he has prepared the summary, he presents it to the accused to read and sign. The accused always signs to acknowledge that this is an accurate summary of what he has told his interrogator.

This is where the problem arose. The arrested elders refused to sign the interrogation records. This likely frustrated their interrogator, Lieutenant Patsula. The signature was a form of contract acknowledging the validity of his prepared report. It also verified that the state-appointed interpreter for the men had done his job in explaining the Russian-language document to the men in their native Romanian. Both state officials risked undermining their own authority if the men would not go along with the mandatory rituals of Soviet interrogation. Yet the report also silences this conflict between interrogator and accused. There is no recorded back and forth between interrogator and accused over the missing signature. Instead, Patsula provided a simple penned-in statement "refused to sign" at the bottom of each page. Given that this phrase was written in Russian, the interrogator, not the arrested men, wrote this as well.

Patsula felt the missing signature was problematic enough to warrant further explanation to his bosses. It violated the criminal procedure rules that governed such investigations. Thus, Patsula included his own memorandum in the case file to justify his inability to obtain consent from the accused. It is notable that this memo chalked up the men's obstinance to their religious beliefs.[24] Patsula seemed to confirm that whatever the men's actions, they were religiously, rather than politically, motivated. And indeed, this is a fairly accurate assessment of why the men refused to sign. Their religion motivated them to have no part in the Soviet system, and that included Soviet documents.

The question of documents sparked the first arrest and now formed a major source of evidence against the men. Testimonials from village informants affirmed their neighbours' refusal to recognize Soviet authority. One such informant, Ivan Dan, served as a local agitator. A young married man and one of the early collective farm members in the village, he also had more education (eight years) than most of his neighbours. His responsibilities included communicating to villagers the requirements of the new Soviet system. Historian Serhy Yekelchyk has written extensively about the role of the agitator in postwar Ukraine. He notes, "In theory, agitators were ordinary citizens who volunteered their time during lunch breaks and after work to prepare the population for voting by explaining the procedure and promoting Soviet achievements." In reality, they were far more than that. Agitators were "intermediaries between the government and the population" as well as "collectors of public opinion." In a village with minimal official presence, agitators were crucial foot soldiers in Sovietization.[25]

On a practical level, this meant that Dan and other agitators spent their free time tracking down their neighbours and explaining the newly imposed civic duties to them. At least in Bila Tserkva, most agitators were, like Dan, relatively young, male farmers. The work was tedious and rarely rewarding. In the best of circumstances, an agitator might make a sincere connection with a local family. He might assist them in resolving some bureaucratic issue, thus earning their trust and by extension, solidifying their faith in the socialist system. In the Russian city of Rostov, one model agitator talked a young woman out of suicide, and he found another an apartment. Most of the work, however, was far more mundane, and one can hardly blame agitators for doing little more than the bare minimum. In Rostov, after one agitator was robbed while going about his work one evening, other agitators asked for the right to arm themselves when venturing out after dark. Overall, there was simply too much work to do, too many homes to reach, and too little time or resources given to agitators. Even with all these limitations, however, they were the eyes and ears of the state and thus a crucial mouthpiece in communicating expectations to its citizens.[26]

The investigation depended heavily on what agitators in the village had to tell the state. Dan was one of several agitators to supply evidence against his neighbours. As it turned out, his work led him to interact with nearly all the arrested men. From his own testimony, we might reasonably conclude that Dan was not a particularly effective agitator, given that his arguments appear to have had no impact on his religious neighbours. And this is true of all the agitators who testified. Yet nowhere do residents frame their interactions as failures of their own persuasive talents. This would have shifted responsibility onto their own shoulders. Nor do they blame the lacklustre product they were selling to their neighbours. This would have required the dangerous suggestion that Soviet power was somehow a hard sell. If agitation did not work, it was because its targets, the Witnesses of Bila Tserkva, were already too far gone to be saved by clever words or an enlightened sales pitch. In Dan's case, he told interrogators how fruitless his efforts had been in convincing the men to carry documents. The men rejected his advice, telling him that Soviet identity papers were "forbidden by Jehovah God." Dan's multiple warnings to obtain a passport had no effect.[27] Neither did fines.[28] The men were not interested in persuasion, and threats and penalties did not appear to move them either.

Dan was not the only villager to approach the men on the state's behalf. A small cadre of local men and women attempted to sell their Witness neighbours on the benefits of Sovietization. They were no more successful than Dan. Agitators who worked with Nutsu Guzo from the neighbouring village of Serednie Vodiane reached a similar impasse. Zhdanov Collective Farm chair Mikhail Popsha told interrogators that Guzo had not only refused to obtain papers but also repeatedly dodged direct summons from the local government, the village soviet, to appear and discuss the matter. He developed the habit of fleeing to the nearby woods whenever police or soviet deputies approached his home.[29]

When agitators did catch Witnesses at home, they were not afraid to call on the power of the Soviet state to pressure the men to obey the law. Although agitators rarely told interrogators that they had threatened their neighbours with punishment, Witness responses to agitation suggest this subtext. When future collective farm chair Peter Porchan knocked on the door of Dmitry Marinchan's home, Dmitry bluntly remarked, "I will never get a passport or a military service card. Let them do what they want to me."[30] This statement makes sense only if Dmitry had reason to fear that officials intended to do something to him, as indeed they did.

Another Witness, the brother of one of the arrested men, was even more direct about the stakes with a village activist who, incidentally, was collective farm chair before Porchan. The man informed the agitator that "even if they send me to prison for ten years, I will remain true to Jehovah God's laws and will never betray them for as long as I live."[31] On a different occasion, this same agitator warned Vasily Bokoch that if he were not careful, he would end up like his brother, Dmitry, the arrested man already serving a five-year sentence for refusing documents. Not surprising, Bokoch seemed unfazed by this comment. He told the agitator, "I am a true follower of Jehovah God and I will never reject his teachings even under threat of death."[32] While such dramatic statements may be seen as rhetorical, or a reflection of the men's theological belief that secular government would always persecute true Christians, they also fit with the realities of Soviet justice in the postwar era. The men knew that disobeying Soviet authorities could carry serious consequences, including lengthy prison terms.

These comments reveal the impending sense of doom among the Witness men in the village. Their friend and brother, Dmitry, was under arrest, and the men in his congregation anticipated that they might soon face a similar or far worse fate. That said, Dmitry only faced a five-year labour-camp sentence. The escalation to possible death reveals that Witnesses were already thinking in terms of much more serious penalties before they became a lived reality. The former chair's testimony suggests that other villagers also understood the full consequences of disobeying Soviet power. The man threatened Vasily with arrest but did not correct Vasily when he proclaimed his readiness to die at the hands of the state. He did not tell Vasily he was overreacting to a simple request for documents, or that he was wrong to fear for his life. Rather, he advised him to get his passport. Clearly, the man thought, as Vasily did, that death was a possible consequence of failure to do so.

Passportization was at the heart of Sovietization. It formalized the new reality that the villagers of Bila Tserkva were indeed Soviet citizens. The state reasonably wanted this basic level of control over its population. While Witnesses and the state literally spoke different languages, this particular conflict was not entirely one of misunderstanding between a government and its new citizens. To a great degree, the Witnesses understood what the state wanted of them, and they simply refused to abide by it. They saw passports as formalizing a relationship between themselves and the Soviet state, and said no. In the years after the arrests, the Society managed to convince Soviet Witnesses of the wisdom of a more moderate approach: accepting state documents in line with the practices of Witnesses worldwide. The passport was one of the "many details" of the faith and its expectations that was unclear in the immediate postwar period. When in doubt about where to draw lines between themselves and the new state authorities, the Bila Tserkva men erred on the side of caution. When they learned that their faith did not require such a sacrifice, they went ahead and got passports.[33]

By 1952 the chief official for religious affairs in Transcarpathia reported that "Jehovists" were now accepting passports. He credited the state's punishment of local Witnesses for passport violations as a major reason for this shift.[34] Other state officials echoed these same findings in later reports.[35] In fact, fear of persecution likely had relatively little to do with the changing attitudes. Rather, Witnesses had slowly been brought in line by their own religious community, a process that took time and education.

From that point forward, the issue never again surfaced as a major concern for Soviet authorities. In this regard, passportization was the most successful feature of Sovietization in this village. Although it took longer than expected, borderland populations formally registered with the state. Witnesses may have entered the postwar period as stateless believers, but they became Soviet citizens in name and deed. As for the seven men, their attitudes changed during this period as well. When Soviet authorities issued reductions in their sentences in 1955, they notified the men in writing of their new release dates. These forms bear the men's signatures.[36]

In hindsight, had Jehovah's Witnesses not already existed in the western borderlands before the war, passportization would likely have made it impossible for them to settle there. Bila Tserkva, a town located in the security perimeter of an international border, would almost certainly have been off-limits for members of an unrecognized religious community. Indeed, the same year as the investigation, the Soviet state initiated the wholesale removal of Witnesses from borderland territories. In 1949 and 1951, two secret operations deported over ten thousand Witnesses to distant outposts in Siberia. Witnesses from western Ukraine, Belarus, the Baltic States, and Moldavia were sent in cattle cars over thousands of miles from their homelands.[37] These particular operations singled out Witnesses, but many other groups met this same fate during the Stalin era. Some belonged to ethnic minority populations, others were labelled rich peasants (kulaks), and many others were marked as politically disloyal for any number of reasons. All told, millions of citizens were rounded up and summarily deported to remote locations in the Soviet hinterlands.[38]

Transcarpathian Witnesses were spared this fate. The few declassified documents that exist on the operations give no indication as to the reason for this decision. That said, there are some plausible explanations. Unlike the targeted territories, Transcarpathia was new to the Soviet experience. It had not been occupied by Soviet troops until the war. As a result, Sovietization began only in the postwar period. Moreover, partisan warfare in the region was more muted than in the formerly Polish territories in western Ukraine. Thus, Transcarpathia garnered less scrutiny than its neighbours along the borderlands. Still, the deportations, even if they did not uproot Transcarpathian Witnesses, had a major impact on these communities. After 1951, they were the sole intact congregations left for thousands of miles. An elder from Lviv could no longer reach out to his fellow believers in Solotvyno. He could not travel to Rakhiv district to convey instructions from the Society or speak at a religious convention. Literature deliveries temporarily slowed in the absence of underground printers who had duplicated the Society's magazines. Transcarpathian Witnesses now had to manage much of this work for themselves and re-establish contact with deported members at the other end of the Soviet Union's vast territory. This was a burden for rural, impoverished communities.

Passportization followed Witnesses into exile. Soviet Witnesses in the resettlement communities had no freedom of movement, no ability to travel to their home villages even for a visit. When finally freed of this restriction in 1965, Witnesses discovered that passports and residential permits dictated where they could and could not live and work.[39] Local authorities were loath to allow religious believers into their towns and cities. As a result, only a handful of Soviet Witnesses ever lived in major metropolitan centres. Few even lived in Uzhhorod, the regional capital of Transcarpathia. The vast majority remained in rural communities or towns in far-flung regions scattered throughout the vast Soviet state.[40] The passport made Witnesses into Soviet citizens, but it did not make them equal under the law. Far from it. This fact may help to explain why nearly all Bila Tserkva Witnesses remained in their home village, even after the investigation. They had nowhere else to go.

3

The Draft

Passportization, however, did not fully resolve the documents question. Sovietization demanded more than just a passport and a residency permit. For men, another set of documents was also required. The state mandated that all adult men register for the draft and obtain a service card vouching for this fact. If Witnesses initially balked at carrying a passport, they likewise refused to comply with this additional imposition. This situation proved to be a more enduring problem for both the state and Witnesses.

Simply put, the Soviet Union needed soldiers. World War II had taken the lives of an estimated twenty-seven million Soviet soldiers and civilians.[1] Roughly 75 per cent of the dead were men, creating a lasting gender imbalance in Soviet postwar society.[2] Ukraine was particularly devastated by the wartime violence. While it is hard to quantify the magnitude of suffering experienced by Ukrainians during the war, George Liber puts the casualty figures into perspective. He writes that Ukraine "experienced a total of 13.8 million human losses, including a net out-migration of 2.3 million, a deficit in births of 4.1 million, and a loss of 7.4 million due to exceptional mortality, including the murder of approximately 1.7 to 1.8 million Jews."[3] The war was a cataclysmic event for the Soviet population.

Moreover, victory came with a heavy price for maintaining the postwar peace. The Soviet Army, the Red Army's successor from 1946 onwards, remained in the territories it had entered long after the fighting stopped. By the late 1940s, the Soviet state had made a long-term political commitment to shore up the newly established regimes in Eastern Europe. Soviet soldiers stood ready to defend these satellite states and keep them within the Soviet orbit. Within its own territory, partisan conflict continued to threaten Soviet control of its western borderlands. Western Ukraine bore the brunt of this guerrilla warfare and its brutal repression by Soviet military forces in the late 1940s. One historian estimates that as many as four hundred thousand men and women were involved in some fashion, either as supporters or fighters, in the anti-Soviet resistance in postwar Ukraine.[4]

At the same time, increased tension with the United States heightened calls for international security and defence. Soviet citizens gossiped openly about a looming World War III. These rumours swelled with the emergence of a new Cold War between the two superpowers.[5] The possibility that this war might suddenly become hot, especially with the advent of nuclear weapons, was all too real for ordinary people on both sides of the Iron Curtain. For the Soviet Union, an overextended superpower, this situation demanded enormous manpower to meet all the state's domestic and foreign obligations.

Universal military service had existed almost since the creation of the Soviet Union. The bloody civil war that followed the October Revolution had generated a demand for young men to serve in the newly formed Red Army. Since that time, every male Soviet citizen was required to serve in the military. Soviet schools offered mandatory training classes to prepare for service, and teenagers were required to officially register with the local draft board. In exchange, they received a military service card. When they reached conscription age, the draft office issued a summons to appear for a medical exam. After the war, the state limited these call-ups to two per year, once in spring and once in fall.[6]

Soviet propaganda championed the military as the protector of Transcarpathia. The Red Army had "brought long-awaited freedom" to the region. No longer would Transcarpathians be made to suffer under the rule of foreigners. The military had reunited them with their Ukrainian brethren; now they shared a single homeland. All this was the result of heroic wartime efforts by Soviet soldiers. Their sacrifice had enabled Transcarpathia to be "forever united with its mother, Soviet Ukraine."[7] Military service was a way for the local population to repay this enormous debt. That not all Transcarpathians fit this narrative of Ukrainian brotherhood did not fundamentally enter into the equation.

Young Transcarpathian men greeted the sudden military obligations that came with citizenship with comparatively less enthusiasm. Draft evasion is hardly uncommon among any military-age population. In this case, the men of Bila Tserkva had barely gotten to know their new government before being asked to defend it with their lives.

Moreover, less than ideal living conditions in the military, including rampant and violent hazing, made service less attractive for all young men.[8] Across the Soviet Union, young men found ways to avoid their military duty. Poor health kept some men out of the ranks and provided a way to legally avoid service. Education could also result in a lengthy deferment. Overall, exemptions were not uncommon for individuals with connections.

The men of Bila Tserkva had no such negotiating power. For a young man from a rural background, with minimal education and a life of farm work ahead of him, there was little chance of avoiding the call of duty. Moreover, as a member of a minority community that did not speak Russian, it was likely that the men of Bila Tserkva would be assigned to a construction battalion, where they would perform hard labour on various infrastructure projects. This service would probably occur far from Transcarpathia, with minimal military training, if any at all. This form of conscription was not a viable route to a career or profession but rather an unavoidable distraction from farm and family right as men entered adulthood. The construction battalion in particular was a dumping ground for the least desirable and least physically fit. For those chronically ill youths who could not get a medical exemption, they might find themselves "assigned to construction battalions to do heavy labor alongside criminals and ethnic gangs." Not surprising perhaps, desperate young men sometimes resorted to self-harm to avoid such a fate.[9]

The Jehovah's Witnesses among them had objections that went beyond concerns over medical risk, lost time, poor living conditions, and potential danger. Military service put them under moral obligations to a secular government and gave that government the power to order them to kill.[10] Neither situation was acceptable to Witnesses. The passport issue had challenged Witnesses, uncertain about what their faith required of them. Military service was a different matter. The Society had taken a clear stance on the matter and proclaimed it loudly in its publications. Its previous president, Joseph Franklin Rutherford, had been imprisoned under the Espionage Act in the United States for his vocal opposition to military service during World War I.[11] Society magazines recounted how European Witnesses risked their lives to uphold "Christian neutrality" in World War II. The *Watchtower* magazine told its readers, "It is far better to die faithful to God and because of faithfulness and receive at the hands of the Lord everlasting life than to compromise with any part of Satan's organization and suffer everlasting destruction."[12] This rhetoric instructed Witnesses to be ready to face death rather than sacrifice their salvation.

This stance did not make the Witnesses pacifists. The Society held that only warfare directed by God could be justified as righteous. The same *Watchtower* article used all caps to make this point absolutely clear: "The covenant people of God are not pacifists, even as God and Christ are not pacifists. God's covenant people are authorized to defend themselves against those who fight against the THEOCRATIC GOVERNMENT."[13] A Society memo circulated among Soviet Witnesses after the war reiterated this view. It advised Witnesses that they were, in fact, soldiers for Christ. Their armour was their Christian character, and it would protect them in the battle against Satan. Even if the men of Bila Tserkva had not read these exact publications, they would surely have gotten the message that true Christians do not take up arms for a secular government. Throughout the war, Witnesses faced arrest and imprisonment for this stance across Europe, including in Transcarpathia and elsewhere in Ukraine.[14]

To remain in good standing with their faith community, Witnesses knew they could not serve in the Soviet Army. The problem of draft-dodging Witnesses was acute enough to come to the attention of district party officials by late 1946. Officials complained that the draft rolls in Bila Tserkva and two other nearby villages were in "poor condition." In Bila Tserkva and the village of Serednie Vodiane, where Nutsu Guzo resided, forty-seven Witnesses had refused to register. The following spring, the party obligated local officials, the draft office, and law enforcement to coordinate "all necessary measures" to get these men on the books. More ominously, it called on the prosecutor's office to immediately take "the harshest possible measures" against men who continued to avoid service.[15]

These early party records refer to "penitent" individuals rather than the more formal "Jehovah's Witnesses" or the Soviet-favoured "Jehovists." The word choice suggests that Transcarpathian officials initially saw the Witnesses through the eyes of local informants who would have used this term when speaking about the faith in Romanian. They may not have immediately drawn connections between the "penitent" individuals and the "Jehovists" already being investigated and arrested elsewhere in Ukraine. At least in 1947, all they knew was that religious believers in the borderlands were a problem for an orderly military enlistment.

This was not the first time that the local men had faced demands to join the ranks. Before the arrival of Soviet power, other states had attempted to call up the men. During World War II, the army in Hungary had ordered Dmitry Bokoch to report for service but then rejected him due to poor hearing.[16] Now in his mid-forties, he could hardly have been of much value to any army. His younger brother, Vasily, served in the Czechoslovak army before the war began, and before his conversion to the Witnesses. He did not serve in World War II, as by that time, he had become a Jehovah's Witness.[17] In the postwar period, Dmitry was likely more concerned about his teenage son, Mikhail, than himself. Now approaching middle age, Dmitry had less to offer the Soviet Army. His son, on the other hand, was just a few years from adulthood.

The rest of the men had similar stories. Nutsu Guzo and Ivan Ona were both in their late thirties by World War II; neither man served in any army in the conflict.[18] Vasily Marinchan served in the Czechoslovak army before the war. Under interrogation, he claimed to have avoided service in the Hungarian army for religious reasons; at trial he acknowledged that he had briefly been enlisted but was discharged for medical reasons.[19] Ivan Nan's lack of any Czechoslovak service is rather unusual. He made no mention of any condition that would have kept him out of the military.[20]

Alone among the men, Dmitry Marinchan left home in World War II. Like his brother, he completed his two years of required service in the Czechoslovak army in the interwar period.[21] During occupation, he entered the Hungarian army as a private in spring 1942. After a brief training period, he joined the infantry, was issued a rifle, and sent marching east. He lasted only six days in combat against the Red Army. A serious wound to his right leg ended his military career.[22] The army evacuated him to a military hospital in Budapest. Then they sent him home. Until Hungary retreated from Transcarpathia, Dmitry continued to receive disability payments from the Hungarian government for his wartime service.[23]

Ironically, their conscientious objection largely spared the other men from questions about what they did during the war. Their involvement in the Czechoslovak army occurred in peacetime and did not require them to engage in combat against the Red Army. The Soviet state was not concerned that the men had not met their obligations to Hungary. Dmitry, in contrast, faced far more scrutiny of his wartime actions. Take note of this particular line of questioning from the second of two interrogations on this subject:

> Q: What was your military rank?
> A: I was a soldier.
> Q: What did you have as a weapon?
> A: I was armed with a rifle.
> Q: Continue your statement.
> A: Once we arrived at the front line of the Soviet-German front, our unit was thrown into battle against the Soviet army. But on the sixth day of combat I was wounded and sent for treatment to a military hospital in Budapest.
> Q: On what part of the front did you engage in combat against the Soviet army?
> A: I don't know.
> Q: What other residents of Bila Tserkva or Rakhiv district served with you in the Magyar [Hungarian] army?
> A: I don't know.[24]

Dmitry's professed ignorance is somewhat suspect. He could hardly have forgotten the other young men from his own village who, like him, had been thrown unwillingly into a global conflict with minimal training. Nor could his memory have failed him on the location. Dmitry's silence was calculated to obscure details as much as possible.

The Soviet state had established an impossible standard for Dmitry and other men in the borderlands. They were required to demonstrate loyalty to a state before they had any knowledge that they would become its citizens. Dmitry had served in the Hungarian army at a time when the village belonged to Hungary. If he had had a choice in the matter, he would not have served at all. Now, four years later, he stood accused of having betrayed his not-yet-motherland in war. The formal indictment in the case put this accusation in writing. Dmitry, the state alleged, "took part in military actions against the Soviet Army."[25] From the state's perspective, Dmitry was now refusing to do for the Soviet Army what he had done for the Hungarian army. It was a no-win situation.

For the rest of the men, their refusal to serve at all was still a problem, even if they avoided tough questions about wartime activities. The act of registering for military service required men to obtain a military service card. As with the passport question, the men refused to obtain this particular document because it was issued by the Soviet state. Also like the passport, this document could be requested by local authorities at any time. The men could have avoided conflict by simply applying for the document since it was unlikely they would ever be drafted. The Soviet state was not in dire need of married middle-aged men to fight in peacetime, but it did demand that they follow the same rules as everyone else. By not going through the motions of compliance, the men were highly vulnerable to arrest.

All the men attempted to explain their position to interrogators. Vasily Bokoch told his interrogator that his religious views would not allow him to accept military documents or service. The state recorded this statement as follows: "As a Jehovist who follows the teachings of Jehovah God, I refuse to register for military service, accept a military service card, or, in the event of conscription, to take up arms and defend the USSR against invasion."[26] The texture of this remark betrays at least some reformulation of Bokoch's words by the investigator. We can hear the collision of secular and sacred language, as "Jehovah God," a term of reverence, comes in contact with the harsh Soviet-speak of "Jehovist." It is equally certain that Bokoch did not say "Jehovist" as it is that the interrogator did not say "Jehovah God." Yet both appear in a single sentence in this transcript.

All the men voiced similar concerns. From the nearly identical wording, we get a sense of what mattered to investigators and the state. As with Bokoch's remarks, these statements were not how the men themselves would have explained how their faith informed their interactions with the state. Rather, the interrogator repackaged the men's theological reservations into something more understandable to the state. In particular, it is unlikely that any of the men volunteered their unwillingness to defend their country in the case of attack. More likely, the interrogator prompted this question because this was important to him and his investigation. This does not mean that the men's recorded answers do not reflect their beliefs. The men did refuse to serve in the Soviet Army. They did not want to take even the basic step of registering for the draft because it required too much interaction with the Soviet government. If war had broken out, they would not have taken up arms and defended the state. The men clearly conveyed this position under questioning from interrogators. The official case file reflects a narrative written by the state as it translated Witness beliefs into the language of Soviet power. In doing so, "Christian neutrality" became treason.

Ultimately, the seven men were not of great value to the Soviet Army. At least two had serious health concerns. All were rather old for military service. The Soviet Union may have wanted the men to register, but absent a war, it had no intention of enlisting them. Why then did the state invest resources into this matter? The answer is that the state felt that it could not afford for a small minority to persuade the rest of the population to follow their example. The men belonged to the pre-war generation, born and raised outside Soviet norms. The state reached out to them, but its chief concern lay with the next generation. It was imperative that they learn Soviet values and not be corrupted by opponents of the new order. Thus, investigators worried far more about what the men told others than what they themselves believed. The men readily admitted that they refused to carry Soviet documents. They also acknowledged that they did not accept passports or military service cards. What investigators wanted to know was how much had the men shared these views with their neighbours. This was more difficult to establish. On a practical level, so-called neutrality was a matter of conscience among fellow Witnesses. As such, this matter was likely discussed in some detail within the community of adherents in the village. A person who had already accepted the basic tenets of the faith and had begun to prepare for baptism would have been exposed to this information as well. Non-baptized individuals were not held to the same standards, and evangelizing chats with neighbours would rarely have broached such matters.

Upon arrest, the men were not eager to divulge such details about faith practices. They quickly recognized that their fates had already been decided. An arrest would lead to conviction and then to a labour camp. There was no route back home. But they were not the only Witnesses in the village, or in the district. To protect those still at large, the men largely avoided questions that implicated others. This meant that the state had to rely on agitators to access what Witnesses said about military service. It is worth noting that among the informants during the investigation, only two men, the school principal and the district party official, were identified as having participated as soldiers in World War II. The latter was also the only informant not native to the region. He had fought as a captain in the Red Army, earning four medals and a Red Star for his service.[27] The rest of the agitators, despite many of them being of prime military age during the war, spent the conflict at home in Bila Tserkva or its neighbouring villages. Dmitry Marinchan's military record was the exception rather than the rule in

Bila Tserkva.

Local agitator Ivan Dan, who had offered much information on the passport question, described the difficulties the Witnesses posed to the local draft office, which had to repeatedly issue summons for young Witness men to appear and obtain military service cards. When the draft office appealed to agitators to assist them in this effort, Dan ventured out to make contact with the recalcitrant parties. His neighbour was one of the holdouts. When Dan arrived at the home, he informed the man that he would need to travel to the district centre in Rakhiv to resolve the matter. The man disagreed with this assessment. He told Dan, "I do not need a passport or a military service card. Jehovah God has issued me documents; I will never accept any others."[28]

Other agitators gave similar accounts of how Witnesses stubbornly refused to listen to reason on this matter. One agitator, Yury Fonduriak, was a rare local member of the Komsomol, the Communist Party organization for teenagers and young adults. His Komsomol affiliation and full eight years of education made him especially valuable to the Soviet state, and they earned him the position of chair of the neighbouring village soviet in Serednie Vodiane. In 1949 he was only twenty-six years old and had already held this title for at least a year. He recounted for the investigator how Nutsu Guzo had brought some corn to the local mill, where Fonduriak worked in early 1948. Rather than discuss more secular matters of concern to the state, Guzo took the opportunity to encourage Fonduriak to consider his own salvation, encouraging him to give some thought to joining the "most just faith on earth." Fonduriak felt the need to inform the interrogator that he did not take Guzo's advice. That fall, as part of his official responsibilities, Fonduriak repeatedly summoned Guzo to his office to get a service card, but to no avail; Guzo did not appear.[29]

For the Witnesses, the passport and military service question were identical: both required them to formally recognize Soviet authority. The actual military was a more abstract danger to their salvation than a printed card with their signature on it. That said, this priority changed along with the gradual decision to accept passports by the mid-1950s. The newfound willingness to sign documents meant that men no longer had any reason to refuse to register for the draft. As long as they did not serve, the Society reassured Witnesses that signing the draft card posed no threat to their conscience. This more moderate stance came with concrete benefits. Rather than face immediate fines or imprisonment for not having the proper papers, young men could delay the inevitable conflict with the state for at least a few more years. Once their draft notice finally arrived, they could also seek exemptions for health reasons, keeping some from having to serve time in prison or in the military. Overall, by carrying with them the documents necessary for lawful citizens, they shielded themselves from some of the regular agitation and harassment from local officials.

Even so, throughout the Soviet Union, military service was the most common reason for Witnesses to suffer arrest and imprisonment. In the case of Dmitry Bokoch, it led to the arrest of his son, Mikhail, just a few years after his own imprisonment. By the time Mikhail entered draft age, he had dropped out of school, which allowed to him to avoid pre-enlistment classes to prepare him for service. Even so, he was already on the state's radar. While many young men successfully avoided service in the Soviet Army, Mikhail was not so lucky. His enlistment order arrived three years after his father's arrest. When summoned to report to the draft board for the biannual conscription, he and several other young Witness men from the village refused; they stayed home instead. Noting the absence of these youth from the call-up, the village soviet demanded that they explain themselves. Although they had not appeared before the draft board, the men did walk down to the village soviet to discuss the matter. The school principal, Alexander Pelladi, who had informed on Mikhail's father, was present at this meeting. He later reported to the state how one of the young men (not Mikhail) had justified himself before the village officials. The man told them, "I am a Jehovah's Witness and I only follow his laws. Therefore, I will not serve in the Soviet Army even if they imprison me for twenty-five years." The other men agreed; the state did not.[30] Shortly thereafter, the men were arrested. Rather than join the Soviet Army, they headed off to labour camps to serve their sentences.[31]

This feature of Sovietization continued to threaten young men until the collapse of the Soviet Union. This was in part because, unlike the documents issue, military service represented a deeply held position by Witnesses in all countries.[32] Indeed, it remains an issue that brings Witnesses into conflict with modern states around the world. According to both the Society and the United Nations, Witnesses make up the vast majority of conscientious objectors in the world in the twenty-first century. Even in Russia today, where Witness men struggled for years for the right to alternative service, what progress was made in the two post-Soviet decades has recently come under renewed threat.[33]

Perhaps the best example of the global situation comes from South Korea, where hundreds of Witnesses faced imprisonment every year for decades over the military service issue. One South Korean Witness, Kim Min-hwan, who served time as a young man, reflected that it was not possible for him to imagine a scenario that would have allowed him to avoid conflict and remain in good standing with his faith. He told reporters, "I was predestined to become a convict because I believed in the creator." These words could have come from any one of the Bila Tserkva men or their sons. Likewise, the men's neighbours were not unique in voicing animosity toward those members of their community who refused to do their patriotic duty, even if they had no personal enthusiasm for military service either. Indeed, that military service was viewed in negative terms made citizens all the more demanding that others not be allowed to avoid it. Again, the South Korean example is instructive. One Witness there noted that "South Korean men don't want to serve in the military if they have a choice, so they get angry if others don't while they have to." Another recalled how when he was imprisoned, even his fellow inmates scorned him as a traitor.[34] The Bila Tserkva agitators, many of them men of draft age, would have related to this sense of a shared burden. In part for this reason, Witnesses both in and far outside Transcarpathia have faced accusations of disloyalty not only from the state but also from society at large.

The example of South Korea is a cautionary one against seeing the Soviet experience as unique. Sovietization was a state-building project. In requiring identity papers and military service, the Soviet Union made demands similar to those of other modern states, including ones with more democratic political systems. In turn, Soviet citizens asked that the state hold everyone to the same standards. Military service was a burden, and citizens wanted reassurance that if they had to shoulder this weight, so, too, would their neighbours. Witnesses' refusal to abide by both state and societal expectations brought them into repeated conflict. While other citizens may have flouted the new border expectations and dodged the draft, the Witnesses' more direct challenge to Soviet norms made them far more vulnerable to state repression.

4

The Ballot Box

While Bila Tserkva residents had no voice in the annexation of their village, the Soviet state promised them that their voices would be heard in the new system through other means. At the local level, this meant the introduction of the "soviet" as the cornerstone of representative government. The term "soviet" simply means council. Its official functions were not entirely dissimilar from the duties of town and city councils across the United States. Each population centre in the Soviet Union had its own soviet that made decisions about governance, infrastructure, and a host of other matters that influenced daily life. Local residents elected the "deputies" who served on the soviet from among the men and women of their communities. Each soviet had a chair to oversee the council.

When village soviets were first introduced after the October Revolution, they struggled to win over the support of the local population. With few communists in rural areas, the state had a hard time finding committed allies in the countryside. Party officials griped that villagers showed no interest in attending meetings or getting involved in Soviet activities. As one historian notes, "simply finding people to work in village soviets, with their tiny budgets, could be extraordinarily difficult." In some locales, no one wanted to serve as chair, a rather thankless job. The position was so unpopular in one village that officials agreed to a rather unorthodox solution: they decided that whoever showed up late for the next session would automatically become chair.[1]

The situation in the rural postwar borderlands was rather similar. Like many Soviet villages in the 1920s, Bila Tserkva appears to have had no Communist Party members. This meant that the village soviet would also have no communists as delegates. Instead, local ballots included a bloc of non-party candidates. These were the most promising activists from among the local population. They would make decisions for their community. Of course, Bila Tserkva residents did vote for party members when they cast ballots for the more powerful soviets at the district, region, and all-union level, and when they selected judges to represent them on the newly established people's courts. In daily affairs, however, their communities were represented by their fellow residents. Like them, these local delegates spoke Romanian, farmed for a living, and had lived most of their lives outside the Soviet system. In this regard, Sovietization was constrained by the realities of the available electorate, which included no industrial workers. Nevertheless, the state invested resources in selecting the best possible options from the shallow pool of candidates.

The Soviet state carefully stage-managed not only the candidates but also the elections themselves. When residents went to vote, they did not encounter competition for seats. Instead, they were asked to trust that the state had already selected the most qualified individuals. Even though no alternative existed to the official bloc of acceptable candidates, it was important that citizens cast their ballots to show their support. The state devoted major resources to crafting a public image of these elections as democracy in action. Elections legitimized the takeover of the region and demonstrated the popularity of the new system. Participating in socialist democracy was a performative affair. Citizens exercised their rights by casting votes for the new government. Jan Gross, writing about elections in occupied Poland in 1939, offers an even darker interpretation. By casting ballots, new citizens "lost their innocence" and became "tainted" by their own "complicity" in the Soviet takeover. He argues that this is precisely what the Soviet state wanted out of its elections. Whether Transcarpathians saw themselves in this light or experienced any "residual feeling of shame" after casting their ballots is impossible to know. Ultimately, the state cared less about private thoughts than about public performance.[2]

Above all, endorsement of the Soviet system meant support for its leader, Joseph Stalin. As General Secretary of the Communist Party of the Soviet Union, Stalin oversaw the implementation of Soviet power in the western borderlands and the imposition of party orthodoxy over the people who lived in these territories. While local citizens did not literally vote Stalin into power, their votes in elections were publicly trumpeted as affirmations of support for him. In postwar Kyiv, ballot boxes were placed directly under giant portraits of Stalin, "effectively turning the moment of depositing the ballot in the box into a kind of symbolic offering to Stalin."[3] The polling place was just one site where local residents would have encountered Stalin. His image was everywhere in postwar life, from newspapers to portraits and posters in public buildings and schools. Later Communist Party leaders would decry the "cult of personality" that existed around Stalin. During Stalin's lifetime, however, there was no such critique. To support Soviet power and communism was to support Stalin.[4]

Newspapers played a major role in selling elections and Stalin himself to the local population. Historian Jeffrey Brooks describes the public selling of Stalin in the postwar period as a bit of bad theatre: "In conformance with public rituals, the players in Soviet public life were a little like a theatrical company of great reputation, compelled to enact a flawed drama repeatedly before a half-empty house." In the year of the investigation, this excessive praise reached new heights as Stalin approached his birthday that December. Workers wrote to newspapers across the Soviet Union to share how they dedicated their labour in honour of Stalin and to thank him for his beneficence.[5] As a reflection of Stalin's wise leadership, every election proved a smashing success and a triumph of Soviet power. Election coverage reflected this reality. Front-page stories declared that an estimated 99.99 per cent of residents cast votes in the village soviet elections in Transcarpathia. The result was a "shining victory for the Stalin bloc." The overwhelming approval by residents of the bloc of communist and non-party deputies demonstrated "the great strength of the moral-political unity of the workers."[6]

The state expected every single citizen to do their civic duty and participate in the electoral process. On the eve of elections in January 1949, the local papers called on workers to show their "boundless love for the Soviet homeland and the great party of Lenin and Stalin." By casting ballots, workers could "demonstrate their love and loyalty to their leader and teacher, the great Stalin."[7] Although voting was ostensibly voluntary, citizens found it nearly impossible to avoid the relentless pressure to participate from local activists and their workplace. In Bila Tserkva, this message would have been conveyed primarily through appointed agitators who spread the word among their neighbours.

Those who assumed positions of power in this new system worked hard to demonstrate that they deserved the party-state's trust. In a public letter addressed to Stalin and published in the newspaper, newly elected deputies from Rakhiv district extolled their joyful embrace of the new political system. They praised Stalin as "our great leader of the Bolshevik Party and the Soviet people, our beloved teacher, father, and friend," and informed him that they would prove themselves worthy of their new responsibilities:

> The election campaign for the soviets of workers' deputies has rallied the workers of our region closer together, just as it has the entire Soviet people, around the Communist Party of Bolsheviks, around you, the inspiration and organizer of the Soviet people's struggle for communism.
>
> Following your example, Joseph Vissarionovich [Stalin], that every genuine soviet official should faithfully and truthfully serve the people, that public service is the highest goal, we, the elected representatives of the people, assure you that we will put all our energies and knowledge into fulfilling the task before us: the building of communism.

Rakhiv's elected officials promised Stalin that they would "keep their word" to devote themselves fully to their new homeland.[8] Employing similar language, the voters also sent messages directly to Stalin through their ballots. The district reprinted some of these patriotic sentiments in the newspaper. Voters scribbled, "I am voting for our homeland, for comrade Stalin!" Others wrote in the margins, "Long live our leader and teacher, comrade Stalin!"[9] At least in the public realm, Transcarpathians were expected to see Stalin as *their* leader and the Soviet Union as *their* homeland.

Postwar elections all proclaimed near universal participation and near unanimous approval of party-approved candidates. The reality was more mixed. We know this because the Soviet state carefully collected information on dissenting views, especially around election time, relying on networks of informants to report back the general tone of public opinion. These reports tell us what Soviet citizens may have privately said but not publicly proclaimed. Informants recorded a whole range of rumours and reservations about the elections. Some citizens dismissed them as an elaborate sham. With only one candidate per position, what was the point? Others wondered if the voter lists were a nefarious plot to identify people for arrest or deportation. Some just did not care much about elections when there were more immediate concerns, such as food shortages on the collective farms. While those who uttered such sentiments probably still went to the polls, these informant reports reveal that sky-high voting rates obscured more ambivalent attitudes about Soviet "democracy."[10]

For districts such as Rakhiv, opposition to elections was a much bigger problem due to its sizable population of Witnesses, who do not vote. This position is universal among Witnesses in both democratic and non-democratic countries. Baptized members are expected to remain neutral in political affairs. Just as they refuse to serve in the military, Witnesses interpret the act of casting a vote as an endorsement of secular government.

The Soviet state knew that Witnesses would be a problem for elections rather quickly after annexation. This information came from the newly formed Council for Religious Cult Affairs, created after the Soviet state made wartime concessions to religious communities that allowed a small number of religious organizations to carve out a legal existence.[11] Keeping tabs on these organizations was the central task of the council. It had to make sure that these communities stayed within the carefully defined boundaries of permissible religious worship.[12] To do so, the council operated overworked and understaffed branch offices in every region of the Soviet Union. Many local officials saw the new bureaucracy as irrelevant and unworthy of respect or support. In the eastern Ukrainian region of Kirovohrad, the commissioner asked to be relieved of his duties, citing "the unbearable conditions" of his job. In previous months he had endured numerous indignities. Local officials pressured him to abandon his one-room office to make way for a barber shop for themselves. When he refused to leave, they simply picked up all his furniture and removed it to a drafty storage room. Writing his complaint letter to his superiors, he pleaded that surely his Red Army service and Communist Party membership ought to afford him "better treatment worthy of a Bolshevik." Other commissioners cited similarly squalid office allotments.[13] Yet despite their limited resources, commissioners amassed an enormous amount of information on legally sanctioned religious life. The council also served a vital second purpose as a knowledge centre for underground religious activities that did not have state sanction. Ironically, by denying legal status to so many religious communities, the state made its own efforts to document religious life all the more difficult. It had less leverage with underground religious believers and less access to their services and clergy.

After annexation, the council opened an office in Transcarpathia and appointed a commissioner. Despite its heavy burden and modest financial support, the council began the difficult work of collecting information about the large number of unregistered religious communities. It relayed this data among the other Ukrainian branch offices and forwarded it to the local soviets and police. Thus, it was the council that alerted others about the potential conflict between Witnesses and elections. It had this information by late 1946, in time for the upcoming elections that December. In a memo sent from its central office to its Ukrainian branch offices, the council informed commissioners that Witnesses were likely to boycott the elections.

The council indicated that the Witnesses' refusal to vote was rooted in a clear hostility to Soviet power. It suggested that Witnesses had a political agenda rather than a sincere set of religious beliefs. The council alleged that Witnesses were now engaged in a campaign of counter-revolutionary agitation with the goal of subverting the electoral process. This was a serious accusation. A government agency had directly identified Witnesses as a specific threat to postwar elections in the borderlands. This allegation had more severe consequences than the question of passports or military service cards, both of which constituted criminal acts of a lesser order. By comparison, counter-revolutionary agitation was a state crime, punishable by twenty-five years' imprisonment and loss of property. Millions of Soviet citizens had already been convicted of this crime and sentenced to toil under horrific conditions in the Gulag.

The memo was revealing for another reason: the council already knew quite a bit about Witnesses in and around Rakhiv district. Along with its general warning to commissioners, the central office provided a list of several major Witness clusters. One was in the neighbouring town of Solotvyno. A second was in Hrushovo, a village just twenty miles farther west. A third hot spot was Bila Tserkva. The central office acknowledged its information was incomplete. For both Solotvyno and Hrushovo, the state provided the name of an individual it believed to be the leader of the community. In Bila Tserkva and one other village in the region, the state was unable to make this determination.[14]

The central office does not indicate where it got its initial information about population clusters and elders. The files of the regional council contain a nearly identical report from around this same time, which dealt with the issue of religious believers boycotting elections, but it cast a wider net. In addition to Witnesses, it identified Adventists and other "sectarians" as a potential problem. "The sectarian underground is rearing its head," the report declared, and it is hostile to Soviet power. Like the central office, it acknowledged "imprecise information."[15] The missing names were clearly an additional reason for the communications between the branch and central offices. In the final lines of its memo, the latter asked that any additional information be forwarded to state security so that it could take appropriate measures.[16]

Yet neither the regional commissioner nor the central office knew who was in charge of the Witness community in Bila Tserkva. Someone, likely within the secret police, had given the council names and locations of adherents in the region, but the commissioner and his staff knew too little about the Witnesses to do much with this information. The men who occupied these positions were not well versed in religious affairs and would have had a hard time just distinguishing a Witness from an Adventist. They certainly did not understand that Witnesses have no formal clergy. In fact, the organization is run at the local level by elders.[17]

Soviet officials were ignorant about much in the borderlands, and this knowledge gap extended to religion. This was particularly so for relatively novel religious communities in the Soviet Union. Witnesses were not present, at least not in any significant numbers, within the pre-war Soviet borders.[18] As such, the state had no road map on how to deal with them. This was a fundamentally new problem, created as a result of Soviet territorial expansion along its western borders. As a general rule, the state reacted more harshly to religious minorities than it did to the Russian Orthodox community in the borderlands. Greek Catholics were singled out for special persecution. Also known as Uniates, Greek Catholics recognize the authority of the Roman Catholic Church and the Pope, but their liturgies and rituals conform to Orthodox practices.[19] One 1950 Soviet pamphlet labelled Greek Catholics "major agents of worldwide reaction" and their clergy "wolves in sheep's clothing." Its author noted that while the Russian Orthodox Church had supported the Soviet war effort and annexation, Greek Catholics took their marching orders from the Vatican.[20] The postwar period was one of relative calm for Russian Orthodoxy, but this respite came at the expense of other faiths, which were seen as a greater threat to order.[21] This was certainly true of the Witnesses, but other religious communities were targets as well.

State propaganda did little to nothing to shine a light on religious minorities. On the contrary, it promoted the notion that everything one needed to know about religion could be learned from reading Marxist-Leninist theory. If Soviet officials wanted to understand the religious situation in their district, they were told to brush up on Lenin's collected works. The council itself took this approach. In a 1947 memo, the chief commissioner encouraged his staff to study more theory. He even included a recommended reading list of Marxist classics. The "minimum" required reading consisted of texts by Stalin, Marx, and Lenin. The official textbook history of the Soviet Union, the so-called Short Course, which Stalin himself had personally edited, also came highly recommended.[22] The list included page numbers to save officials from skimming the entire text for mentions of religion. A "further reading" list advised yet more works by Marx, Lenin, and Stalin. Even the specialized section on "sectarianism" was hopelessly narrow and theoretical. Of the six works listed in this section, four were about Tolstoy, and three of these works were written by Lenin.[23]

There were no Tolstoyans in Bila Tserkva. There were few Tolstoyans anywhere in the Soviet Union by 1947. A careful review of Lenin's writings about them would have not helped officials in Transcarpathia. They needed accurate information about the real, existing religious communities in their villages, but this information was not forthcoming in the late 1940s. Communication with the central state about local religious life was particularly spotty in Bila Tserkva. While nearly every village in Rakhiv district provided forms to the council about registered churches, synagogues, and prayer houses, Bila Tserkva did not.[24] When the investigation opened in 1949, the state remained unclear about the structure in the congregation. Local informants dutifully named the arrested men but also many others in the village. In sum, elections put the Bila Tserkva Witnesses on the state's radar, but without more information the state could not immediately act to respond to this threat.

As it turned out, the state's early concerns about an election boycott were well founded. When the state did eventually investigate, informants repeatedly turned to this issue in condemning their neighbours. As it turned out, none of the arrested men voted. Not only did the men not cast ballots, they were also vocally opposed to the elections. Agitators provided investigators with a litany of failed efforts to bring their neighbours to the polls.

They also painted a detailed portrait of how electioneering worked (and, to the great concern of the state, sometimes did not) in the Soviet Union. Soviet electioneering bears little resemblance to the door-to-door campaigning with which so many Americans are familiar. Agitators exhausted only minimal effort in singing the praises of specific candidates. Nor did local candidates themselves make the rounds, kissing babies, shaking hands, and politely asking for people's votes on election day. Given that political parties did not exist and competition was non-existent, Soviet citizens never wondered who would win if they did not cast a ballot. Even so, aspects of Soviet electioneering might not be quite so foreign to Americans in swing states: the unwelcome knocks at the door, the eager sales pitches by young people, the repetitious visits, and the repeated reminders to go to the polls and do one's civic duty.

During election season, a villager could expect at least one visit from a local agitator. Assuming the villager had no objections and voiced a clear intent to vote, the campaigning may have ended there. In Bila Tserkva, agitators were far too precious a commodity to spend most of their time preaching to the choir. On the day of the election, the villager would get a return visit to ensure they had actually gone to the polling station and cast a ballot. This was especially critical for individuals who seemed less than fully committed or reliable. Theodore H. Friedgut describes the agitator's relationship to his assigned voters as rather dependent on their goodwill:

> The agitators on their part are anxious to see "their" voters at the polls. They cannot go off duty until the last person on their list has been accounted for. They therefore become impatient with those who have not voted by mid-morning and begin to knock on doors, pleading, "Come and vote. I too have a home and a family like you, and want to spend the day with them" ... The general opinion is that if you are a decent fellow, you vote early and free the agitator, incidentally saving yourself increasingly frequent and importunate visits as the day wears on.[25]

Bila Tserkva agitators quickly learned to focus their efforts on their Witness neighbours, who received most of these increasingly frequent visits on election day. The agitators' success hinged on their ability to bring these religious believers to the polls. Agitator Yury Kogut was assigned to this task in Bila Tserkva. He was twenty-four years old, and with eight years of schooling and a job in a nearby village, a bit more worldly than some of his neighbours. He recounted one particular encounter with Witnesses during his electioneering work.

> On 18 January 1949, I was an agitator for the elections to the People's Court. Agitator Vasily Iurevich Stan and I went to the home of Vasily and Dmitry Marinchan and Nutsu Dan to explain to them the significance of the current electoral campaign and to encourage them to vote.
>
> Vasily and Dmitry Marinchan, and Nutsu Dan responded to our explanations about the need to take part in the People's Court elections and the significance of elections by stating that they had already voted for their god and would not vote for anyone else, as this would go against their laws.
>
> All of our attempts to explain the necessity of taking part in the vote were met with the answer that they (categorically) will not vote: "Do with us what you like, but we will not vote." When I told them that I would stop by their home again, they declared, "You can visit us one thousand times, but we will not vote." On 30 January 1949, none of the men took part in the election.[26]

Kogut did not visit them one thousand times. It seems his first attempt to even broach the subject occurred less than two weeks before the election itself. His efforts, such as they were, did not prove effective. Agitators such as Kogut were eager to prove to investigators that they had done their duty and that only the most wilful resistance had prevented electoral success in the village. Their testimonials stressed the difficulty of their task.

In theory, the small, rural location of Bila Tserkva should have made it easy to ensure perfect attendance at the polling station. Everyone knew where their Witness neighbours lived, and agitators had already marked them as unreliable voters. The village itself offered few spots for disinclined citizens to hide. Assigned agitators were supposed to track them down at home and bring them to the polls. In light of this fact, many local Witnesses simply left town, likely choosing any number of alternative routes through fields and forests. Vasily Stan, the collective farm worker who accompanied Kogut on his trip to the Marinchans, told investigators that the brothers left the village on election day. They returned only after voting had ended. Stan also corroborated Kogut's version of events at the Marinchan home. In his retelling, the men affirmed, "We voted for our god long ago and are not going to vote for anyone else. Do what you want with us, but we will not serve two masters. Service to our god comes first."

Stan added an additional detail to this conversation. He claimed the men also told the agitators, "You have your work, and we have ours. We do not need your work at all."[27] It is impossible to know if the men did make such a statement, but it fits with the general tenor of their refusal. The Bila Tserkva Witnesses did not intend to legitimize the Soviet system by participating in the selection of its leaders. The phrasing here suggests that the men understood the goals of the Soviet state but saw them as separate and even incompatible with the demands of their faith. Of course, it is also possible that Stan inserted this language to emphasize the stubbornness of the men and the impossibility that any effort he exerted would have brought them to the polls. If the men did not show up to vote, it was through no fault of the agitators.

Other informants echoed Kogut and Stan. Agitator Ivan Dan painted a picture of the Witnesses as long-time opponents of elections. He told the interrogator that not a single Witness in the village voted in any election. As a result of this boycott, elections had "repeatedly failed" over the past three years.[28] When agitators asked Witnesses why they refused to vote, they often recited the same phrase that Stan referenced in his statement: "we cannot serve two masters." Maria Lumei, a youth activist, and Nutsu Tsiple, a young collective farm worker, both recalled hearing these words. So did others in the village.[29] The phrase does not originate with Witnesses. It refers to a biblical parable, in which Jesus Christ tells his disciples: "No one can slave for two masters; for either he will hate the one and love the other, or he will stick to the one and despise the other. You cannot slave for God and for Riches."[30] Although many agitators mentioned the phrase, none explained it. It is not an obscure passage in the Bible, so it is possible that its origins were considered common knowledge. Alternatively, the villagers may have simply taken it at face value as a literal explanation of Witnesses' views on church and state. Regardless, the Witnesses appear to have used this verse to clarify their position to their neighbours.

Overall, the agitators' descriptions of such interactions are consistent with how Witnesses worldwide have reacted to pressure from state authorities to cast ballots. The story of Nasho Dori is a useful comparison in this regard. In the pages of the *Watchtower* magazine, he recounted how he handled the 1946 elections in his village in Albania, also under communist rule in the postwar period:

> Election day arrived, and government delegates came to our house. They began calmly, "Oh, let's have a cup of coffee and talk. Do you know what today is?"
> "Yes, today elections are being held," I answered.
> "You'd better hurry, or you'll be late," one officer said.
> "No, I don't plan to go. Our vote is for Jehovah," I replied.
> "All right, then come and vote for the opposition."
> I explained that Jehovah's Witnesses are absolutely neutral. When our position became well-known, greater pressure was exerted upon us.[31]

The situation is virtually identical to what the agitators of Bila Tserkva recounted: the agitator, the home visit, the encouragement to vote, the refusal, and the reference to neutrality. This version, however, is from a Witness himself, rather than an agent of the state.

Encounters between agitators and Witnesses had one clear outcome. Both sides had a chance to hear each other's views and defend their own. The state ultimately concluded that the arrested men had conducted anti-Soviet agitation against elections, but the case file suggests that both sides agitated to each other and both without much success. In this regard, agitation had the unintended outcome of provoking difficult conversations about Sovietization with skeptical villagers. The situation was deemed serious enough to warrant a more interventionist approach by officials outside Bila Tserkva. It was this matter, among others, that brought Ivan Baider, the district party official, to the village. Baider concluded from his involvement that pressure from the "Jehovist" men had undermined the elections. In his testimonial to investigators, he claimed to have visited in early 1949 at least some of the men, who told him that they would not vote because Jehovah God forbade them.[32]

While Witnesses may not have welcomed the intense political scrutiny of their voting practices, it did lead to opportunities for evangelism. For agitators, knocking on doors was a tedious but necessary component of integrating themselves within the new social and political order. For Witnesses, knocking on doors was a religious mandate and a sign of faith. Dmitry Marinchan's daughter recalled that the men "had all been happy that they could serve God" through their imprisonment. Her father told his children, "If we had not been sent out there [to the Gulag], who else would have evangelized so far out?" The life was hard, she noted. Still the call to evangelism gave their suffering a sense of purpose.[33] This mirrors the common view of evangelism by Witnesses worldwide, then and now. All Witnesses engage in door-to-door ministry for this reason. When the Society issues its annual membership reports, it counts individuals only if they have been active in evangelism over the past year. While in recent years, Witnesses have broadened their ministry to include street stands, a website, and other tools, the door-to-door approach remains an essential component of their identity.[34] A 2006 PBS documentary on Witnesses was simply titled *Knocking*.[35]

In this instance, Witnesses were the ones answering the door, but still, agitation unintentionally opened up space for evangelism. Villager Mikhail Ona recalled this discussion with one Witness:

> On 2 April 1949, near the village soviet in the village of Velykyi Bychkiv, I met with the active sectarian-Jehovist Vasily Iurevich Ona. In the course of this conversation, he told me, "We will soon have a new world. If you are going to treat people poorly, you will perish under the new authority of Jehovah God." I asked V. Iu. Ona to explain why he thought that the world would change soon. Ona responded, "Jehovah God is stronger than Soviet power. So he is going to establish his own authority on earth soon and defeat Soviet power."[36]

Obviously this explanation did not win over Ona to Witness theology. Even so, it suggests that villagers were exposed to alternative visions of the world and that Soviet officials had no monopoly on how individual citizens interpreted Soviet power. Agitators knew better than most residents that not everyone bought into the new Soviet political vision. At least some of these individuals thought the Soviet system might be rather temporary and felt compelled to share this view with others.

The year after the men were arrested, the villagers of Bila Tserkva again went to the polls. The village was determined to showcase itself as a paragon of civic participation. It proudly proclaimed itself the first village in the district to cast its ballots. It was a rare moment when the village made headlines for its positive achievements. Although portrayed as an organic display of enthusiasm, the external pressure was evident. Outside agitators from nearby Solotvyno visited the village for weeks in advance to raise awareness about the elections. The day before the big event, they organized a mass demonstration. Workers, students, and collective farm members marched down the main road through the village. Some followed on horseback. The demonstrators carried banners and portraits of Communist Party leaders. Music played. Newspaper reports described villagers as like children waiting for Father Frost on New Year's Eve. Residents were so excited to vote that "hardly anyone slept the night before 12 March. Every voter wanted to be the first to cast his vote for a happy future." Before the polling stations even opened the following morning, crowds had gathered. Collective farm director Peter Porchan told reporters, "I am voting for the great Stalin, creator of a happy life on the collective farm." After an early morning of casting their votes, the rest of the day was spent enjoying concerts, dancing, and performances by local artists.[37]

This glowing report was at least partly false. Seven men had been removed from the village, but by the state's own estimates, this left nearly two hundred Witnesses in Bila Tserkva. It is improbable that they warmed to elections in less than a year. Moreover, internal state documents suggest that they did not. In early 1950, the regional commissioners for the religious council in Ukraine hosted a conference to address ongoing opposition to elections by underground religious communities. The council was disturbed enough by the pessimistic reports from regional commissioners that it sent a follow-up memo to its staff with instructions. Every region, it stated, must have a clear plan going forward to deal with religious believers who obstruct voter turnout in elections. It called on its commissioners to review in particular the issue of "fanatical" sects, including "Jehovists," but also Shakers, Pentecostals, and others. Any information about these groups was to be shared immediately with state security.[38]

Further evidence that state-run newspapers publicly presented a much more positive spin than what officials acknowledged in private comes from how the press covered another postwar campaign. The same summer that the men were arrested, the state was in the midst of a unionwide campaign for world peace. The following year, it launched a massive effort to garner signatures for the Stockholm petition, an international effort to draw attention to the dangers of nuclear war. The Communist Party promoted itself as the global protector of peace against the warmongering capitalist world.[39] Once again, agitators were sent out to rally the population. They now had seven fewer men to visit, but many more Witnesses remained in the village. On the surface, the campaign went splendidly in Bila Tserkva. The school principal authored a newspaper column on how workers worldwide had already begun to vote for peace.[40] By that time, the petition had nearly a hundred million Soviet signatures.[41] A subsequent editorial in the regional newspaper declared triumphantly that the entire adult population had signed.[42] As with the election announcements, this was simply not true. Private discussions among party officials indicate that Witnesses refused to participate in the Soviet petition campaigns for peace.[43] Records from other case files in Ukraine also affirm this fact.[44] While these are sources produced by the Soviet state, Witnesses themselves have confirmed this conflict with state authorities. One Ukrainian Witness, who later recalled the difficult circumstances of his life under Soviet power for the Society's *Awake!* magazine, recounted how his refusal to participate in the Stockholm petition had dire consequences: "On 3 July 1950, I was asked to sign the Stockholm Appeal, an appeal against nuclear armaments that was reportedly signed by over 273,000,000 people, mainly citizens of Communist countries. When I refused to do so, explaining that I was politically neutral, I was once again fired. Following this incident I was arrested, tried, and sentenced to 25 years' imprisonment in a labor camp."[45] These outside sources from Witnesses themselves give additional reason to be deeply skeptical of official accounts of Witness participation in elections and other state campaigns.

Last, the 1952 investigation of Bila Tserkva resident Vasily Dan challenges the notion that Jehovah's Witnesses participated in local governance and state campaigns after the arrests in Bila Tserkva. Informants in this case told state officials that Witnesses remained an issue for election agitators. Some of these men were the same individuals who had reported to the state in the previous investigation. High school principal Alexander Pelladi, who had penned the newspaper column about local support for the Stockholm petition, was one of these informants. He recalled stopping by to talk with several Witnesses about elections; they were not responsive. One man told Pelladi that he had already chosen God as his leader and had no intention of selecting a different leader anytime in the future. Another Witness was even more direct in his opposition. If he were to vote, the man claimed, it would violate God's laws and he would be destroyed as an unbeliever. Other Witnesses made similar remarks to Pelladi as he went door to door, agitating in advance of the coming election.[46]

In short, once investigators closed the case, the village went right back to painting a rosy picture of Sovietization for outsiders. This allowed it to avoid state scrutiny by isolating the "problem" to a marginalized community of religious deviants. This also benefited the state, which could continue to proclaim the success of Sovietization without devoting significant resources to its rural territories. Thus, for years after the men's arrest, the state privately acknowledged its inability to resolve the election issue, even as its newspapers publicly declared the triumph of the Soviet political system. To be sure, Sovietization brought the vast majority of newly minted citizens to the polls, where they cast ballots to demonstrate public support for the new system. The entire affair was carefully choreographed, complete with music and festivities, to showcase the triumph of the state. The refusal of a small minority of villagers to participate in elections only partly disrupted this pageantry and threatened the state's careful narrative of joyful citizen voters.

5

The State Bonds

The new political system had other tasks beyond elections. Passports had made villagers into citizens. Identity papers formalized this relationship and allowed the state to make more demands. Elections required villagers to show that they approved of the new system. The local soviet now had to govern, and this meant further intrusion into the private lives of residents. It also needed money for a host of new expenses. A border fence had to be built, guards hired, passports printed by the thousands, and offices staffed to monitor compliance. This was a significant undertaking and only one small component of Soviet power.

Overall, postwar Sovietization was expensive, and the state intended for its citizens to help finance the new order. Beyond the bills associated with new Soviet institutions, the Soviet Union also needed funds to pay for its victory in World War II. The state required huge resources to rebuild entire communities destroyed by the war. Millions of Soviet citizens had lost their homes, their schools, and their workplaces. Some of this devastation occurred in Transcarpathia; much of it did not. As new members of Soviet society, however, residents were expected to contribute their fair share to assist their fellow citizens.

To pay for reconstruction and infrastructure in its annexed territories, the state ran several bond campaigns in the first postwar decade.[1] In essence, the state asked citizens to lend money to the government, which promised to return their investment. On the surface, this was an entirely normal request. Many governments issue state bonds, and many individuals buy them as a stable investment. The US Treasury even encourages citizens to buy them as gifts for friends and family.[2]

The Soviet government was well within international norms, then, when it established a bonds program only a few years after the revolution that brought it to power. During the investigation year, local authorities were in the midst of the fourth state bond campaign. The state issued twenty billion rubles worth of bonds and earmarked these funds for agricultural investment.[3] As in other Allied countries, all bond drives were allegedly voluntary.

The funds collected were championed as selfless and spontaneous acts by patriotic Soviet citizens. Most famously, a beekeeper who donated a large sum of money for the war effort became a poster child for citizen fundraising. Newspapers featured a personal thank-you message from Stalin to the beekeeper. The money went to fund a plane inscribed with the man's name and flown by one of the army's ace pilots. The beekeeper later became a central figure in a massive effort to have citizens donate their savings to the war effort.[4]

The reality behind such civic generosity, however, was more complicated. Certainly Soviet citizens, as elsewhere in Allied countries, bought bonds in part because they wanted to help their country, especially in the midst of a war for survival and its immediate aftermath. That said, we cannot characterize these drives as entirely or even mostly voluntary in nature. Soviet citizens were expected to buy bonds, which were sold to them by their employers. When they went to work, their supervisors pressured them to do their part by signing away a portion of their paycheque. It was hard to ignore such requests, since they came from individuals with significant power over their income and work conditions. No one wants to be on bad terms with their boss, and refusing to buy bonds was a sure way for that to happen. For those workers who stood their ground and said no, pressure did not end at the factory door. Agitators circulated in the community to sell bonds door to door.

In Bila Tserkva and other rural locales where factories did not exist and nearly everyone was a farmer, agitation was the primary mechanism for meeting state-set bond quotas. Agitators dedicated the first week of May to selling bonds door to door. They made the rounds of the village, pestering stragglers to chip in and support their newfound homeland. In some cases, agitators resorted to threats and violence to strong-arm their reluctant neighbours. These tactics made the bond drives akin to extortion and were especially common in outlying rural areas.[5]

Newspapers carried enthusiastic reports of the bonds campaign. *Soviet Transcarpathia* printed a large photo of peasants eagerly poised to lend a helping hand. A villager eagerly proclaims, "We are not the same people as we were before Soviet power." Life had become better, the paper told readers, and the bonds would provide needed fuel for further improvements.[6] In a triumphal article on the campaign's success the following year, the paper declared, "Signing for a bond in our country is a demonstration of loyalty to the workers of our great homeland and of their infinite trust in the Soviet state, the Communist Party, and Comrade Stalin." Over sixty-five million Soviet citizens were now bondholders, including more than two hundred thousand residents of Transcarpathia.[7]

Like many aspects of postwar Sovietization, buying state bonds was voluntary in theory but mandatory in practice. As with elections, the state expected universal participation, but not everyone was enthusiastic about the idea. The campaign atmosphere around bond sales both obscured and revealed that citizens were reluctant to part with their hard-earned money on behalf of the state. They had just experienced the upheavals of a world war and were often barely able to provide for themselves. Few had so much disposable income that they could afford to give it away for an unlikely reward in the distant future. It took sustained pressure to persuade them otherwise. Even in the capital city of Kyiv, shortfalls in subscriptions reached "crisis" levels by 1948.[8] Agitators stepped in when appeals to civic duty failed to do the trick. In one village in the Kursk region, local Soviet officials even brought in the parish priest to help persuade residents to buy bonds. With his help, the village quickly met its subscription goals but also earned a reprimand from central party officials.[9]

In Bila Tserkva, the village ran into problems with bond sales and did not apparently turn to religious clergy to drum up support. Witnesses presented one obstacle to this campaign. They refused to finance a state that they did not recognize as legitimate. Thus, agitators trudged to the homes of Witnesses, as they had on numerous other occasions, hoping to convince them to change their minds. They were not the only villagers to need extra persuasion. The very presence of agitators indicated that not everyone saw the value of these bonds. At the same time, if citizens felt pressured to buy bonds, agitators felt equal responsibility to sell them. Sovietization campaigns demanded universal participation; opting out was not a viable option. If nothing else, agitators had to at least show a good-faith effort to achieve the state's lofty benchmarks. The lack of party members in the village meant that it was always the same overworked agitators sent on these errands. If the Witnesses resented the intrusions, these agitators cannot have been particularly enthusiastic about such visits either. There was scant hope of convincing their devout fellow villagers to abandon religious principles in a half-hour conversation. If it were any consolation, the men could at least save time by addressing multiple issues with their neighbours in a single visit. Most agitators took this approach. A visit to a Witness might ostensibly be directed at the bond issue, but it also frequently implicated other problem areas of Witnesses' relationship with the state. In short, as long as he had the man at the door, the agitator might as well inquire about the state of his passport and registration.

First, however, agitators had to catch the Witnesses at home. This proved surprisingly difficult. Nutsu Guzo had already taken to hiding among the trees to avoid these chats. Likewise, Ivan Dan visited Witnesses' homes during the bond campaign but found them empty. He speculated that the families had decided to hide out in the woods that week. As long as agitators could not find them at home, they could not be pressured to sign for the bonds. Shifting blame from himself for the faltering bond campaign, Dan pointed the finger at his Witness neighbours. Their refusal to participate had ruined the activists' diligent efforts in the village.[10] This interaction is also revealing for how informants shaped the conversation with interrogators. In some reports, the interrogator appears to ask only a few general questions. In other instances, the questions are more detailed. This reflects that the report was written at the end of a conversation between the interrogator and informant. In the case of Ivan Dan, he clearly disclosed detailed information about the bond campaign. This is reflected in the report:

> Q: How did the aforementioned active sectarian-Jehovists in Bila Tserkva regard the fourth state bond campaign for the restoration and development of state agriculture in the USSR?
> A: I am well aware that during the fourth state bond campaign for the restoration and development of state agriculture in the USSR, not a single one of the aforementioned sectarian-Jehovists signed up. As a rule, none of them were home during the distribution of bonds on 3–9 May 1949. They all hid in the woods to avoid signing up for bonds. That is how this important political measure was derailed in Bila Tserkva by sectarian activists and the rank-and-file participants of the sect who followed their lead.[11]

In his testimony, Dan made clear that he thought the bond campaign had not been successful in his village. He placed the full blame for this situation on his Witness neighbours. He must have thought that this information would be of value to investigators because he included it in his statement. In other informant summaries, interrogators rarely asked about the bond campaign. The question appears in Dan's record because Dan told them he had information on this matter. This is true of all the interrogations. The investigators asked informants to provide evidence of anti-Soviet activity by Witnesses in the village. Informants then offered a range of actions of their neighbours that they decided fit within this category. The bond campaign was frequently on this list, but informants did not regularly provide the same level of detail as Dan.

Dan was not alone in judging the bond campaign a failure. By the time of the arrests, it had already drawn unwanted attention from the district. The matter was deemed problematic enough that the party intervened in the efforts. This was not the first time the party had poked its nose into the village-level actions of agitators. A few months earlier, it dispatched one of its own men, Ivan Baider, to the village to look into election irregularities. At the time, Baider was a district commissioner for political and agricultural affairs in Rakhiv. He did not last long in this position. Appointed in fall 1948, he stepped down in May 1949. He was the highest-ranking official interviewed during the investigation, and the only member of the Communist Party. Baider's short-lived term in office can be understood as a sign of a broader party weakness in the rural borderlands. Baider was an outsider. A Ukrainian by nationality, he grew up in Voroshylovhrad region (now Luhansk) in the eastern part of Soviet Ukraine. As a young man, he joined the party, completed an engineering program, and served in World War II. Now based in the nearby mining town of Solotvyno, he struggled to connect to the local population. Most problematically, he did not speak Romanian.[12]

As a result of his limited language skills, it is unlikely Baider could have been effective in communicating Soviet power to the villagers of Bila Tserkva. At no point in his statement to investigators did he mention how he conversed with the men, who did not speak Ukrainian or Russian. The language barrier may help explain why Baider began his intervention in Bila Tserkva by recruiting a group of village activists to assist him. The men's familiarity with the local terrain quickly came in handy. They led Baider outside the village to a spot where locals led their sheep out to pasture but also where Witnesses were known to congregate in secret. The ploy was successful. The men soon stumbled across a startled group of Witnesses. Before Baider and his band could approach them, however, the men scattered.[13]

Not all Witnesses, of course, hid from their neighbours. Others remained out in the open, or simply got too exhausted to hide from all the men and women knocking on their door day after day. One man found Dmitry Marinchan at home and willing to discuss the issue, but uninterested in compromise. Marinchan remarked, "I cannot give money to the state. I can never do this because Jehovah God forbids me."[14] Another villager managed to catch Nutsu Guzo at his home. Guzo was even more forceful, telling the bond salesman that the "the state would never get a kopeck [or cent]" from him.[15] The school principal, Alexander Pelladi, tracked down Ivan Ona, whom, he claimed, had stated bluntly, "I have money, but I am never giving it to the state because Jehovah God forbids it."[16]

In theory, village informants should not have been needed to confirm that the men had not signed for state bonds. The state had its own records of state bond sales, which they could have consulted. That said, no such documentation appears in the records, and there is no evidence that interrogators requested this information from other officials. Instead, they relied on local residents to assess the bond campaign and the Witnesses' participation in it. The state could not charge the Witnesses with refusal to buy state bonds since this was not a crime. Unlike the passport question, the bonds were not a requirement under Soviet law. In fact, though the bond issue featured in the arrest orders and the investigation, it did not appear in the August indictment. As Ivan Dan indicated, the crime was not in the refusal but in the disruption caused by Witnesses to the broader campaign. His testimony called attention to the fact that "sectarian activists" undermined state efforts, and ordinary congregants followed suit. Much of the case hinged on whether or not the men had communicated their beliefs on Soviet power to others. Agitators were in the best position to provide evidence that this had happened. Informant testimony was vital in demonstrating that the men represented a danger to broader society.

The unwillingness of a few hundred men and women in a border village to sign forms and buy state bonds was hardly enough to challenge Soviet territorial control over the region. Certainly the money lost in bond funds could not have made a significant impact on the

Soviet financial system. Even without a "single kopeck" from Witnesses, the Soviet Union rebuilt its damaged infrastructure in the postwar period. What was at stake in Bila Tserkva was something less tangible but still important. Sovietization required not only territorial integration of Transcarpathia but also total social and ideological integration. Such a goal left no room for outsiders who wished to remain on the lands but outside this nascent society.

From the perspective of Witnesses, this refusal to join in the Soviet project put them at great risk. Escalating Soviet demands made it imperative that they know for sure they had made the right decision in refusing to co-operate. This was not unique to the Bila Tserkva Witnesses. The requirements of Sovietization challenged congregations across the western borderlands and sent elders scrambling to provide answers. Outdated religious publications were insufficient to address perplexing aspects of the strange new world of the Soviet Union: Was all this conflict with the new government really necessary? Did their faith truly require them to accept such dangers, or was there room for a more flexible interpretation of scripture? In an attempt to clarify matters, local elders sent queries to more senior members of their faith abroad. For Ukrainian Witnesses, this meant reaching out to the Society's representatives in Łódź, a city in central Poland and a good deal west of the new international border. Ukrainian Witnesses asked Łódź elders to advise them on how to navigate Sovietization.

The answer, the so-called Ten Points memo, arrived as early as late 1947. Possibly it was drafted in eastern Poland, and then crossed the Polish border into western Ukraine. This region had a large community of Witnesses, including some of the most senior elders on Soviet soil. Once the memo arrived, it took time to filter this information across the scattered communities in the Ukrainian borderlands. At some point in its circulation, the memo fell into state hands.[17] When arrests of Witnesses began in Transcarpathia in the late 1940s, investigators translated the document from Ukrainian and included it in their case files. Thus, a copy of it appears at the end of the Bila Tserkva file. That said, there is little evidence that it had a major impact on the investigation, as interrogators never asked the accused about it. Likewise, it never came up at trial, nor did the prosecutor cite the memo. The file does not indicate when or how investigators received this document, and it is possible it arrived only at the end of the investigation, or even after its conclusion.

Is the memo authentic? Certainly the name "Ten Points" is assigned to it by Soviet investigators. A major KGB operation just a few years after the Bila Tserkva investigation, code named "Termites," systematically infiltrated the Ukrainian Witness communities. At this same time, the KGB liquidated the Łódź office in Poland, seizing a treasure trove of internal Witness documents. These two events meant that by 1951 (and quite possibly earlier) the KGB convincingly forged materials that could appear genuine to Witnesses. We cannot rule out the possibility that the Ukrainian state security also forged documents for its investigations a few years prior.

There is also reason to suggest the Ten Points memo may be an organic artifact of the Ukrainian Witness community. Witness histories of Ukraine and Russia both describe instances where Soviet Witnesses appealed for guidance to more senior individuals abroad and received written responses. This included guidance from Polish Witnesses to Soviet believers across the border in this exact time period. Polish Witnesses advised Ukrainian Witnesses about seeking legal registration in 1949; this effort failed.[18] As such, a memo from Poland to Ukraine in this time period would have been entirely in line with the organization's other activities. The content and tenor of the memo is consistent with Witnesses' beliefs and practices; if forged, it would have been done by someone with extensive knowledge of the faith. Perhaps most important, the memo's guidance does little to advance Soviet objectives. It offers some caution and moderation, but not enough to fundamentally shift relations between Witnesses and the state.

Ultimately, it is impossible to establish the memo's origin through the case file records. In the investigation itself, the men of Bila Tserkva do not address the document or its authenticity. Moreover, it is unlikely they would have seen such a document, real or fake, because the Society did not mass-produce such instructions but rather circulated them to a discrete group of responsible elders. Regardless, the memo is worth a close read because it may reveal how residents of the western borderlands grappled with how to interpret their new circumstances. This was a particular challenge in Transcarpathia where, unlike for residents of western Ukraine, Sovietization was a fundamentally new experience. They would have wondered how best to navigate all these new institutions and rules, how to protect their families, and how to make the best possible life for themselves in these conditions. For the Witnesses, the answers to all these questions could be found in religious dogma, which they saw as a faithful guide through the perils of Sovietization.

The Ten Points memo is an interpretation of that dogma. Its goal was to help Soviet citizens understand what their faith did (and did not) require of them. It begins with a lengthy introduction that stressed the need for Witnesses to draw themselves closer to their faith for protection:

Serve Jehovah with Joy!

"Shout in triumph to Jehovah, all the earth. Serve Jehovah with rejoicing. Come into his presence with joyful shouting."
Psalm 100:1–2

Beloved Brothers in Theocracy

The present-day "signs of the times" increasingly confirm that Jesus Christ rules among his enemies. *Psalm 110:1–2* Theocracy is spreading far and wide, despite the fact that its enemies, i.e., Satan and demons, through their representatives on earth, are using all their powers to prevent it.

Still, they are not successful because, with the help of the Lamb, God's people throughout the world have shown their loyalty and faithfulness during the cruelest of trials, neither fearing prison, nor torture, nor concentration camps, nor death.

The firmness of God's people has pushed the devil's organization into this endgame, as the victory of the Lamb is assured. *Revelation 17:14* To bring this war to its victorious conclusion, we must arm ourselves with the armor of God, so that we can offer a rebuff at the decisive moment (in which we now live) and remain standing. *Ephesians 6:11–24.*

Every soldier of Christ must now ensure that he has put on the armor of God, *Ephesians 6:10*, and eliminate any shortcomings in faith, love, heroism, and courage, and in Christian character because the final war is already at the door and Armageddon is ready to explode, and only those individuals will be victors and survive this war by almighty God. Only those who are fully under the will of God and Jesus Christ, and especially those who are fully in agreement with God's views on difficult questions, will prove Satan a liar and the enemy of truth, justice, and love, while

> Jehovah is the only source of life, the God of justice and love, and Jesus Christ is the true ruler of the world.

The language of "theocracy" reflected that the Society had shifted its organizational structure to "theocratic" governance under its second president, Joseph Franklin Rutherford, in the interwar period.[19] For Witnesses, theocratic government was the gold standard for how human societies should be organized, while secular government offered nothing of value.

The apocalyptic tone of the memo envisioned Soviet rule as a temporary reality before the inevitable destruction of secular institutions at Armageddon. "God's people," i.e., Witnesses, were to expect persecution during this period and prepare for it. This warning was in line with Society publications during this period, which regularly stressed that persecution was inevitable, and that true Christians should expect the wrath of corrupt secular officials. A 1933 *Watchtower* article, for example, told readers to face this suffering at the hands of evil actors with courage:

> Satan's organization is powerful and wicked beyond the description of words. That organization is fatally bent on the destruction of Jehovah's witnesses. Satan and his agents use all the power they possess to accomplish that wicked end. Doubtless the enemy will succeed in killing some of the faithful, but not even that fact will in any wise deter the faithful witnesses from rendering full obedience to the Lord.[20]

In this regard, both the memo and other Society publications acknowledged that Soviet Witnesses were in dangerous opposition to the current order. While we cannot know exactly which publications any individual Witness in Bila Tserkva would have read, they could not have missed the repeated references to persecution of Christians by secular authorities in this time period; they were ubiquitous.

The rest of the Ten Points document, however, tempers much of this rhetoric. It advises Witnesses to not compromise their faith but to do so in a manner that does not unnecessarily antagonize the state. This is evident from the very first of the ten points in the memo, which cautions: "For our general guidance, it must be understood that compromise never upholds Jehovah God's name. Therefore, one must avoid compromise. It is a godly inheritance to endure in the name of truth with a sincere heart. But we should pay great attention not to endure in vain or when not necessary." What did it mean to suffer "in vain" or "when not necessary?" Other points provide some clues. Point four notes the need to make all necessary payments, including taxes, to the state. Point eight regards the question of identity papers and registration for the draft. The Łódź Witnesses admit that they do "not have an answer yet" on this issue, suggesting that even they grappled with the implications of this new reality under Soviet rule. The lack of clarity probably also meant that the Łódź elders had themselves sent questions to more senior individuals in the Society and awaited a response. In the meantime, they felt confident enough to offer advice in the interim: avoid conflict with the state whenever possible "so that they [the authorities] do not ensnare all of our brothers and deprive them of freedom, denying them the ability to uphold Jehovah God's name." This answer clearly suggests the need to acquire passports, the lack of which had already led to the arrest of men in the community.

Most important, Witnesses were not to allow these issues to sow division between them. Even in offering support for identity papers, the memo notes that if someone does not feel comfortable with this position, he should not be criticized or his faith questioned. The memo explains, "The unity of God's organization is the greatest asset that God has provided." It would be a mistake, it admonishes, to create artificial barriers for believers seeking to remain true to their faith. Such an action would weaken the organization. That, above all, must be avoided.

While the state signalled to residents of the borderlands that they accept, even celebrate, the arrival of Soviet power as a permanent transformation of their social order, the Ten Points memo advised readers that Sovietization would not survive much longer. The final point reminded its audience that their suffering would give way to reward:

> Historical events are coming to a close. This period of tribulation, sorrow, and temporary misfortune, will be followed by joy and mirth in the world, as well as happiness and material abundance.
>
> Jehovah will wipe the tears away from the eyes of those who love him. *Revelation 21:3*. In the near future God will awaken his men to life so that they may prove to him their loyalty ... [ellipses

> in original] We must be patient and decisive, and everything that Jehovah has foretold through his prophets will come to pass.

Were the Bila Tserkva residents aware of this instruction? As noted earlier, we should not assume that because it appears in the file, it came from this particular community. More likely, since it appears in identical form in the files of other Witness defendants across Ukraine, it originated elsewhere and was added to the case file at some point. Moreover, there is evidence to suspect that the Bila Tserkva residents had not been told about this information, or had been told to disregard it by others in their community. Ironically, by strengthening border security, the Soviet state hampered its Witness citizens in moderating their views. Given the tense and repressive climate, which fractured communications with the Polish office, not everyone trusted that the Ten Points memo came from Society representatives on the other side of the border. They worried that the Soviet state might have forged this document to encourage Witnesses to betray their faith. Society representatives struggled with this issue of trust in both the postwar Soviet Union and Soviet bloc countries, a fact acknowledged in their own publications.[21]

The view that the memo was a fake was held by some of the most senior Witnesses in Transcarpathia. One of them, Dmitry Shelever, rejected the Ten Points until further clarification could be offered. As Mikhail Bokoch, the son of one of the arrested men, later described the issue, Shelever was a "good organizer," but there were "some misunderstandings" regarding how to respond to the imposition of Soviet power.[22] This directly affected the Bila Tserkva Witnesses because Shelever occupied a position of authority as circuit overseer for the Romanian villages in Transcarpathia.[23] As overseer, Shelever was responsible for articulating the Society's message to the Bila Tserkva Witnesses. His hardline stance placed these Witnesses in more direct opposition to Sovietization than was true elsewhere in the western borderlands, where other congregations more readily adopted the recommendations outlined in the Ten Points. Shelever also put himself in great danger. The state had already identified him as a threat and issued an arrest warrant. Other Witnesses sheltered Shelever, enabling him to continue to function as circuit overseer until his death.[24]

A year before their arrest, the men had a chance to hear Shelever speak directly at a large gathering of Romanian Witnesses from Bila Tserkva and neighbouring villages. Shelever, who delivered a talk at the event, could not have ignored the pressing questions about Sovietization in his remarks. This would have been an opportunity for him to discuss the Ten Points memo, but as he had rejected it, those gathered would likely have heard a more rigid position on Soviet power. While the state did not get wind of the gathering in advance, it did learn about it later from village informants. One of them, Mikhail Ona, relayed second-hand knowledge he gleaned from conversations with a neighbour who attended. Ona told interrogators that Shelever had instructed the audience not to take part in the measures of "Satan."[25]

With Shelever on the run, part of the state's motivation for the Bila Tserkva investigation may have been to gather evidence on this fugitive leader. Interrogators certainly hoped that the investigation might lead to his capture. They questioned the men about their ties to Shelever but got little information from most of them. Dmitry Marinchan told his interrogator, "I know only about myself. I know nothing about other people." He said simply that his faith would not permit him to betray his fellow believers.[26] Only Ivan Nan admitted to knowing Shelever. He acknowledged having attended meetings led by him, including at least one large gathering in the nearby woods. Yet even he refused to discuss what Shelever had told the crowd. If he had any idea where Shelever was hiding, he declined to say so.[27]

At least in regard to elections, however, Shelever's influence would not have had a major impact on changing minds in Bila Tserkva. The Ten Point memo did not argue for any moderation of the community's position. Point five is clear that no compromise is possible on this matter. It notes that "in regard to elections, you yourselves know the view of God's people in all countries." There was no solution that the organization could offer that avoided conflict with the state, short of modifying its worldwide standards for the faithful. The best it could do was circle back to its message of righteous suffering for one faith. To bolster this interpretation, it offered an anecdote about a female Witness who had been tortured for her faith but whose torturer was later accidentally shot and killed. It concluded, "in this instance, God's miraculous help is demonstrated."[28] It is hard to know how comforting such an anecdote would have been to Witnesses facing similar hardships in Bila Tserkva.

In the immediate postwar period, Soviet officials integrated Bila Tserkva and the surrounding region into the Soviet political system. They ostensibly gave residents a voice in politics by allowing them to choose their own representatives in new elections, accompanied with much fanfare and pageantry. In reality, the state's primary concern was that the elections affirm that Sovietization fundamentally reflected the will of the people. Thus, it was important that citizens buy bonds to demonstrate their support for the state and for Stalin, and that they show up to the polls to endorse the system and its leadership. Seen in this light, the state could not afford to allow Witnesses within its communities because they did not accord with this glowing image. For their part, Witnesses had to determine how to respond to growing state demands in light of their faith. In this regard, Sovietization required believers to adapt their beliefs and practices to new circumstances, altering their communities in the process. While they struggled to do so, however, state officials moved quickly toward extreme measures to eliminate this perceived threat.

6

The School

The first of September marked the start of the school year in the Soviet Union. It was always a festive date on the official calendar. Children brought flowers for their teachers. Parents took photographs of their beaming children. And schools welcomed their pupils with enthusiasm and speeches exhorting them to study hard and do well. These ritual events often extended beyond the schoolhouse into the local community. To celebrate the new school term in Uzhhorod, over a thousand students gathered in a local park. One child reportedly exclaimed, "We will study so that Stalin says, 'Thank you, children!'"[1] Bila Tserkva was no different. The year the men were arrested, their children marched off to school alongside the sons and daughters of villagers who had denounced them. All were expected to praise Stalin for this wonderful opportunity.

The newspapers provided cheery news coverage of the festivities around the country. Readers gazed at pictures of happy schoolchildren in newly pressed uniforms. They read articles about young boys and girls eager to start the new term. The press also had a deeper goal. The first day of school was the perfect time to make clear what the state expected of both students and teachers under Soviet power. Teachers were to mould their pupils into loyal citizens and communists, and the pupils were to embrace the worldview imparted by their teachers.

The regional paper recounted the earnest proclamations of schoolteachers as they busily readied themselves for the exciting new learning adventure in the year ahead. A teacher from Uzhhorod told reporters that her job was to "instill communist views in students." There was no better day to teach this message than at the start of the school year. She gushed to her new students about how happy they should be now that they could study in the Soviet Union. The new generation would not know the hardships faced by their parents. This opportunity, she noted, is all thanks to the Communist Party and "the great leader comrade Stalin." She instructed her students to repay the favour by working hard to make Stalin proud.[2] Another schoolteacher outlined his personal goals for the coming months. He would master Marxist-Leninist theory so that he could impart it properly to his students. He would make sure students understood the heroism of the Russian people. And he would teach his students to become "fervent patriots of the socialist homeland."[3] Certainly the teachers would also instruct students on the traditional three Rs, but the newspapers wanted parents to appreciate the ideological content their children would be expected to absorb.

No other institution offered the state the same opportunity to instill its values. In the postwar period, patriotic instruction was heavily centred on the wartime valour of the Soviet Union and on a millennium of pre-revolutionary Russian history that extended back into the medieval period. Such lessons frequently equated "Soviet" with "Russian," as is evident in the schoolteacher who wanted his students to recognize the heroism of the "Russian" people. A 1949 memo on how to encourage patriotism in the classroom told teachers: "The history teacher's direct task is to explain, on the basis of historical examples, all of the noble qualities of our country's peoples, with the Russians coming first."[4] For a classroom full of Romanian-speaking children who had no knowledge of Russian history, this was a particular challenge.

At the schoolhouse, children would learn what the state wanted them to learn. They would become "Soviet" and grow to appreciate the special contributions of Russians to this noble project. Ideally, they would carry these lessons into the home and win over the older generation whose views were shaped in very different circumstances. In contrast, these children would grow up within the Soviet system and, the state assumed, would have less reason to question it or reject it. They would become the next generation of workers, officials, bureaucrats, party activists, and educators. If the system was to take root in village life, the school had to properly nourish young minds. The state felt confident that it could raise children better than could their own parents who lacked the necessary education and political maturity.[5]

A happy childhood was therefore far more important than just an empty platitude, repeated in newspapers, official speeches, posters, and banners.[6] It represented the Soviet state's promise to its citizens. Catriona Kelly writes about the importance of childhood happiness to the Soviet state. She notes:

> Childhood happiness was thus not only (or even mainly) a goal of Soviet culture but also a legitimating sacred value. The state's ability to guarantee happiness to children was both a key instance of the country's status as a kind of earthly paradise (in the loose sense), and a way of assuring adults that, whatever else might be unsatisfactory, at least one section of the population was well looked after.[7]

Nowhere was this more true than in the newly annexed borderlands where the state promised parents that their children would have a far better life than they had known.

With this goal, the Soviet state dramatically expanded the school system from its pre-war scale. When the Red Army arrived in the region, Transcarpathia had 543 schools, but many had been shuttered during the war. Those that remained open under Hungarian occupation primarily offered instruction in the Hungarian language.[8] In Rakhiv district, a few dozen Ukrainian-language elementary schools existed before annexation.[9] These schools did not extend beyond basic education. In short, until the arrival of Soviet power, most villagers would have had the chance to learn to read and write at a rudimentary level but probably not in their native language; more than a few did not even gain this basic degree of literacy.

Sovietization undeniably invested more resources in education. Within four years, the region added nearly three hundred more schools. The vast majority of these new schools gave instruction to students in a language other than Russian.[10] By 1948 Rakhiv district alone had established four secondary schools to offer a full high school equivalent education. Even so, Rakhiv remained a rural farming district, where schooling opportunities did not necessarily match parental expectations for their children. Perhaps not surprising, nearly all the district's approximately ten thousand children dropped out of school before entering high school. Only a few hundred enrolled in the eighth through tenth grades offered at these new institutions.[11] Thus, while the state extended its education system to ten years in the cities in Transcarpathia in 1950, the villages continued to offer no more than seven years for rural children.[12]

Bila Tserkva was part of this massive and uneven expansion in education. All children seven years of age and older were required to attend school.[13] The village built a new schoolhouse so that children could complete the required years of schooling without travelling outside the village. Equally important, they could learn in their native Romanian language.[14] The new school system meant that children would now be able (and expected) to surpass their parents in education. This was true for both the Witnesses and their neighbours. A few of the village informants had completed eight years of education, the highest level possible within Rakhiv district before annexation. Most villagers had dropped out earlier. At least one informant was illiterate, and others had only three or four years of schooling. Before the war, the district did not have a single complete high school, and only two incomplete secondary programs.[15] Children had to travel outside the district if they wanted to finish secondary school. Even if some of Bila Tserkva's residents had wanted this for themselves or their children, almost no one could afford it. Moreover, for a district that relied on farming and logging, there was little incentive for parents to pay for such luxurious pursuits.

The most educated man in the village, Alexander Pelladi, had completed high school. This is a reflection of his background. Unlike the other villagers, he had grown up in the nearby town of Solotvyno and is listed as Ukrainian in the case file.[16] After high school, Pelladi had married and started a family. When the Red Army arrived in Transcarpathia, he enlisted in the Red Army and served until the war ended.[17] Returning home, he settled into village life as the local school principal. It was his duty to make sure that the next generation received a better chance to learn than their parents had. On another level, he was responsible for ensuring that students received an ideologically sound education that fit with the state's goals for the annexed region.

Although the village now had a new school and a new principal, it remained a rural community where parents and children laboured in the fields for much of the year. Farming had taken precedence over school in the parents' childhood and some now kept their own children home for the same reason. They needed the extra labour during the planting and harvest seasons. Frequent absences of rural children occurred despite generous praise for the new educational opportunities. In response, the district instituted fines for truancy. The heavy monetary burden was meant to discourage families from keeping their children in the fields. Akseniia Nan received a fine a year after her husband's arrest when one of their children missed a month of school. She was hardly alone. Over a dozen other village families were hit with penalties that same month. Not all of them were Jehovah's Witnesses.[18]

Nor did the educational system always live up to parental expectations. Lack of resources and trained staff created a large gap between state propaganda and lived reality. The press may have published images of smiling, eager children, but not everyone was quite so happy about the school system. Villagers aired numerous grievances about the local kindergarten. A year after the investigation, a visit to the kindergarten detailed a deplorable state of affairs. Staff were rude and mistreated children, some of whom were found kneeling in the corner and crying under the harsh disciplinary methods of the director.[19] Not surprising, most parents withdrew their children, leaving the schoolhouse more than half empty by the following year. Nor was this problem unique to Bila Tserkva. Inspections of other kindergartens in the district reported that villages had not allotted enough space or provided sufficient toys, leaving children bored and idle. In some instances, the kindergartens were also unsanitary, with children forced to sleep on dirty, unwashed linens.[20]

Likewise, adult education was supposed to be a priority, but state investment did not always match official enthusiasm. Soviet propaganda frequently compared the harsh conditions of life before annexation with the world of opportunities available under Soviet power. Even though the state invested the greatest effort in the youth, the parents were not supposed to be left behind. Literacy was a frequent measure of how the pre-war generation had progressed since the war. Some villages proudly proclaimed themselves entirely free of illiteracy. The newspapers eagerly extolled the achievements of such model communities. Bila Tserkva was not among them. In fact, the entire Rakhiv district was singled out for criticism.[21] Still, it apparently made some improvements soon after. A few years after the arrests, the village claimed to have achieved substantial progress on this front. It recorded only 143 illiterate or functionally illiterate residents on official charts, two-thirds of them women, and noted that every single one of the illiterate individuals was enrolled in some form of adult education. There is reason to be skeptical of this official statistic, given the unlikelihood of total participation in literacy classes among an older, sometimes elderly and infirm, population.[22] Nevertheless, Soviet education clearly set ambitious goals for overcoming the "backwardness" of its rural residents.

In theory, reading huts and village clubs were meant to build on more formal classes for adult education. They offered informal settings for citizens to acquire Soviet culture. These modest establishments provided a space for residents to read the local newspaper, browse through new issues of the major national magazines, or enjoy a good novel, all free of charge. Soviet officials envisioned that these "cultural enlightenment establishments" would reach into remote, rural areas. They would also attract older citizens who had long since aged out of the school system. In essence, Soviet power proclaimed that it would leave no citizen behind. Even a village as remote as Bila Tserkva was expected to put in the effort to construct sites of Soviet culture, and so it did.

The results, however, left much to be desired. The village set up a club, but it was hardly a civic centre for cultural enrichment. The building was rarely ever open, except to host weekly dances. The club director was hard to track down, a drunk, and belligerent to patrons on the rare occasions when he showed up to unlock the club doors.[23] The reading hut was little better, earning public scorn in the district newspaper.[24] Perhaps the most pathetic was the village library. The local soviet saw the structure more as a useful storage site than as a place of enlightenment. After a month-long effort by the village to spruce up the building, the village soviet chair undid these earnest efforts. Instead of investing in further repairs, he gave the collective farm permission to use the library attic for its grain harvest. The enormous weight of the grain was more than the library could bear. The ceiling buckled under the strain, threatening both the grain and the few books the library contained. Additional support beams saved the building from immediate destruction, but the money that should have been spent on filling the library shelves was now gone. Rumours spread that, having ruined the library, the chair now had designs on the village club as an alternate grain dumping location.[25]

Local families, therefore, encountered many promises from authorities about the cultural bounty offered by the new Soviet system, but delivery remained to be seen. A year after the investigation, then village collective farm chair Peter Porchan visited a much more impressive collective farm in another region. He promised Bila Tserkva residents that their children too would eventually enjoy athletic facilities and organized recreation. He brought back a soccer ball and volleyball as tokens of this goal.[26] In the meantime, Witness parents and children shared with their neighbours a distrust of the new cultural institutions, which were modest at best and dirty, even dangerous, at worst. As was clear from the kindergarten, parents were willing to withhold their children rather than risk their safety and happiness. Previous decades under other regimes had taught families that they could use the schools to impart basic skills but also ignore them when necessary. The Soviet system, in contrast, demanded that families relinquish control of their children's education to the state. Adjusting to the reality of Soviet universal education took time and did not occur without conflict.

As did other parents in the village, Witnesses sometimes kept their children at home. They had farms to maintain, but they also had other concerns about the content of the education itself. Indeed, the investigation revealed as much frustration on the part of village officials about when Witness children attended school as when they stayed home. Recall the schoolteacher from earlier in this chapter, who stated that one of his central goals was to teach his students to love their homeland. Even reading and writing lessons were designed to instill patriotism. Children learned to how to read from stories about Lenin and how to write from essays about the heroic deeds of Soviet soldiers and Bolshevik leaders. Their music lessons included songs about Stalin and the Communist Party. In short, the state's ideological goals were fully integrated into the curriculum. Children who refused to embrace this aspect of their education presented a serious obstacle to the goals of Sovietization.

Investigators were clearly concerned by how religious students threatened their newly established school system. At the same time, school administrators were eager to avoid drawing attention to the lacklustre performance of the new educational institutions. As a result, when investigators interviewed both Principal Pelladi and two of his schoolteachers, neither mentioned the broader challenges in postwar education: the lack of funds for construction and supplies, the need for competent staff, and the wariness of parents who found the new system both intrusive on their rural way of life and underwhelming in its quality.

Instead, the village informants painted a more convenient picture that absolved both them and the state of responsibility. They outlined a quality school curriculum systematically undermined by the religious beliefs of some of the children and their parents. Principal Pelladi, who arguably bore the most responsibility for the current state of affairs, was likewise the most eager to deflect blame. He described how Witness children "categorically refused" to accept the official ideology imparted by their teachers in the classroom. They kept silent when asked to sing the Soviet national anthem with their classmates. They would not learn about Communist Party leaders or the Soviet Army. They did not memorize patriotic poems. They even refused to recognize the Soviet Union as their homeland. When asked what country they lived in, the children told him that they lived "on earth" rather than "in the Soviet Union."[27]

These complaints echo the concerns of school officials worldwide about Jehovah's Witnesses in the classroom. We need not look further than the United States in the twentieth century for a parallel example. When American Witness children refused to recite the pledge of allegiance in public schools, the schools responded by expelling them in the 1930s. Billy Gobitis, one of the two children whose expulsion triggered a protracted court battle, addressed his local school board about the matter in 1935:

> I do not salute the flag because I have promised to do the will of God. That means that I must not worship anything out of harmony with God's law. In the twentieth chapter of Exodus it is stated, "Thou shalt not make unto thee any graven image, nor bow down to them nor serve them for I the Lord thy God am a jealous God visiting the iniquity of the fathers upon the children unto the third and fourth generation of them that hate me." I am a true follower of Christ. I do not salute the flag not because I do not love my country but I love my country and I love God more and I must obey His commandments.[28]

Billy's words parallel the voiced concerns of Witness schoolchildren in Bila Tserkva. In Billy's case, the controversy ultimately reached the Supreme Court in 1940, which ruled in favour of the schools in *Minersville School District v. Gobitis*. It concluded that the schools had lawfully required children to participate in such patriotic activities. If students refused to do so, the school was within its rights to remove them. As a result, Witness children remained at home, unable to attend public schools until the Supreme Court reversed itself three years later.[29] In this regard, Sovietization shared some of the same policy goals as more democratic states in the modern world. As with military service, the Soviet Union promoted the inherent good of state-sanctioned patriotism. Children were expected to reflect these values when they entered the classroom.

Seen from this angle, the actions of Bila Tserkva school officials reflect a broader conflict in modern states over accommodating religious children without sacrificing civic goals. For their part, Witness children in Bila Tserkva took a stance similar to their fellow believers elsewhere in the world. They attended school but did not participate in activities that would seem to require them to endorse the official ideology. This would have been a tall order in any school, as evidenced by the difficulties that American Witness children faced in a much more democratic political system. Soviet school staff and the state assigned an inaccurately political motive to a theologically based decision by Witness children, but they did not invent such accusations. On the contrary, they reflected the deeply held beliefs of Witnesses about the separation of Christians from a world they saw as corrupted and doomed for destruction. Witness parents everywhere send their children to school to learn the three Rs but require that this education be free of political bias. Inevitably, this position leads to conflict, the degree of which varies enormously based on the flexibility of the state, the local school district, and individual teachers.[30]

For the school staff in Bila Tserkva, politically neutral education was an impossibility. When Witness children balked at the political content of their learning, blame fell on their parents' shoulders. If the children refused to become little patriots and communists, it was because their parents had instilled in them values antithetical to the Soviet state. Pelladi told investigators that the parents raised their children in a "reactionary, fanatical, anti-Soviet spirit."[31] This explanation reduced the very real obstacles faced by the school system to a single point: the threat of a religious minority. Dmitry Marinchan's eldest daughter, Maria, recalled that the persecution of her family seemed to start first in the school system. From the perspective of an elementary-school child, the trouble began when she and her siblings refused to sing certain songs or recite certain poems. The teachers blamed her father, even though the children refused to say that he was responsible. She could not have known that the battle between her father and the state went far beyond what happened in her classroom.[32]

The school made clear that the Witnesses endangered not only the curriculum but also the integration of the Communist Party into village life. Given that the village had no party members, it was of paramount importance that the next generation fill in this gap. All Soviet children were expected to join party youth organizations. The littlest children became "Octobrists," and earned a shiny star-shaped pin with a picture of a cherubic young Vladimir Lenin in the centre. Elementary-school students joined the "Pioneers." They did after-school projects, sang songs, played games, and sometimes went to state-sponsored summer camps together.[33] Teenagers signed up for the "Komsomol" and remained members through early adulthood. Membership in the Komsomol was a requirement for admittance to a university. It also positioned young men and women to apply for admission into the party, a necessary badge of honour for many coveted jobs and positions in the Soviet Union.[34]

Octobrist and Pioneer membership were nearly universal. As with the pageantry surrounding election day, induction ceremonies celebrated the new system. In Soviet cities, this ritual was conducted in so-called Pioneer Palaces, special clubhouses specifically built for members.[35] Even in rural areas, which lacked such fancy spaces, schools made these events into a formal affair. On induction days, each chosen student recited a formal oath, vowed to "always be prepared," and was awarded a bright red scarf, folded like a bandanna and worn around the neck. Teachers looked on with pride as the next generation publicly joined the ranks of the Pioneers. For some students, the scarves were an exciting rite of passage, and the ceremonies a fun celebration and break from the normal school routine. For others, they were a minor annoyance, as teachers now expected them to remember to wear the scarves in school each day.[36]

For Witness children, the scarves were a bigger problem. Witnesses were not supposed to join civic organizations, and certainly not organizations run by the Communist Party. This prohibition extended to children. As such, membership in the Pioneers was an impossibility. Pioneer induction ceremonies put Witness children on the spot to defend their faith and reject the Soviet system, and to do so in a very public fashion, often in front of the whole school. Even after the formalities ended, Witness children were marked as different. As their classmates took their seats each day, the red kerchiefs tied around their necks, Witnesses stood out for their bare collars. Several weeks before the arrests, this crisis of conscience played out at the Pioneer induction ceremony in the new school. A second-grader, who had been invited to join along with his classmates, had spoiled the festive event for his classmates. For the school staff, the ceremony should have been a chance for celebration of Soviet accomplishments and pride in the next generation. Instead, it turned into a fiasco.

School officials brought the incident to the attention of investigators because the child in question was the son of Ivan Nan. The school apparently did not anticipate the conflict between the boy, his faith, and the Pioneers. Otherwise, it is hard to imagine that staff would have staged this event in front of all the other children. As a second-grader, he could have been delayed admission to the Pioneers. It would not have been unusual to simply postpone consideration of membership for another year. That the school did nominate Nan's son suggests that this was a relatively recent issue as educators implemented new Soviet rituals among their students. Whatever the reasoning behind the decision to include the boy, events began to deteriorate when it came time for the teacher to present each new Pioneer with his or her scarf. Principal Pelladi describes in detail what happened next: "In April 1949, the son of Jehovist Ivan Vasilevich Nan, a second-grade student, was admitted into the Pioneers organization. During the reciting of the solemn oath and the distribution of the Pioneer scarves, the son of I.V. Nan threw off his Pioneer scarf. He turned pale and shouted, crying, 'Don't! Don't! Take it off!'"[37] This scene was hardly the ringing endorsement of Soviet power envisioned by the school.

School officials disagreed in their explanations for how such a young child could have already turned against the state. The boy's teacher, Yury Pop, had also witnessed the entire scene. Like his principal, Mr Pop had been born outside the village and completed high school, making him one of the few qualified individuals in the village for this particular job. That said, Mr Pop was still in his early twenties, which is to say of Komsomol age, but was not a member of this organization. Perhaps he was not a particularly ambitious young man, or perhaps he had an indifferent attitude toward the Communist Party. Either way, he was hardly the go-getter schoolteacher described in the newspaper reports from September 1. The investigation was a chance to demonstrate some loyalty to the new system. In doing so, Mr Pop gave a rather different version of events to investigators than had his principal:

> In February 1949, our school conducted its induction into the Pioneer organization. Along with other students, the son of Jehovist Ivan Nan was admitted into the Pioneers. When we began to recite the solemn oath and distribute Pioneer scarves, the sister of the Nan student threatened him from a window. As a result, the boy started crying. Later, they began to call him a "son of the devil" at home.[38]

In Mr Pop's retelling, the event took place a few months earlier, and involved a sister who meddled in the ceremony. In this version, the boy did not necessarily reject the scarf at all. Indeed, he appears to have been successfully inducted into the Pioneers because otherwise there would be no basis for his family to mock him afterward. Principal Pelladi makes no mention of the sister or the family as instigators, which seem like valuable details to include in an investigation of the family patriarch. Overall, Pelladi's version is less flattering to the school, which appears unable to control the situation or win over the boy. Given that Pelladi would have no reason to embellish the story to make his institution appear worse than it is, this is the likelier of the two stories. In contrast, Mr Pop may have reasonably felt the need to shift responsibility for the incident on to someone else outside his own classroom, in this case the sister and the family. Otherwise, the state may have wondered how he had lost control of his students, and not even noticed when one of them got involved with an anti-Soviet religious community. As a young teacher, he might also have felt greater pressure to convey a useful narrative that kept him in his job.

Even if the two men disagreed on details, they both painted a similar portrait of the overall situation in the school, in which staff were frustrated by their inability to establish authority and control over their classrooms. Witness children, who refused to even acknowledge the Soviet Union's existence, made up a significant portion of the student body. Their presence in the classrooms frustrated educators in imparting the new Soviet curriculum to other students, who watched as their classmates challenged the system. A relative of the arrested Bokoch brothers, a fourth-grader, allegedly told Mr Pop that she could not read Soviet poems or sing the national anthem. When asked to explain, the girl replied with words that echoed her parents' views on involvement with Soviet power. She stated, "The Bible says so. We cannot serve two masters." Mr Pop reported that he heard similar comments from other students.[39]

Both Principal Pelladi and Mr Pop voiced serious concerns about the corrupting influence of parents and faith on the schoolchildren. For the state investigator, of equal concern was what the children and their parents learned outside the schoolhouse. The Soviet state intended to have a monopoly on the dissemination of culture, and churches threatened this position. One of the first decrees by the fledgling Soviet government after the October Revolution of 1917 was the "separation of church and state, and church and school." Before the revolution, the Russian Orthodox Church had been a major partner in primary schools, particularly in rural areas. The 1917 decree barred clergy from continued involvement in education.[40]

In the Stalin era, Soviet legislation further restricted what religious communities could legally do and subjected them to strict regulations in exchange for registration. By law, believers had the right to petition the state to recognize their community, granting them space to worship and the ability to gather in prayer and conduct religious rituals such as baptisms. In practical terms, the system was not nearly so easy to navigate. Believers were at the mercy of local officials who had little motivation to approve such requests. Few soviets wanted their town or village known as a hotspot for religious belief. It was easier and safer for one's political career to simply say no. Even if believers did win recognition, registration came with a long list of restrictions. Religious organizations could not carry out charitable work, hold children's services, or evangelize their faith outside designated houses of prayer. Moreover, the state exercised oversight over internal affairs that were traditionally the purview of the congregation. In doing so, the Soviet state hoped to keep religion behind closed doors where it would not interfere with public life or influence others.[41]

Regulation of religious life was a necessary component of Sovietization. A 1948 list of registered religious associations in Rakhiv district identified only nine in total: four Catholic and five Baptist churches. Neighbouring Solotvyno had both a Catholic and Baptist church. Bila Tserkva had neither.[42] A chart of all religious buildings in Rakhiv district, which included both designated houses of worship and pre-war religious structures, listed nothing at all for Bila Tserkva. The village had not submitted any data, unlike the vast majority of villages in the district.[43] The extraordinarily low level of official religious life should not be taken to indicate that the population was largely secular. Few officials wanted their town flagged as having a high number of churches. In contrast, local governments wanted to claim to have fully eradicated religious prejudice. Acknowledging a church meant acknowledging a certain lack of cultural enlightenment among the local population. Religion could easily become yet another item on the checklist for agitators to address as they made their rounds among their neighbours. In addition to getting out the vote and selling bonds, agitators would be expected to spread atheism.

While this aspect of Sovietization is not mentioned in the case file, and only rarely in other archival documents from this time, later documentation provides additional reason to doubt that the villagers had suddenly become atheists overnight. In the postwar era, Greek Catholic churches in the region were forcibly integrated into Russian Orthodox churches, leaving them without any recognized existence on Soviet soil. Yet this process did not fully eliminate Greek Catholic communities. A much later report from the regional religious council acknowledged the presence of "former" Greek Catholics in the village. It noted that the local priest, now a "former" Greek Catholic himself, had resettled in neighbouring Solotvyno. By the time this document was written in 1955, the village had no functioning church, ostensibly because the Russian Orthodox Church reported no local interest. Yet this same report acknowledges that the "former" priest had been visiting other "former" Greek Catholics, and that some "former" believers had shirked state-mandated military service.[44] Thus, one can reasonably assume that at the time of the investigation, Greek Catholicism remained a factor in village life, even if it no longer had an organized presence.

Overall, Bila Tserkva's unwillingness to acknowledge any religious activity in the village is not entirely unusual. Jehovah's Witnesses could not have expected to earn legal status in this environment. Elsewhere in the Soviet Union, other Witness congregations did seek registration and were denied. The state extended the carrot of registration only to certain faiths, primarily the Russian Orthodox Church, but also Baptist congregations and some other mainstream Protestant denominations, along with some synagogues and mosques. More marginal communities were entirely excluded. This included Greek Catholics, various Old Believer sects, which had broken from the Russian Orthodox Church in the tsarist period, and Pentecostals, among many others.[45]

Given that Jehovah's Witnesses were a new phenomenon in the postwar period, the state did not initially have a clear policy on this community. Nor did the international organization of Jehovah's Witnesses have a full understanding of what registration entailed or even how to obtain it. Thus, only a few weeks after the arrests in Bila Tserkva, three Witnesses from western Ukraine walked into the offices of the Ministry of Internal Affairs in Kyiv. They carried a petition for registration of the entire Soviet Witness community. The document explained the basic tenets of the Witness faith and its history. It also detailed the specific activities that Witnesses conduct in democratic countries. All these actions would have been in violation of Soviet religious legislation. In particular, the petition noted that Witnesses proclaim their faith through public evangelism and radio, publish and distribute religious literature, and hold private Bible studies.

Although the petition reassured officials that Witnesses had no political intentions and were "loyal citizens of the USSR," its content suggested otherwise. A call to evangelize religion in a secular society, and to do so in public and in private homes, was anathema to Soviet norms for religious communities. Moreover, it suggested to Soviet officials that whatever the petition might claim about its political neutrality, the Witnesses' objective was to replace Soviet ideology with religious dogmatism. Indeed, the Witnesses appear to make this basic point in the petition, when they declare: "The Kingdom of Jehovah under Christ is the only means for the liberation and salvation of humankind." This statement rejected the notion that communism could create such a system. It is not surprising that when the petition was forwarded to the Council for Religious Cult Affairs, officials underlined this particular passage.[46]

A parallel petition by Estonian Witnesses a month earlier was even more direct in its message: "We demand that Jehovah's Witnesses be released from prison and that the persecution against them be stopped. Jehovah God's organization, by means of the Watchtower Bible and Tract Society, should be permitted to preach, unhindered, the good news of Jehovah's Kingdom to all the inhabitants of the Soviet Union; otherwise, Jehovah will utterly destroy the Soviet Union and the Communist Party."[47] For Witnesses, the claim that "Jehovah would utterly destroy" the Soviet state would have been meant as a theological statement of faith. For Soviet officials, however, its meaning was far more sinister. In their view, an illegal organization, composed of dangerous criminals (after all, their members were in prison), had threatened war with the Soviet state. The notion that such a group should be granted legal standing was unthinkable. If anything, the petitions likely brought the Witnesses greater scrutiny by the state. Both petitions were rejected and forwarded to other officials to review. The men who had delivered the petition in Kyiv were arrested shortly thereafter.[48] The first registration of a Witness community in Ukraine did not happen for over forty more years.[49]

Meanwhile in Bila Tserkva, the congregation was not registered and therefore had no legal right to exist at all. There is no evidence that it sought registration in the village. Given the uncompromising stance taken by local Witnesses, it is unlikely this option would have appealed to them. Even if the congregation had sought legal status, the state would have refused, just as it had in Kyiv. Thus, Bila Tserkva Witnesses had no officially designated "house of prayer," or what Witnesses worldwide would have called a "Kingdom Hall." These are typically modest one-storey structures built by volunteer labour. With no altar, sacred objects, or statues, they look similar to a union or town hall. When the Witnesses first appeared in the village, the congregation had constructed a modest Kingdom Hall, but it did not survive the war, nor did the hall in neighbouring Solotvyno.[50] These buildings only appeared in the mid-1930s, and they are not mentioned in any of the postwar records.

By the postwar period, Witnesses had taken to gathering in private homes for services. Most were small affairs; the circle of attendees might be just relatives and close friends. After all, village dwellings could hardly accommodate larger crowds. Rather than view these meetings solely through the prism of worship, it is useful to consider how local officials understood them. The Soviet state had mandated that all religious life take place within the walls of officially sanctioned churches, but given that Bila Tserkva had no registered churches, it appears that officials were not entirely clear on what to do with activities that occurred outside these boundaries.

There is some evidence that in the first few years of Soviet power, local officials ignored religious services in private homes. This information comes in part from the later trial of Vasily Dan, when he is asked how he pleads to the accusation of anti-Soviet activity. Dan responded as follows:

> I do not consider myself guilty of having transported and distributed anti-Soviet religious literature. I only transported religious literature, for example the magazines "the Watchtower" and "Infor-

> mator." I did not keep anti-Soviet literature at home. During arrest, they confiscated a Jehovist book in the Romanian language entitled "Riches," and that is it. I never engaged in anti-Soviet agitation, and I never attended illegal gatherings. Until 1948, I attended a Jehovist congregation, which still met openly at that time. I admit my guilt on the remaining charges.

Prosecutors underlined this curious comment by Dan that he had never attended an illegal meeting because before 1948 they had been essentially legal.[51] The son of one of the Bila Tserkva men likewise recalled "a bit of freedom" after the war. As he remembered it, Witnesses were able to freely gather and to evangelize in nearby villages. Some even did so in Romania because the border had not yet been established.[52] Of course, this is not entirely accurate given that the Witnesses never received the required state approval to meet and that evangelism of religion was not legal in the Soviet Union. It is quite possible, however, that neither local officials nor Witnesses in those initial years entirely understood what was and was not allowed. Alternatively, officials did understand but chose not to fully enforce the law, either because they did not want to or lacked the resources to do so. Certainly, that Dan admitted to "openly" attending unsanctioned religious services is suggestive of this fact.

More broadly, Dan's comment reflects that Soviet regulation of cultural life came only gradually to the village. It took time for both Witnesses and officials to learn the new rules of the game. During the state's investigation of Dan, local activists, including some of the same men who had earlier testified against the other Bila Tserkva defendants, acknowledged they had monitored meetings by Witnesses in the early postwar years. At one meeting, agitators stood by and listened while Witnesses read from the Bible and an elder delivered a talk about the reading.[53] At another, a Komsomol member watched as Witnesses read from religious literature, and elders warned that believers must follow Jehovah or face destruction at Armageddon. The latter event was attended by over thirty people, a rather significant crowd.[54] In all such instances, the onlookers made no attempt to halt the proceedings, and no attendees were detained or arrested. A Witness like Dan could reasonably assume that the state did not approve but was not prepared to prevent their community from coming together to worship.

Whatever brief détente existed between Witnesses and Soviet officials did not last long. The state had designated official sites for cultural activity in the village. The reading hut, club, library, and school offered controlled spaces for citizens to learn approved information about their world. Likewise, the newspapers and radio (when it eventually reached Bila Tserkva) interpreted and promulgated events from an official perspective. Many residents may have found them dull, outdated or otherwise lacking, even if only a minority belonged to the Witnesses, but there were few alternatives. The state invested a great deal of effort into selling culture to its citizens. Allowing citizens to create their own spaces, and their own meaning, was a direct threat to this system. Sovietization required the destruction of such alternative communities. Thus, the investigation devoted increasing attention to tracking when Witnesses came together outside sanctioned spaces.

Although the Witnesses began to take precautions to avoid attracting the attention of authorities, it is worth noting that village life makes it rather hard to keep secrets. This was not a large town but a small, rural community, with houses and fields near one another. Homes were clustered along one major road through the village. Residents knew who came and went from their neighbour's residences. They also knew when outsiders arrived. Since the Witnesses had previously met in the open, neighbours would have remembered who had hosted and who had attended in the past. Moreover, gossip and rumour spread quickly, especially since there was little else of interest to do in Bila Tserkva, with its shuttered club and half-shuttered library. Not surprising, numerous informants kept close enough track of their neighbours that they could tell interrogators exactly who visited whom and when.

Witnesses took risks, therefore, when they gathered in small groups, and even more so when they invited the uninitiated to these illegal events. Perhaps the boldest example of this evangelism comes from the testimonies of Anna Porchan, the wife of the collective farm chair, and her sister, Todora Moish. Anna was a lifelong resident of the village, twenty-six at the time of the trial, and illiterate. At the same time, she was also employed at the local kindergarten, though the case file listed her as having no profession and labelled her a "housewife." This suggests that she may have not worked full-time in this job. Interrogators were highly interested in Anna's testimony because, alone among the informants, she claimed to have been recruited into the "sect." Nearly the entire interview with her focuses on this issue:

> Q: Did you previously attend illegal meetings held by participants of the illegal anti-Soviet sect of Jehovists in the village of Bila Tserkva, Rakhiv district, Transcarpathia region?
> A: Yes, in 1948 I attended illegal meetings of the sect of Jehovists in the village of Bila Tserkva.
> Q: Tell us about this in detail.
> A: In February 1948, I do not recall the exact date, Dmitry Mikhailovich Marinchan, one of the leaders of the sect of Jehovists in Bila Tserkva, came to my home. He told me, "If you want to be our sister and believe in Jehovah God, come to our meeting at my apartment where you will learn everything in detail." Then D.M. Marinchan added, "A time is coming soon when people who have not found faith will perish. Therefore, everyone must follow our God."

After attending six more meetings over the next several weeks, however, Anna regretted her actions and stopped responding to future invitations. Her sister confirmed this basic information.[55] This anecdote reveals much about Witness evangelism in the village. First, assuming the two sisters' information is truthful, it is remarkable indeed. A Jehovah's Witness appealed to the wife of a local official and convinced her to join a religious gathering; this woman did not immediately denounce the man to authorities. Witnesses seemed to have taken minimal precautions to shield themselves from official notice. Second, Anna's testimony suggests that small group gatherings were frequent and could include non-believers. These groups would be consistent with the Bible study groups conducted by Witnesses with potential converts worldwide. In just two months, Anna had attended seven such gatherings. Given that she was not yet a full participant in the faith, it is likely that this figure represents only a portion of the times these individuals met during this time period. Third, Witness religious services featured a book not available in the dilapidated village library: the Bible. Given that many villagers had only basic reading skills, and Anna had none at all, such meetings would have offered a rare chance for them to interact with religious texts.

Not all gatherings were so modest. In 1948, the year before arrest, the congregation had taken the risky step of hosting a large-scale event at which nearly the entire congregation was present. The rural location made it slightly easier to pull off such a feat. Still, neighbours definitely noticed when hundreds of men, women, and children disappeared into the nearby forest. More than one informant referred to having seen Witnesses in the woods that spring. Mikhail Ona spoke with the owner of the estate near to which the event had taken place.[56] Further, though none of the informants mentioned this detail, the investigator already had outside confirmation of this gathering. A border patrol had submitted a report about the event to the state investigator, estimating that five to six hundred individuals were present, all of them Romanian speakers from Bila Tserkva and nearby villages. It is unclear from the memo if the patrol actually witnessed this event, or merely recorded information it heard from another source. However, in a separate report, a fighter battalion detained fifty-four of the men on their way home, none of whom had passports, including the Bokoch and Marinchan brothers, and Ivan Ona.[57] This was also not the first time the Witnesses had used the woods as cover. Mr Pop recalled stumbling upon a large group of them while taking a shortcut back to the village from neighbouring Serednie Vodiane.[58]

During interrogations, the state investigator made clear that he saw such activities as evidence of an illegal underground organization. In response, all men tried to minimize the extent to which they had practised their faith in concert with others. When the interrogator accused Ivan Ona of holding religious meetings at his home, Ona attempted to explain his actions:

> It has been nearly three years that my wife has been in poor health and confined to her bed. During this period when my wife felt very ill, neighbours, acquaintances, and other villagers of Bila Tserkva came to visit her to check on how she was doing. During these visits, I, as a Jehovist, read Jehovist literature to my wife, and her visitors listened to me do so. I read this Jehovist literature so that Jehovah God would improve my wife's health.

When asked if he ever explained what he had read aloud to these visitors, he responded no. In his version of events, Ona had simply shared a private religious moment with his wife. If others happened to be in earshot, this was not his problem or his responsibility.[59]

Not all the men were so creative in brushing aside these particular accusations. On a practical level, the men understood that their neighbours had already testified to this fact in some detail. It was of little use denying that they had met as a community in such a small village, where everyone tended to know everyone else's business. Nutsu Guzo, as a resident of nearby Serednie Vodiane, found it even more difficult to enter the village without attracting attention. When brought face to face with one of his accusers, who claimed to have seen him visit Bila Tserkva residents on multiple occasions, he admitted that he had done so, but only "as acquaintances," not as part of an illegal religious gathering.[60] Such deflections carried little weight with interrogators. Even so, they suggest that by 1949, believers understood the new system of religious regulation well enough to know that meeting in private homes was a serious crime.

Alone among the seven men, Ivan Nan found it impossible to deny this particular action after weeks of sporadic interrogations. He had a wife and seven young children to worry about back at home. Perhaps he hoped that greater transparency would somehow result in his quicker return to them. The interrogator sensed this vulnerability when Nan recounted how Dmitry Bokoch had baptized him and several others in the Tysa River in 1942.[61] After this point in the record, the interrogations of Nan suddenly shifted from infrequent and rather short sessions to an all-night marathon the following night. It began at ten o'clock in the evening and wrapped up at five o'clock the next morning.

It is difficult to interpret this interrogation record, which stands in stark contrast to all the others in this case file. It begins with a monologue from Nan, directed more at his fellow believers than at the interrogator who recorded it. The text of the statement cannot have been transcribed verbatim, but nor could a regional interrogator, who had no knowledge of Witness theology, have created it entirely out of whole cloth:

> During the interrogation on 25 July 1949, I named several participants of the illegal anti-Soviet sect of Jehovists in Bila Tserkva, and also named Dmitry Todorovich Bokoch, who baptized me as a Jehovist.
>
> By these actions I have committed a great crime against Jehovah God and will be punished for it at Armageddon. I have violated the sacred oath of the Jehovist, that a Jehovist should not inform on a fellow Jehovist or on the activities of the Jehovist sect. Thus, from this day forward I do not consider myself a Jehovist.[62]

The interrogator underlined the entire passage in red pen. What can we make of this rather odd comment? As noted in earlier chapters, Nan would not have referred to himself as a "Jehovist." He certainly would not have done so only moments after carefully uttering "Jehovah God," the specific term Witnesses believe is God's proper name. The state would have been eager for Nan to cave under pressure and betray his fellow Witnesses, but this passage does not justify this optimism. Instead, it suggests that Nan struggled with the competing demands of theology and state, and saw no viable route to bring the two into harmony with each another. The interrogator would have had little reason to invent this inner conflict, which only undermines the state's strongest evidence against the men.

The rest of the interrogation affirms this interpretation. Nan refused to name any more names. This likely disappointed the investigators, who clearly anticipated a much more pliable informant. It may also help explain why the interrogation lasted so long, as investigators tried to capitalize on Nan's previous interrogation. Instead, Nan attempted to carve out a middle route, in which he provided general information about Witness activities but did so without implicating anyone by name:

> Q: Provide the names of those whom you know to have participated in the anti-Soviet illegal sect of Jehovists in Bila Tserkva.
> A: Other than those whom I named on 25 July 1949, I refuse to give out any further names to the investigation.
> Q: Describe the organized activities of the anti-Soviet illegal sect of Jehovists, of which you are a participant.
> A: I want to say the following about this question: in March 1949, Jehovists of Bila Tserkva were told to gather on a given day for an illegal Jehovist gathering near the village of Dibrova, Tiachiv district.
> Q: Who called this gathering of Jehovists?
> A: I refuse to answer that question.
> Q: Continue your statement.
> A: In the forest at the designated location, about 200 Jehovists gathered, mostly from Rakhiv and Tiachiv districts.
> Q: Name the Jehovists of Bila Tserkva who were present at this gathering.
> A: Among Bila Tserkva residents, I was present at this gathering, as were other Jehovists, whose names I refuse to provide.

Q: Who led this gathering of Jehovists?
A: The Jehovist Dmitry Shelever led this gathering. He is currently on the run.
Q: What topics were discussed at the gathering of Jehovists?
A: At the Jehovist gathering, Shelever read the Bible and other Jehovist literature, and then gave a speech. I do not recall the content of the speech.
Q: How long did this gathering of Jehovists last?
A: I cannot say.
Q: Besides Shelever, who else led this Jehovist gathering?
A: Several other Jehovists spoke at this gathering, but I do not know their names.
Q: How many times were you present at Jehovist gatherings led by the wanted man Shelever?
A: I refuse to answer that question.[63]

Nan's careful answers to questions suggest that whatever he might have divulged the previous evening, he did not want to harm his fellow congregants in Bila Tserkva. The state already knew about Shelever, and Nan likewise knew that at least for the moment, Shelever was out of the state's grasp. While Nan confirmed one forest gathering, he refused to place his fellow defendants at this event when told to do so.

Despite what he might have said in his initial remark, Nan clearly still considered himself a Jehovah's Witness. Since his arrest, he had refused to sign the interrogation records because, like the other men, he considered his signature on an official form an acknowledgment of Soviet power. On the day when he allegedly declared himself no longer a man of faith, he still refused to sign. Twelve hours later, when he was brought back in for a quick and fruitless follow-up interrogation, the state did not find a man who had rejected his faith at all. Instead, the investigator recorded a man unwilling to go further in providing information. In fact, Nan retreated from this earlier statement and expressed regret about having mentioned Shelever. He couched his early statements in stark theological terms: "Today I want to inform the investigation that I renounce my earlier statements because when I gave them, I was not in control of myself; I was possessed by a demon. I did not speak with my own tongue but rather a demon's who had entered into me." This is the last sentence of the final interrogation of Nan. The statement that follows reads, as it did on all other interrogation records: "refused to sign."[64]

Neither the state nor Nan had gotten entirely what they wanted out of this exchange. For Nan, the interrogations had led him into dangerous waters that he felt ill-equipped to navigate on his own. His theology taught him to view state hostility as a test of faith, and his answers left him shaken as to whether he had passed this examination. The state eagerly latched on to Nan's uncertainty, misreading it as a sign that Nan had renounced his beliefs and was ready to fully cooperate with investigators against his fellow believers. Ultimately, Nan may have given the state valuable information, but he did so without endorsing the underlying worldview of the Soviet system. This distinction may have mattered little to the state, but it mattered a great deal to Nan.

The state needed Nan to confirm that Witnesses met as a community because this transformed the Witnesses from individual believers into an underground anti-Soviet organization. These meetings provided spaces for citizens to exchange unauthorized information and ideas, some antithetical to the Soviet project. Sovietization meant the creation of designated sites of official culture: the school, the library, the club. There, and only there, were Soviet citizens supposed to learn what to think and how to behave. At least some villagers, such as Anna Porchan, may have found Witness meetings interesting enough to attend, even if they were not committed to religious conversion. If nothing else, the Witnesses clearly intrigued their neighbours, who watched them go about their daily activities, and sometimes even stopped by their homes to see for themselves. State institutions did not want to compete with such informal, unsanctioned cultural life.

The state voiced particular concern over competition for the hearts and minds of the next generation. Soviet legislation placed firm limitations on children's access to registered churches. It did not allow them to host youth events, such as Bible studies or Sunday schools. Registered churches felt pressure to keep children out of regular Sunday services.[65] For the state, if a diminishing number of aging citizens still clung to an antiquated set of beliefs, that was an unfortunate but tolerable reality until religion ultimately withered away. The same could not be said for the next generation of Soviet citizens, who were expected to embrace state ideology. At least until they became adults, the state intended to shelter them from the dangerous influence of religion, hawked by the old and ignorant to a naïve and innocent youth.

In violation of Soviet law, Witnesses provided tailored activities for children and took turns hosting these events in their homes. Local activists broke up one gathering at the home of Ivan Bokoch. When they arrived, roughly twenty children sat listening to Ivan's brother, Dmitry. A month later, the police disrupted a study session at another home, this one led by Mikhail Bokoch, Dmitry's son.[66] Mikhail, only a teenager himself, had stopped attending the local school after the sixth grade. At the impromptu Bible study, he taught the children to memorize Bible verses, read passages from the *Watchtower*, and other simple tasks.[67]

This was a dangerous position for Mikhail. While school officials blamed parental meddling for children's actions in the classroom, the state was more than willing to prosecute teenagers for serious crimes. On a practical level, state crime statutes allowed for the prosecution and imprisonment of minors under the age of sixteen.[68] Moreover, it was hard to expect young children to keep quiet about what they did after school. Some of the information about these youth gatherings came from the children themselves. One child told Mr Pop, his teacher, that he and some of the other children had met to read the Bible. The teacher conveyed this information to investigators.[69]

Police and school officials worked together to enforce the state's control over acceptable cultural activity. When local police got wind of a children's lesson one week, Principal Pelladi accompanied them on the raid. Arriving at the home, the men found Mikhail and two dozen young children assembled. The officers demanded that the children tell them who was in charge. Luckily, the children had enough sense to remain silent. Finally, Mikhail took a calculated risk and spoke to the men. He explained that the children were studying the word of God. This would have been of little comfort to the authorities.[70] His father was arrested soon after this incident.

The investigation placed much of the blame for the Bible school on Dmitry Bokoch, which spared Mikhail a similar fate. This was also made possible by Dmitry himself, who did not deflect responsibility on to his son. Instead, he transferred authority for the school on to Jehovah himself. This was a common tactic among the men. The state expected prisoners to name names of other individuals. This would lead to further arrests, while doing little to lighten the burden on those already imprisoned. To the likely frustration of the interrogator, therefore, the men repeatedly cited Jehovah as a chief accomplice or co-

conspirator, while avoiding the names of friends and family. Thus, the interrogator recorded a rather mangled testimonial about the Sunday school from Dmitry, which combined Dmitry's obfuscations with Soviet language: "Jehovah God ran the Jehovist lessons with the children. I never ran any such lessons." Asked to explain why his children had never been involved in the Pioneers and refused to sing the national anthem, Dmitry responded, "Jehovah God directs my children."[71]

The men repeated this strategy when faced with direct rebuttals from the school staff. In a face-to-face interrogation, Principal Pelladi confronted Vasily Marinchan about his alleged sabotage of the school system and indoctrination of his children. In Pelladi's version of events, Vasily had adopted a hostile ideology, and then imparted it to his children, who accepted these dangerous ideas without question. Vasily had a different understanding of his role. He denied that he had instilled in his children an anti-Soviet attitude. Moreover, he retorted to Pelladi that he did not "teach" his children in the same way that Principal Pelladi instructed the children in the schoolhouse. Rather, they learned through observation. He read the Bible, and his children listened. He had no control over what they did with that information when they entered the school.[72] At trial, Pelladi repeated his accusations, but also acknowledged the parents' view of events. He told the judge that the parents had repeatedly informed him that their children "have their own ideas."[73]

It is worth noting that both sides expected a great deal of children. For the Soviet state, children were the standard bearers of a new Soviet way of life. For Witness parents, children were Christians who must learn to defend their faith against a hostile world, just as the adults in the community had. Neither side allowed much space for common ground or neutrality. The enormous pressure placed on rural communities to choose between their faith and state ideology was overwhelming even for adults. Nan struggled under this strain. Children had even less capacity to cope with it. While promised a simple, happy childhood by the new Soviet system, few Witness children experienced it.

Finally, it is worth considering how it would have felt for the other village children in the school. They could not help but notice how some of the boys and girls did not sing along at music time or did not recite the patriotic poems. They would have heard the children talk about Jehovah and why they could not be part of a corrupt "system of things." A classmate might even have made a bold attempt to evangelize to them about joining the faith. Although nearly all of them grew up to embrace, or at least accept, the Soviet worldview, they would have known that some who lived in their community did not. In this regard, the school system could never have total control over its message because children offered one another alternative views. Meanwhile, adult members of the community carved out informal spaces for airing these same views in private homes and in forest glens. In such a small village, everyone knew at least one neighbour who did not abide by the new rules of the Soviet system.

7

The Farm

Postwar annexation by the Soviet Union had a direct impact on the villagers' economic livelihoods in Bila Tserkva. Only a few regional industries existed to offer employment; everyone else worked on the land. At the same time, the local topography, with its abundant forests and mountainous areas, made farmland hard to come by.[1] Wartime border shifts added new complications to the land issue. Hungary's wartime control of Transcarpathia extended south of Bila Tserkva across the Tysa River. For Bila Tserkva residents, that meant that the international border just south of their village no longer existed. The lack of a border allowed villagers to expand their farms on to the southern bank, near the river town of Sighet. Some residents more than doubled their lands in this manner. While a bridge provided steady access to fields on both sides of the river, the Tysa was often shallow enough to walk across the natural pathways created by stones at narrow points. In a pinch, farmers could also swim from one bank to the other with relative ease.[2] This new farming situation did not last long. With Allied victory in World War II, Hungarian expansion was quickly undone. The Red Army arrived in Bila Tserkva and moved to re-establish border control. The river no longer separated Czechoslovakia and Romania, but rather the Soviet Union and Romania. Villagers eventually found the river off-limits entirely, behind a barbed wire fence.

The construction of the new Soviet order required physical labour, which the state was loath to pay for despite its necessity. The devastation of the war had also left the state in a weak financial position. The bond campaigns were intended to collect some of this capital, but it was not enough. To meet the growing demand for a local workforce for various infrastructure projects, the state instituted mandatory labour for residents in Transcarpathia. Village officials were expected to distribute the burden among the villagers, exempting the disabled and those with full-time state employment. The state included women from eighteen to forty-five years old in this requirement, and men from sixteen to fifty-five years old. In theory, a teenager could find himself trudging away to a forest camp for a few weeks of felling trees. If residents owned horses or oxen, they could be required to bring them along. State workers could only return home once they had completed their designated work for the season.[3]

Given that the work was poorly paid (if at all), and often entailed hard physical labour in the woods, residents often dodged these summons from the state or stole away early. Mikhail Bokoch, the son of Dmitry, recalled that he once skipped town with some other young men in the village, but was caught and taken back to the forest by truck.[4] At a village soviet meeting the year of the arrests, the village admitted that it was far from meeting state demands for mandatory labour. It had too few available residents, and it managed to round up only a small fraction of the requested individuals. Frustrated with the poor quality of work performed by those who did show up for work, the soviet resolved to inform the state authorities about those villagers who left without completing their work.[5] Failure to report for labour duties could result in criminal charges, but fines were a more common penalty. Bila Tserkva issued fines to seventeen residents who had shirked the latest round of mandatory labour. The list of guilty individuals included a sixty-year-old man, suggesting that the village ignored the state's own regulations in selecting whom to send on these brigades. Even heavy fines, however, were insufficient to generate the necessary participation of the villagers.[6]

Several of the informants note the arrested men's avoidance and opposition to mandatory labour requirements. Yury Fonduriak, the chair of the neighbouring village soviet in Serednie Vodiane, told interrogators that he had sent a summons for Guzo to report for labour duty the prior fall, but Guzo never showed. Ivan Baider, the district party official, affirmed that most of the men had been listed on the labour rolls for that season, but none of them had ever arrived at the labour sites.[7] While the informants ascribed a political motivation to this refusal, this explanation is problematic. Witnesses do not have a theological opposition to physical labour, and indeed manual labour is a common profession of Witnesses worldwide.[8] Bila Tserkva Witnesses might have been wary about offering their labour to a state authority, concerned that this violated their Christian neutrality.

That said, it is equally possible the men simply did not want to leave their homesteads to engage in exhausting forest labour. This reason seems particularly likely given that the men were never accused of making theological arguments about this issue. While agitators were able to recite plenty of concrete statements by Witnesses about their opposition to various party measures, none could come up with similar examples with regard to mandatory labour. This suggests that while Witnesses may have avoided labour because it required them to participate in a state effort, they also did not need this justification to stay home.

State involvement in the local economy extended far beyond short-term labour roundups. If the local population had had more engagement with Soviet rule before 1944, residents might have predicted that they would face many of the same radical transformations as villagers in the Soviet heartland nearly two decades prior. Forced collectivization violently and irrevocably transformed the Soviet countryside under Joseph Stalin. Intense opposition from peasants, including armed resistance, was no match for the power of the state. Well over a million peasants were deported to Siberia.[9] Some deportees were wealthy, others resisted collectivization, and many others were targeted for any number of reasons irrespective of their political beliefs or land ownership.[10] Those who remained became state agricultural workers, with only small private plots of their own. In the aftermath of this upheaval, deadly famines further decimated the countryside.

The Soviet Union pursued similar land reform in its newly conquered western borderlands in 1939–40. A non-aggression treaty between Germany and the Soviet Union in August 1939 secretly carved up lands on the Soviet Union's western border. Shortly after signing this document, Germany invaded western Poland, which set off the global conflict. The Red Army, meanwhile, exploited its treaty provision. It occupied eastern Poland and the Baltic States, and, somewhat later, portions of eastern Romania. These territories experienced the rapid and brutal introduction of Soviet institutions and practices. Industry was immediately nationalized. Land confiscations stripped monasteries and landowners of their estates and redistributed it to peasant households that lacked sufficient land. State officials has just begun to establish state-run farms when Germany launched its invasion of the Soviet Union in June 1941. The non-aggression period was dead, and so was the process of collectivization, at least for the duration of the war.

Even so, it is remarkable that the Soviet Union committed resources to agricultural reforms while the world around it engaged in total war. In short, the state stood committed to collectivization as the model for agriculture despite its costs. In the face of widespread opposition, it had introduced it on its own territories, and maintained it even as millions died through famine. In the borderlands, it had moved quickly to implement this model in newly annexed territories as war broke out across Europe. Collectivization was an integral and essential Soviet institution. Any Sovietization project in Transcarpathia would have to include it.[11]

The full contours of this broad agricultural vision for Transcarpathia's future were not apparent on the ground level immediately after the war. Instead, the state moved forward cautiously with its economic reforms in the initial months. To set targets for its economic plans, the state began to collect data on crops and harvests. It founded the first machine tractor stations to eventually provide the industrial equipment and skilled labour for a more modern agricultural system.[12] It nationalized what industry existed in the region and drafted the first plans for industrial output in 1946.[13] The state also set limits on the amount of land a single household could own, reducing this figure over time and redistributing "excess" land first to poor peasants and then to the local collective farms. While large estates and church lands were confiscated, many Transcarpathian villagers continued to retain ownership of modest farms.[14]

For nearly three years after the war's conclusion, collectivization was a largely voluntary, ad hoc process, and one that attracted only modest interest from local residents.[15] Rural residents were understandably skeptical. They worried about what would happen to their land once they joined a collective farm. This concern was well justified, since the allotted private plots they would receive were no more than a half hectare (roughly one and a quarter acres), a fraction of the lands many farmed as individuals.[16] Villagers also expressed trepidation about the workload demanded by the state. They sent in their questions and concerns to the newspapers, which printed answers to some of them.[17]

Soviet authorities publicly expressed early confidence that collectivization could remain voluntary and still attract the vast majority of peasants.[18] Peasants simply needed to be sold on the idea that collective farms offered a better life. The state farm model undoubtedly appealed to some, particularly those with meagre plots of land or no land at all. However, it had less appeal for everyone else in the rural communities who stood to lose both land and livestock. Given that a voluntary approach had not succeeded in the Soviet heartland in the 1920s, the state undoubtedly knew that collectivization would take much more than a well-worded sales pitch. Moreover, there was almost no one to deliver this message in many villages, given the lack of local party members.[19] In this regard, the party faced an even more difficult challenge than it had in its earlier collectivization efforts. In the Soviet heartland, it had relied heavily on young activists to carry out collectivization by brute force. In the face of violent opposition, they responded with their own crude methods, burning down homes, humiliating and assaulting local resistors, and even using marching bands as they rounded up alleged kulaks (or rich peasants) for possible deportation.[20] In Transcarpathia, the state had far fewer trained party activists at their disposal, and even fewer who spoke Romanian.

It did not take long for the enthusiasm to wear off and reality to set in. Party officials noted with frustration the haphazard and ineffective propaganda efforts in rural Transcarpathia. A newspaper editorial in June 1948 was blunt in its criticism. The state farms had attracted a steady trickle of individuals but no interest on a broader scale. Party activists seemed to view collectivization as a seasonal activity. At the spring sowing and fall harvest, they showed up, made a few speeches, and figured that they had done their duty.[21] The party pushed for more dedication and more creativity in marketing the state farms to the masses. It suggested that agitators try engaging in conversations with local villagers or organizing field trips to a successful farm in a neighbouring region.[22]

Even positive reports on early collectivization betrayed the tenuousness of local support. The regional newspaper sung the praises of the new state farm in Berehove. The coverage included a large photograph of the farm's inaugural meeting. Despite the enthusiastic descriptions of the event, the photograph captures little of this alleged grassroots energy. At the far right of the frame, the farm chair delivers a speech to the crowd. Yet the reader's gaze is drawn not to him but to an older woman in simple dress at the centre of the frame. She sits with her arms folded and face slightly downcast. The man next to her timidly steals a glance at the photographer. In the row behind, two men stare sullenly at the camera. The shot suggests acquiescence to the inevitability of collectivization, but little else.[23]

The initial collectivization effort yielded mixed results. A mere handful of collective farms formed in the two years immediately following the war.[24] The state had the most success in low-lying and urban areas with a relatively strong party presence. In the district of Uzhhorod, seat of the regional capital, and in nearby Berehove and Mukachevo, most peasants entered collective farms relatively quickly. By 1949 collectivization was largely completed in these regions. Even the rural Tiachiv district directly west of Bila Tserkva had collectivized over one-third of its households.[25] The situation in Rakhiv district looked far less positive by comparison. By the end of 1947, the entire district contained only one collective farm, named for the thirtieth anniversary of the October Revolution. Four additional farms followed soon after.[26] In the span of the next twelve months, the party managed to persuade nearly 10 per cent of district households to sign on to the state farms.[27] Even so, that meant that nine out of ten locals had chosen *not* to join.

Party officials may have framed membership in the state farms as a voluntary decision for individuals, but this autonomy could not last much longer. Sovietization required collectivization of agriculture; those who had not already joined must be compelled to do so. The 1948 fall harvest ushered in a marked change in the official tone. Party propaganda continued to portray the farms as so clearly superior that no reasonable peasant could claim that they would not be better served in this system. But now, if some peasants still disagreed, the state made clear its intent to act in their best interests.[28] The campaign for full collectivization launched that fall. The timing gave local activists the winter to organize farms and sign up members in advance of the spring sowing season.[29] The year 1949 would be the "Year of Collectivization."[30] The state left no room for error or a more gradual approach: each and every peasant household would enter the farm system. On the surface, initial reports gave reason for optimism: already in early February, party activists proudly reported that 78 per cent of villages and 51 per cent of households in the region had been collectivized.[31]

This statistic obscured that farms were far more successful in some areas than in others. Rakhiv district, already lagging behind, got its collectivization drive off to a rocky start. When the district soviet met to discuss the issue in late December, it quickly concluded that not much had been done since the harvest. Local authorities invested minimal effort organizing new farms or promoting them among the villagers. Most glaringly, just a few kilometres down the road from Bila Tserkva in the neighbouring salt-mine town of Solotvyno, both the chair of the town soviet and his deputies evaded joining the local farm. In fact, they still had not joined even as collectivization picked up steam in the final days before the New Year.[32]

That spring, with the sowing season fast approaching, while the rest of the region hovered at just over 60 per cent collectivization, Rakhiv district reached only half that level. Some farms refused admission to qualified households that had petitioned to join. Others admitted everyone, regardless of social origin. Still others in the more mountainous areas of the district had not even bothered at all, claiming rather plausibly that a collective farm would never work because of the terrain. The district party secretary declared that a grand total of two farms in the entire district could be considered functional. The rest existed "only on paper." At the same meeting, the official in charge of agriculture offered an awkward blend of negativity and optimism in his remarks: "Comrades! Our farms are still in a state of embryonic development. Spring 1949 will be the spring of the collective farm!"[33]

In fact, it turned out not to be the spring of the collective farm in Rakhiv district. The summer proved little better. If anything, collectivization slowed down further in advance of the fall harvest.[34] When harvest time arrived, the party singled out Rakhiv as an underperforming district. Since farm membership was still ostensibly a voluntary decision, much of the blame fell on the local activists for their failure to win over the hearts and minds of peasants.[35] The paper voiced similar complaints again in December. Not only had many peasants refused to acknowledge the superiority of the collective farms, but also the farms themselves did not live up to expectations and suffered under poor leadership.[36] As the New Year approached, collectivization was far from complete in Rakhiv.

Bila Tserkva mirrored the broader flaws in the full collectivization campaign in Rakhiv. During the first few postwar years, the village had done little to generate interest in a state farm model. Only after the launch of the campaign during the 1948 harvest did it take its first steps. Activists gathered on 31 October for the inaugural meeting of the village's first collective farm. The farm initiators numbered less than two dozen, almost all men. District party representatives stood on hand to carefully direct the ostensibly spontaneous event. They told their meagre audience that "every farm worker will live well on the collective farm" and would be given the very best land in the village.[37] The village soviet immediately confirmed the creation of the farm. Its name, "New Life," seemed perfectly chosen to reflect the aspirations of the postwar Soviet project in Transcarpathia. The Soviet allotted the fledging farm 40 hectares of arable land and an additional 35 hectares of garden space.[38] A year later, the Soviet resolved to allot the remaining available land in the village to the collective farm. Principal Pelladi spoke in favour of this resolution. The comment, recorded in the notes from the meeting, embodies the official rhetoric of collectivization at this moment of transition:

> Collective cultivation of the land has been proved to be the best means to cultivate the land. This was recognized by our Bolshevik Party under the leadership of Lenin and Stalin. Therefore, we, the intelligentsia of the village, together with the agitation collective, should find all ways to implement full collectivization of our village. It is the only path that will lead us to a better future and to the full victory of communism.

Despite its unwavering optimism, Pelladi's comment a year after the arrival of full collectivization suggests that progress had been slower than anticipated. Moreover, in its original form, the comment, written in Russian with a healthy dose of spelling errors, reflects the growing power of the central state in village affairs. Almost no one at the meeting was fluent in Russian, and most did not speak it at all. Certainly, either Pelladi or the transcriber struggled with the language, or perhaps both did.[39] Even so, despite the clear primacy of Romanian in private life, official business began to take place in the language of the state. This meant that few villagers could access any of this information.

The district newspaper hailed New Life as the newest member to the collective farm system. The farm, it proclaimed, had formed in response to grassroots efforts. Thus far, twenty-two households had chosen this new life.[40] Left unsaid was that over three hundred households remained outside the farm.[41] The press continued its cheery coverage of New Life that spring as the farm approached its first sowing season. Ever the farm cheerleader, Pelladi penned a triumphal column on the farm's progress for the district newspaper. Already, he noted, the farm had a thresher, two mills, a few draft animals, and twenty plows, among other necessities. Eager members had entered the fields ahead of schedule to spread manure on the soil. Pelladi exclaimed that this harvest would be a first-class effort and would finish its sowing early. With any luck, he bragged, New Life would harvest enough onions this year to keep the entire district supplied![42] Once again, since the newspaper printed these rosy declarations in Ukrainian, few villagers would have been able to read them.

Behind the happy façade, however, New Life already faced serious problems. As the initial statistics suggest, few villagers had signed up in time for the spring sowing season. That left New Life with a severe labour shortage. In fact, so little of the farmland was being used that the much larger settlement of Velykyi Bychkiv, a few kilometres east down the road, began to eye the village's lands for its own use. In March it petitioned the Bila Tserkva village soviet to let it annex some of this land. The soviet demurred but recognized that they needed to get out there and sign up more peasants. Otherwise, it would be hard to ward off a future seizure of land by the village's more motivated neighbours.[43]

New Life management also left much to be desired. Without party presence and with only minimal buy-in from locals, authorities had no choice but to select an inaugural chair from among the available candidates. As it turned out, there were no great options available in this remote area. The man they ultimately chose, Todor Moish, was a disappointment. A middle-aged man and native resident of Bila Tserkva, he had a full six years of education and a background in family farming.[44] With no other professional skills and no party membership, these were the extent of his qualifications. In the postwar era, this was sufficient to earn him a position of considerable trust and responsibility in the village. Moish showed little interest in achieving full collectivization. Instead, he spent most of his short-lived tenure as chair in attempts to profit from the farm and minimize his own personal losses. With plenty of New Life land unoccupied and unused, Moish rented out modest allotments to non-members. This obviously did little to pressure villagers to join the farm, since they could now farm the land themselves for a modest fee. Moish himself seemed less than eager to commit himself or his family fully to the new agricultural system. While he did become a New Life member, he made sure to divest himself of his livestock before he did so. His son took the family horse to market and sold it for cash.[45]

Party officials sensed that something was amiss at New Life by early 1949. Moish had not yet contracted with a machine tractor station for the upcoming spring sowing season. This fact meant that the farm did not have any equipment lined up to prepare the soil and plant crops. Complaints surfaced that Moish had allocated some of the farm funds to an independent farmer. When farm members gathered for a meeting in early June, the discussion centred on Moish's many dubious practices. Nearly every villager in attendance had something to say against the chair.[46] Moish's tenure was over. The district prosecutor opened a formal investigation shortly thereafter. He found a host of serious violations on the farm. Outside assessors struggled to piece together the exact activities on the farm during its initial several months, as Moish had left few accounting records.[47]

As New Life struggled for survival, activists at the farm and in the village noted the intransigence of some of their religious neighbours to collectivization efforts. For the Bila Tserkva Witnesses, collectivization was something fundamentally new, and their religious magazines had not prepared them for how to respond. Certainly Witnesses had written passionately against entanglement with state authorities and secular institutions, but what were Witnesses to make of requests, and then demands, to pull their farmlands into co-operative ownership? Witnesses struggled to agree on an answer that seemed in line with their faith and how to live it under the circumstances of postwar Sovietization. The Ten Points memo was critical in this regard because it was a rare instance in which the religious organization directly addressed the issue. The memo advised Soviet Witnesses to remain apart from state institutions, while taking measures to minimize state repression. Point Nine described the farms in harsh terms:

> Regarding the farms, as you, my dear brother, have described in your words this entire situation, these people are entirely enslaved and have indeed become instruments of enslavement (slaves) and no longer have any ability to leave to follow a different manner of existence.
>
> According to our understanding, one must use all opportunities to find another path that would allow for freedom of action. This is the only way that a person will be able to establish contacts (or connections) with other people to help them understand the truth. However, in this situation, do not issue mandates and let all

> brothers make their own decision. Let every brother decide for himself if he wants to join such a collective farm and be an example for others on his modest plot, or to retain for himself the freedom of action on a bigger scale.

In short, the Ten Points memo told Witnesses to avoid the farms whenever possible. A major concern was that farm membership would entrap residents on the land and make it impossible for them to conduct the sort of evangelism that was detailed in the previous chapter.[48]

In this regard, the Witnesses did indeed conform to at least some of the accusations levelled against them by state investigators. Bila Tserkva Witnesses were opposed to the farm and refused to join it. Interviews with surviving relatives of the arrested men reinforce this fact. On a basic level, they confirm that the men had been opposed to the collective farm for theological reasons. As Dmitry Bokoch's grandson put it in one such interview: "there was much that they [Witnesses] did not understand" in the early Soviet period about what God required of them. He elaborated that these misunderstandings led them to make difficult choices against the Soviet system. "So many details" had yet to be worked out between the faithful and their leadership, and so the community preferred to risk prison rather than potentially jeopardize their salvation.[49]

For local activists, the Witnesses offered an opportune chance to deflect responsibility for New Life's fumbling missteps at Sovietization. The two events—the investigation of the Witnesses and the botched collectivization—were directly linked in time and place. Farm members went from long informant sessions with state officials about their Witness neighbours to heated farm meetings about Todor Moish's failed leadership. Moreover, the Witnesses provided an easier scapegoat than Moish. Just two days before the arrest warrants for the Witnesses, regional party officials criticized the dismissal of Moish as farm chair. The party had not been informed of this action and questioned its legitimacy. Farm members sharply defended their actions. One man griped that the party was itself to blame because "they are not interested in what is going on in the villages." He noted that as a farm composed entirely of the Romanian minority, "our farm ... needs more help than others." The party chose to let the farm's decision stand.[50]

The Moish incident, an event that overlapped with the state investigation of the Witnesses, taught the farm members important lessons. First, it demonstrated the state's relative ignorance of the situation on the ground in many far-flung rural communities. Second, it revealed the state's willingness to accept local versions of events as long as they fit within the limits of Sovietization. Third, it demonstrated the relative value assigned to citizens in the new system: Moish was a loyalist to the state, a valuable individual in a region with so few willing cadres. The Witnesses were much more expendable. Villagers had to persuade the state to allow them to remove Moish. At the same time, the state was asking the villagers for help in ridding it of Witnesses. When investigators summoned local farm members to talk about the arrested men, the farmers provided a consistent narrative: if Sovietization had not happened as the state wanted in the village, it was because their Witness neighbours prevented it. If New Life was not yet a success, it was because Witnesses sought to destroy it.

More than anyone else, Todor Moish had reason to point the finger at the arrested elders. He may have felt that doing so would protect him from a similar fate. In fact, he was removed as chair only a week later. When he sat down with interrogators, he was eager to divulge what he knew about his Witness neighbours. In his testimony, Moish immediately outlined the grave threat of the Witnesses to the broader Soviet project:

> As a resident of Bila Tserkva and as chair of the collective farm, I am aware of the following information about the anti-Soviet activities of the sectarians-Jehovists: the sectarian organization of Jehovists (in local jargon: *pocăits*) has existed in Bila Tserkva at least since 1935. With the arrival of Soviet power in Transcarpathia, the sectarians-Jehovists turned down a directly hostile anti-Soviet path with regard to Soviet power and embarked on anti-Soviet sectarian activity.

Moish then proceeded to offer a list of residents whom he blamed for this state of affairs. With regard to the farm, he was equally clear about where responsibility should stand:

> Given that the vast majority of the residents are kulaks in terms of their property ownership, they continue to agitate against and categorically refuse to join the collective farm. Moreover, having not joined the collective farm, they also refuse to allow the poor peasants among them, who are economically dependent on them and live on the same street, to join the farm.

> As a concrete example, in fall 1948, Nutsu Todorovich Stan joined the collective farm. The aforementioned individuals mocked him and refused to leave him alone. They made fun of him until Stan abandoned the farm and stopped showing up to work on it until he was kicked out.

Moish's version of events adhered closely to the party line that peasants, not the state, were the motivating force behind the recent collectivization drive. If Bila Tserkva villagers had not been keen to sign up, it was not because they did not want to join. It was because Witness activists advised them not to and put strong pressure on them to stay away from the farms.[51] Moish and other collective farm members blamed these men for using their positions of authority to turn their communities against the farms. Other local activists affirmed this view, detailing how Witness intransigence had impeded collectivization. One New Life member, a former deputy in the village soviet, told investigators that full collectivization was "breaking down" in the village because of the Witnesses. He repeated this fact more than once during his conversation with an interrogator, who underlined these portions of his testimony in the case file.[52]

Just days before his promotion to New Life chair, Moish's successor, Peter Porchan, also met with investigators. At face value, he appeared to have no more qualification for his job than Moish. He, too, had only six years of education, no professional skills, and no party membership. Other than being significantly younger than Moish, Porchan brought little new of value to the equation. What seemed most important was that he lived in the village, knew its lands, and was willing to take on the responsibility. He also claimed to have some knowledge of the Russian language, which would have eased communications between him and state officials.

While the state had extended its trust to him, Porchan also understood that this was contingent upon his ability to deliver. It could also be undermined by his answers to investigators. His wife, Anna, after all, had claimed to briefly attend meetings with the Witnesses, and gave separate testimony two days after her husband. The state could reasonably question the extent of Peter's commitment to the new Soviet system given his inability to convince his own household of its superiority. With an infant son just added to the family, Peter needed to reassure authorities that the removal of Witnesses would solve the underlying problems with the farm. Even so, his testimony about the farm is as vague as it is direct. Echoing his predecessor's comments, he noted: "The leaders of the sect of Jehovists in Bila Tserkva, mostly from among the kulak element of the village, whom I have named above, have been the most active sectarian-Jehovists from 1946–49. They carry out sectarian-Jehovist, criminal, anti-Soviet sectarian activities among the population. They do not recognize a number of Soviet laws and boycott party measures and the Soviet government." Peter's inexperience left him unable to provide much in the way of evidence of kulak agitation. Rather, Peter asserted their kulak status as a self-evident fact and then proceeded to provide a laundry list of other defamatory statements about Soviet power he overheard in his work as a village agitator.[53]

Given that the state championed collectivization as reflecting the will of the majority, local agitators carefully recounted their efforts to inform neighbours about the benefits of the farm, and their frustration when an allegedly recalcitrant minority hindered this process. In Bila Tserkva, agitators had gone door to door to sell their neighbours on New Life. While most villagers had evaded joining the farm at this point, activists stressed the actions of Witnesses as the critical factor. Mikhail Ona, one of these agitators, made his sales pitch for the farm at the home of Ivan Bokoch, the brother of the arrested men. Ivan told Ona, "Let them hang me, but I am not joining the collective farm." He advised Mikhail not to visit again.[54] Undeterred, Mikhail caught up with other members of the Bokoch family a few months later. The result was equally disappointing. Vasily Bokoch told him, "Don't be a fool. The current system of things is about to collapse. Armageddon is about to occur and those who do not believe in Jehovah God will all perish. So why should I join the collective farm when the collective farm will soon perish?" When Ona recounted this incident to the investigators, he accused the men of seeking to undermine Soviet power. Investigators highlighted his comments in the margins of the case file.[55]

Mikhail Ona likewise visited the Marinchan brothers that December. They refused to even consider the farm, telling him: "We will never join the collective farm because it is not God's organization but rather Satan's organization."[56] When the interrogators brought Vasily Marinchan and Ona face to face, Vasily denied having used these exact words but did not object to the general characterization of his beliefs. He had indeed refused to join the farm and would continue to do so because, he noted, his faith required this of him.[57]

These comments may have been modified by informants to appear more aggressive and menacing toward Soviet power. Still, they reflected the real, deeply held religious beliefs of Witnesses. Rather than focus on the immediacy of Sovietization efforts, Witnesses preferred to look forward to what they believed was the impending dawn of Jehovah's millennial kingdom. The Society promised that true Christians would inherit a paradise on earth, one that would last far longer and be much more satisfying than the socialist "utopia" offered by the Soviet Union. Vasily Bokoch questioned Ona about why he bothered to talk about the collective farm when he and his fellow Witnesses "await a new era that will soon arrive for us."[58] The farm paled in comparison. When Ona stopped by another Witness home in April, the man made it clear that he was wasting his time: "As long as I have a head on my shoulders, I will not join the collective farm."[59]

Witnesses may have rejected collectivization on theological grounds, but agitators also suggested that Witnesses voiced other criticisms of the farms. In this regard, they likely reflect the prevailing reasons for New Life's unpopularity. Todora Moish, the sister-in-law of farm chair Porchan, lived next door to a Witness who was not arrested but frequently mentioned in the interrogations. Todora's sister, Anna, was the villager who had briefly attended Witness services for a few months the previous year. Todora was twenty-three years old and, like her sister, a homemaker when she gave her testimony. Unlike her sister, she had some education: three years at the local primary school. She also made clear that that in contrast to Anna, she had never been involved at any level with the Witnesses. The previous fall, her Witness neighbour had told her that he would sooner go to work in the forest than labour on the farm. This was a serious statement. The forestry industry offered one of the few alternative sources of employment in the region.[60] As noted earlier, it was also not the most desirable of professions, and so this statement was likely meant to indicate how much this neighbour did not want to join the farm. He would take a difficult forest job before he would do that. This same man griped to another informant that New Life was organized for and by poor peasants.[61]

Another Witness vented that the farm had seized much of his land. The agitator pressured him to join or lose access to his farm entirely. The Witness was not convinced.[62] Two of the arrested men allegedly told the visiting party member from a neighbouring town that they worried they would starve to death if they joined. Vasily Marinchan told him that "the collective farm is a bad deal. Everyone who joins will die of starvation."[63] This was no idle fear; it reflected the harsh conditions at New Life that spring. Just days before the arrests, the farm had begun to distribute corn flour to members in dire need of basic foodstuffs.[64] Beyond Bila Tserkva itself, the food situation was far from stable in the western borderlands. A devastating famine had swept across Ukraine just a few years prior, killing over a million Soviet citizens.[65] One did not have to share the Witnesses' belief system to consider it ill-advised to trade individual farming for a risky venture.

That nearly the entire village had rejected collectivization, however, was a far more problematic notion for the state than that a fanatical minority had derailed a noble cause. Local activists struggled to explain to the state why so many non-Witnesses had also not signed up for the farm. One farm member speculated that Witness elders had turned the entire religious community against the farm, leaving it with only seventy individuals.[66] The district party representative gave similar statistics. He noted that once his office initiated full collectivization, Witness activists pressured their congregations not to join. The boycott had resulted in only sixty households joining out of 420 total in the village.[67] In fact, both men may have been too optimistic. The village, with a population of just under two thousand people, had succeeded in signing up less than forty households by 1950.[68] Given that Witnesses almost certainly made up less than a quarter of residents, this means that most holdouts were not Witnesses. It is unlikely that this reluctance was primarily motivated by exhortations from their religious neighbours. A more probable explanation is that Witnesses and their neighbours disagreed on theology but agreed that New Life (and by extension the party-state) had failed in its goal of convincing ordinary citizens of the superiority of the Soviet farming system.

In the earlier Soviet collectivization efforts of the late 1920s and early 1930s, the state had targeted kulaks as the primary threat to the campaign. While poor and middle peasants were encouraged to join the new collective farms, the state saw kulaks as a deadly adversary that had to be eliminated entirely. Beginning in 1929, alleged kulaks had been driven off their lands and forced into exile in remote locations in Siberia. They lost everything. Their children accompanied them into exile, as "dekulakization" affected the entire family. Yet what classified a person as a kulak was murky at best. Sheila Fitzpatrick has described kulaks as an "elastic category."[69] The term, which technically means "fist" in Russian, was open to broad interpretation by local officials. What made a man rich in one village might not make him so in another village. When local officials labelled someone a kulak, they did not always mean that this individual was better off than their neighbours. More often, the label was a way of identifying troublemakers or marginalized individuals with no powerful friends to protect them. Peasants who opposed collectivization or did not get along with local officials were far more likely to be considered kulaks, regardless of how much land they owned or money they had. After all, officials knew that they had to find kulaks among local peasants; it was just a matter of deciding on whom to pin this label.[70]

Getting rid of kulaks also freed up much needed land for the newly formed collective farms. In postwar Transcarpathia, this land grab was a top priority for local officials seeking to form viable collective farms. Village soviets compiled official lists of kulaks, their household members, land holdings, livestock, and use of hired labour. District newspapers pinned the widespread apathy or opposition to collectivization on these nefarious individuals, who allegedly convinced poor and middle peasants not to sign up at the farms. Newspapers described the kulak as a "bloodsucker" and "our enemy."[71] When farms failed, it was the fault of the kulaks.[72] Yet the press also cried foul when these allegedly rich peasants joined the farm themselves.[73] In Transcarpathia, local efforts against kulaks failed to impress party officials. The press regularly named villages for their lacklustre performance in dekulakization.[74] In March 1949, the soviet in Rakhiv district echoed these complaints. It called on village activists to expose their local kulaks and remove them from the farms.[75]

Thus, Bila Tserkva, with its meagre arable land and shoddy collective farm, was presumed by the state to contain kulaks. Yet it is not clear that the labelling of local villagers as kulaks was solely the result of state policy, begrudgingly adopted by local activists. Even before the formal investigation into Witnesses, villagers had applied this terminology to its religious minority. This suggests that villagers had already singled out the Witnesses for removal from their village. Starting in 1947, the village prepared lists of male heads of household who allegedly fit the "kulak" designation. Witness names appear to make up a disproportionate number of the list.[76] In Bila Tserkva, dekulakization benefited both local and state objectives: it satisfied the state's demands for kulaks, and it reimagined local opposition as the work of a resolute minority of class enemies.

Not surprising, what made Witness families "kulaks" was clearly not their status as rich peasants, since few fit that description. Most owned less than five hectares of land and a modest number of livestock. Nearly all had forfeited significant farmland on the other side of the Tysa River. One Witness landowner, for example, was left with two hectares of arable land and half as much pasture on the Soviet side of the border. He owned one horse. Yet the kulak list that contained this rather modest accounting of property noted that the man, his wife, and two children, were Witnesses and hostile to every aspect of Sovietization.[77] Similarly, the arrested men had less than three hectares of land apiece, with the exception of Guzo (who owned five). Vasily Bokoch had a single cow, a pig, and less than half a hectare of land.[78] Yet the village labelled four of these men as kulaks in their 1949 records: Dmitry Bokoch, the Marinchan brothers, and Ivan Nan.[79]

The villagers worked hard to convince investigators of their assumption that Witness were by definition kulaks. Paperwork submitted by the village soviet to investigators detailed the property of the men, listing them as either "kulaks" or "rich peasants."[80] Testimony from neighbours before the arrest made the kulak issue a central part of their accusations.[81] With the investigation underway, however, the kulak label did not fully stick. Perhaps investigators found it unnecessary to maintain this fiction any longer given the wealth of other damning evidence. Thus, while the initial arrest warrants for nearly all of men identify them as kulaks, the interrogation materials did not always affirm this fact, tacitly acknowledging that the men's property hardly elevated them above their neighbours. Vasily Bokoch went from being a middling kulak at arrest to simply the son of poor peasants by the end of the first interrogation. When asked, Bokoch described his socioeconomic background as that of a "middle peasant." In theory, his brother Vasily should have had the same background. Yet Vasily went from "kulak" on the arrest warrant to the son of middle peasants; a label that, like his brother, he agreed with. Most of the other arrested men underwent a similarly sudden demotion. Ivan Nan had perhaps the biggest fall, moving from "kulak" in the arrest warrant to "seasonal labourer" in interrogations. All this suggests that the impetus for labelling the men as kulaks on the basis of their religious beliefs came at least partly from villagers themselves.[82] Moreover, even the villagers did not always agree. Deputy chair of the village soviet Maria Chuban asserted that nearly all of the men were kulaks, but claimed that Nutsu Guzo, the one man not from her village, was a poor peasant.[83] Ironically, he owned slightly more land than the others.

Overall, despite the clear efforts of the village to make the farm a central feature of the investigation into their neighbours, the state ultimately articulated a broader case based on the men's statements against the entire Soviet project, their refusal to obtain passports or register for military service, and their evangelism to their neighbours. The indictments hardly mention the farm or collectivization at all. In this document, the state again adjusted its categorization. It listed Guzo as a kulak and described the remaining six men as middle peasants. For three of them, it further identified their "social position" as that of kulak. This designation indicated that while that the men themselves owned modest land, they allegedly came from families with more substantial holdings.[84] At trial, the court records offer a further window into the weakness of the "kulak" accusation. Required to provide a brief biographical sketch of each defendant, the court listed all seven men as "middle peasants" even as village kulak rolls declared otherwise. When asked, Vasily Bokoch testified that he had not joined the farm because God would not allow him to do so. Yet the verdict itself makes no mention at all of collectivization or kulaks.[85]

The state and village both won in their joint goal of removing these particular men from their homes. The village continued to designate other Witnesses, including the men's families, as kulaks, holding firm to its interpretation of events. Even so, at least a few Witnesses appealed this designation. The village soviet heard appeals by two of these families in early 1951. It rejected the first family's appeal by noting the family's religious beliefs. The second family was no more successful. This was the family of Ivan Nan, one of the convicted men. With Ivan serving time, his wife and seven young children struggled desperately to survive. Yet here, too, the deputies underlined the family's religious faith and previous use of hired labour. Ivan's conviction was noted as further evidence against the family. It deserves mention that the two other petitioners discussed that day, both not current Witnesses, received a favourable decision.[86]

The removal of Witnesses had another important benefit for the farm: it brought much needed land and livestock. With each arrest, authorities arrived to conduct a thorough inventory of personal property. Every single item of value was dutifully recorded. Village soviet chair Yury Moish accompanied the police on each search to examine all the goods the village would inherit given that a guilty verdict was a foregone conclusion. Dmitry Bokoch's son, Mikhail, recalled the presence of Moish at his family's home during the property assessment. Security officers and Moish strolled around the property, making a list of goods. Seeing a large sow in the yard, the chief officer remarked, "That's some good pork fat (*salo*)." Moish responded, "That's not good pork fat. That's good meat." Bokoch's wife and children stood by, watching as the men openly divided the spoils.[87] Some of the men had little to offer the state. Officials listed no property at the home of Vasily Bokoch.[88] Vasily Marinchan had a single female sow, two piglets, and a scythe.[89] The other men owned more, but nothing out of the ordinary for a village peasant. They had modest wooden homes, livestock, and assorted tools and furnishings.[90] After conviction, the farm took nearly everything. No one fared worse than the family of Ivan Nan. With seven young children at home, the confiscations left Ivan's wife barely able to feed her family. Unable to afford soap, the children got skin infections and lice.[91]

The farm, however, did not immediately spring to life once the men had been removed and their possessions confiscated. The new chair, Peter Porchan, inherited a struggling farm with few members and even fewer records. A few days into his new role, Porchan worried openly about the farm's readiness for the looming harvest.[92] None of these problems made it into the press. Instead, the district newspaper cheerily issued updates on the progress of the fledgling farm through the fall. In August, it reported to readers that New Life was the first in the district to send out its threshing brigades. At around the same time, the farm began to harvest its first yields from its vegetable gardens.[93] Village soviet chair Yury Moish himself penned a short blurb for the paper in mid-September to inform readers of the hard work of his local farmers. Many had already completed their work requirements. He encouraged those who wanted to learn more about New Life's early accomplishments to visit the newly installed photo exhibit in the village reading hut that had been put together by the local Komsomol.[94]

As New Life approached its one-year anniversary, district journalists brightly described the farm and its inhabitants as unrecognizable, but Porchan privately begged to differ.[95] Everything on the farm was behind schedule. The farm should have planted the winter grains by now. Yet the fields had not even been plowed, and this was because the yearly corn crop was still there, unharvested.[96] When the Ukrainian

Council of Ministers passed a resolution in early fall to allow Transcarpathian peasants to relocate to the more land-rich Izmail region, the frazzled Porchan wondered aloud at a village soviet session whether perhaps an entire collective farm could be resettled.[97] At least a few members thought this a viable solution. Seemingly without irony, Yury Moish told those gathered at a farm meeting the next day that the whole New Life farm could resettle in Izmail and "start a new life." Ultimately, the farm voted for a more moderate plan to allow those who wished to pursue resettlement to do so.[98]

In the months and years that followed, collectivization did happen in Bila Tserkva, in Rakhiv, and in Transcarpathia. It did not happen in 1949, as the party had initially intended. In fall 1949, Ukrainian party chief Nikita Khrushchev boasted that in three annexed regions of Ukraine, collectivization had already reached over 90 per cent of households.[99] In comparison, most households in Rakhiv remained outside the collective farms through the following January; some villages still had no collective farm at all.[100] It took another two years for Rakhiv to approach full collectivization.[101] Even within this underperforming district, Bila Tserkva was behind. The district singled out the village in early 1950 for its slow progress, berating its farmers and chair for their poor efforts.[102] Within a year of this pessimistic report, New Life was declared non-viable, and consolidated with larger surrounding farms.[103]

Both Witnesses and their neighbours gradually adjusted to collectivization as an unavoidable long-term reality of Soviet power. Although Witnesses continued to view farms as a corrupt institution run by a corrupted state, Vasily Bokoch's wife joined in 1950.[104] The wife of Ivan Nan joined as well and became a milkmaid.[105] When the men finally returned home, a few, but not all, worked on the farm.[106] For those increasingly left with no other option, the farm became a permitted way to survive under Soviet power until the promised millennial kingdom.

Historians have noted the rather muted response to collectivization in Transcarpathia. Pre-war collectivization in the Soviet heartland had sparked a violent peasant war. By contrast in Transcarpathia, many delayed membership as long as possible, but the vast majority ultimately gave in to the pressure to join the collective farm in their village.[107] David Marples describes the rather "passive" region as having adopted a "relatively quick pace of collectivization" in the postwar period.[108] This characterization obscures the deep ambivalence felt by the local population to this aspect of Sovietization. In Bila Tserkva, a clear majority of residents avoided the farm at first, including nearly all Witnesses.

Witnesses provided a unique and convenient cover for villagers to disguise the depth of this indifference and animosity to collectivization and Soviet power more generally. Faced with a failing farm and state scrutiny, village activists scapegoated their neighbours and obscured underlying problems of corruption and land and livestock shortages. When state investigators began an investigation into the Witness community, activists deflected blame for the lacklustre collectivization rollout on to a religious minority. While their actions may have mimicked state propaganda, residents also displayed clear initiative by pushing the state to recognize the arrested men as kulaks. In doing so, villagers removed an unpopular minority community and dodged potential criticism of unmet goals, while the state avoided an uncomfortable truth: the state farms did not perform well and were unpopular with much of the local population.

8

The Trial

Nearly two months after the state interviewed its first informants, it concluded its investigation. All seven men remained in Uzhhorod to await trial. After dozens of interrogations, the state was confident that it had gleaned all it needed from the men and their neighbours to bring the matter to court. It was unwilling to wait for more information to come to light. This rush to judgment occurred despite the fact that village informants had provided a much longer list of active Jehovah's Witnesses. The state's original case named four additional men as co-conspirators. This included Ivan, the brother of Dmitry and Vasily Bokoch, and Vasily, the brother of Ivan Ona, whose names came up repeatedly in statements from neighbours.[1] In this regard, local activists created space for a much wider investigation than the state ultimately delivered.

In part, the more limited scope of the investigation reflects the constraints of state power in the borderlands. Across the region, and especially in the newly annexed territories in Ukraine, the state hunted down alleged collaborators and partisans for years after the war officially ended. Some of these men and women were imagined enemies and reflected official distrust and even paranoia about the local population. Other borderland residents, however, were indeed engaged in a life-or-death struggle against Soviet power. It was a battle they would ultimately lose, but not without significant bloodshed and repression. In this regard, the seven men in Bila Tserkva were a relatively minor threat. None was accused of armed activities against the state. Moreover, guerrilla activity seems muted, if it existed at all, in the Romanian villages that dotted the far eastern portion of Transcarpathia. That said, the case against the men of Bila Tserkva cannot be understood without considering this backdrop. Fear of divided loyalties, connections to western organizations (even if religious), and western intervention defined postwar justice in Ukraine. While the men saw themselves as representative of millions of adherents of a worldwide faith community, the state saw them as collaborators with the capitalist West.

After police carried out the initial arrests, many of the remaining Witness men in the village had gone into hiding and could not be located during the investigation. Without better information about where to flush out these hidden Witnesses who had largely fled to other villages in Transcarpathia, the state could not reasonably eliminate the religious community. Instead, the state created a separate file for the alleged co-conspirators to eventually be located and brought to justice. That said, the state did make one last effort at confirming some of the salient details raised by its informants before it went to trial. In particular, informants had alleged that three local men had been "recruited" into the faith the prior year. The former New Life chair, Todor Moish, even suggested that this helped to explain why the farm had struggled. He claimed that one of the men had joined the collective farm, but that pressure from the Witnesses had led him to rescind this decision.[2] Moish obviously had good reason to explain the farm's troubles in a manner that did not involve his poor leadership.

These were serious accusations. To determine their veracity, the state issued summons for each of the three men to travel to the state-security office in Uzhhorod and meet with the chief investigator. Local activist Mikhail Ona was tasked with delivering these orders, but he came up short. The state managed to locate only one of the three men, who informed officials that, no, he would not be travelling to Uzhhorod. On the back side of the summons, the village soviet chair wrote that the man "is a sectarian and Jehovist. He refuses to accept the summons." The other two, both from Bila Tserkva, could not be found.[3] Given that these individuals were local farmers, if they had been at home, it would have been rather easy to track them down. The inability to do so strongly suggests a few possibilities. Perhaps the other two men could not corroborate this alleged "recruitment" story and were not Witnesses at all. Alternatively, they were Witnesses and had followed the example of others in their community by going into hiding outside the village. Perhaps most likely, they simply avoided local officials but otherwise remained in the area. If so, their non-appearance reflects the lack of enforcement mechanisms in such a remote location. Like the work summons, the village soviet did little beyond asking residents to co-operate with it, fine them if they did not, and lodge complaints with the authorities when the two other measures failed. The failure to find these material witnesses for the prosecution does not seem to have particularly bothered the investigator. Rather than further delay the case, he declared himself satisfied with the results.

With the investigation stage formally at an end, state procedure required that the investigator acquaint each defendant with the case materials against him and certify that he had no complaints or additional information to offer in his defence. This was a pro forma policy meant to sanction the legality of state actions. It was not an opportunity for defendants to have a say in the matter or to provide alternative explanations or exculpatory evidence. In this case, however, the investigator was unable to complete this necessary, if empty, gesture because the men continued to refuse to sign any state documents. As they had done throughout the investigation, the men withheld their signature on these official forms.[4]

Ultimately, with signature or not, the state had made clear its intention to prosecute the men. It issued its indictment the following day. This statement neatly summarized what the state felt were the most important details at the heart of the case. It concluded that the men were, first and foremost, anti-Soviet traitors:

> The investigation has determined that Vasily Bokoch, Dmitry Bokoch, Vasily Marinchan, Dmitry Marinchan, Nutsu Guzo, Ivan Ona, and Ivan Nan, being hostile to the existing Soviet order in Transcarpathia, and under the guise of their religious convictions as Jehovists, conducted active anti-Soviet sectarian work among the population directed at the rejection of Soviet power and its laws and the obstruction of Communist Party and Soviet state measures.[5]

This document makes clear that religion was not a satisfactory explanation for the men's actions. The men did not stand accused of believing in God. Their crime was not a matter of private faith or theology. Instead, the language of the indictment places the emphasis on how the men's personal decisions impacted the broader state project. Religion itself was no more than a "guise" to cloak the alleged political motivations that drove the men into conflict with the state. In this view, Witnesses violated the law when their faith began to inform how they saw their world. More specifically, they became anti-Soviet criminals when they attempted to win over others to this same understanding of the world. This view allowed the state to refashion the Witnesses as political opponents of Sovietization. It provided a necessary tool for both officials and local residents to compartmentalize opposition. Witnesses represented a minority opinion that could be easily identified, targeted, and, at least in theory, neutralized. Blaming Witnesses avoided the need to acknowledge broader weaknesses in Soviet control. It also shifted responsibility away from local activists and regional officials.

The indictment detailed how each of the accused had subverted the official order, even as it left vague the specifics as to exactly what "sectarian work" they had conducted among their fellow villagers. It singled out the military service issue, illegal religious services, and evangelism for particular mention. The case against Nutsu Guzo provides a useful illustration:

> Nutsu Guzo, being an active participant in the illegal, anti-Soviet sect of Jehovists, refused to register for military service or obtain a passport, declaring that in the case of conscription into the Soviet Army he would categorically refuse to take up arms and defend the USSR from invasion.
>
> He conducted anti-Soviet agitation among the population, directed at the obstruction of Communist Party and Soviet state measures. He did not obey the local organs of Soviet power, slandering Soviet reality. As a Jehovist, he recruited new individuals into the sect of Jehovists and attended Jehovist meetings.[6]

A few of the men had additional accusations levelled against them, though all were couched in similar rhetoric: Vasily Bokoch had declared that non-believers would be destroyed. Vasily Marinchan had slandered the collective farm.[7] The investigation classified Dmitry Bokoch as a man of particular authority in this community:

> Since 1942 Dmitry Bokoch has been a leader and preacher in the illegal, anti-Soviet sect of Jehovists in the village of Bila Tserkva. As such, he conducted anti-Soviet activity to recruit new members into the sect of Jehovists, baptized these individuals, and organized illegal gatherings of these individuals where he conducted anti-

> Soviet agitation aimed at destroying the power of the Soviet government.
>
> Together with other Jehovists in the village of Bila Tserkva, he organized illegal instruction on the principals of Jehovism among school-aged children, isolating them from Soviet reality and the Soviet educational system.[8]

This was an important development in the case because it assigned Dmitry greater responsibility than the others. While all the men allegedly conducted anti-Soviet propaganda, the state asserted that Dmitry had directed these actions from a position of particular leadership in the congregation. Although Ivan Nan had recanted his testimony, the state used his earlier statement to allege that Dmitry had carried out baptisms without sanction from the state.

In the end, the state's heightened charges against Dmitry mattered little in terms of practical consequences. In the postwar Stalin period, penalties for state crimes drew little distinction between minor and major offenses. Nearly all political prisoners during the Stalin era were convicted under just one criminal statute, the notorious Article 58. In Ukraine, the criminal code was numbered slightly differently, which meant that the Bila Tserkva men were charged under Article 54 instead. Jan Gross has written that "Soviet police interrogators had an easy job" in Article 54 cases because the statutes were written so broadly that anyone could be found guilty of this crime. Gross notes, "'Dokazhi chto ty ne verbliud' (prove that you are not a camel) was a popular saying that described the status of law and order in the Soviet Union better than the most learned dissertations on the subject."[9] How does a person prove that they are not a camel? How could these seven men prove that they had never said a single word or taken a single action against Soviet power? Like nearly all others accused under Article 54, they could not possibly meet this requirement. Defendants were presumed guilty even before arrest, no matter how outlandish the charges.

Article 54 had multiple components. Article 54-10 prohibited anti-Soviet propaganda and agitation. Article 54-11 banned participation in a counter-revolutionary organization. The men were accused of both crimes. Technically speaking, the penalty for either crime was death. In the late 1930s, the Soviet state executed hundreds of thousands of individuals under this statute and equivalent statutes in the other union republics. There was little to no chance for appeal, and the sentences were carried out shortly after the pro forma trials.[10] Two years before the men's arrest, the Soviet Union suspended the death penalty for such crimes.[11] This left a maximum sentence of twenty-five years' imprisonment. In practical terms, it might as well have been a death sentence. Poor nutrition, inadequate health care, and back-breaking labour made it unlikely that a middle-aged adult would survive over two decades behind barbed wire. When the men were arrested, this was the fate that awaited them. It applied to equally to Dmitry and the others, even though he was judged to have more responsibility in the community.

It is important to note what the men were *not* charged with. Many Stalin-era trials for state crimes involved fantastical accusations of espionage and elaborate political subversion. If the state had wanted to label the men as spies, it certainly could have done so, just as it had in plenty of other cases where no such evidence existed. In the case of Bila Tserkva, it would have been even easier to accuse the men of high-level espionage, as the men *did* belong to an international network. They were Jehovah's Witnesses, and that meant they were part of a global organization with branch offices all over the world. Moreover, this organization was headquartered in New York City, the financial centre of the United States. In later Soviet propaganda against the Witnesses, they were frequently accused of disloyalty to the state because of these international ties and connections to the United States. A 1959 article in the national Communist Party newspaper, *Pravda*, declared that "from its very beginning, the sect known as the 'Jehovah's Witnesses' has been in the pay of the most reactionary circles of American capital."[12] This interpretation of the Witnesses was remarkably enduring. State publications spoke of Witnesses as double agents for American imperialism until nearly the collapse of the Soviet Union.[13]

Moreover, an accusation of foreign allegiance would have been especially salient in the immediate postwar period. As the Soviet state moved to reassert control over its territories after the war, it singled out those who had been exposed to foreign influences for particular scrutiny. Returning veterans found themselves thrown into prisons. Scientists who shared research with foreign colleagues, citizens married to foreigners, even aficionados of American music and films found themselves at risk of repression.[14] Soviet Jews were disproportionately targeted by a state campaign against so-called cosmopolitanism, a thinly veiled cover for state-sponsored anti-Semitism. Jews were removed from high-level positions, arrested as traitors, and even secretly murdered.[15]

Yet the case record includes no such rhetoric. The men were never labelled "spies" or "saboteurs." The investigators never claimed that the men had plotted with conspirators abroad to destroy the Soviet Union. For a group of defendants who belonged to an illegal underground, albeit one with religious goals, the investigation was surprisingly local in its focus on events within Bila Tserkva and the surrounding district. One explanation for why the state chose not to use this weapon against the men is that it did not need to do so. The men had already committed the most serious crimes possible against the state. The Witnesses of Bila Tserkva were indeed outside the boundaries of legal activity in postwar Transcarpathia. Sovietization had restricted officially sanctioned religion to a handful of registered churches, none in Bila Tserkva. Jehovah's Witnesses were not part of this system, making any attempts to gather as a community into a crime. Recognizing that the men were arrested for crimes they did commit means acknowledging that men and women in the postwar borderlands often violated the rules of the new official order. They carried out seemingly simple, everyday actions with devastatingly serious consequences.

Moreover, the men had confessed to much of what they had done and held to their confessions decades later, even if they pushed back firmly against the characterization of these activities as anti-Soviet. In the hyperbolic criminal justice system of the postwar Soviet Union, simply attending religious services could earn a man a life sentence. Once the men had done that, and a whole lot else besides, conviction was a foregone conclusion from the state's perspective. We know from the indictment that investigators wanted a speedy outcome, even if it meant reducing the potential number of defendants. Adding in more complex allegations of subterfuge might have derailed this goal. Instead, the state favoured a straightforward investigation and trial.

In addition, if we assume that the state legitimately saw Sovietization as under threat in Bila Tserkva, investigators had every reason to focus on this information. Given that informants provided it in spades, investigators' primary role was not to fabricate bogus charges, but rather to mould what they already had into usable evidence. They needed to take a mountain of documentation showing that these men were active participants in an illegal religious community, and reshape it to prove that these activities were, in fact, the workings of an anti-Soviet underground. This strategy left investigators highly dependent on their local informants. In postwar Bila Tserkva, several hours outside the regional capital, it could not have been otherwise. The state did not yet have enough presence in the village to know any differently. Nor did it invest much time trying to rectify this situation. It stayed just long enough in the village to interview informants, and it returned only briefly to arrest the men before transporting them back to Uzhhorod. The men themselves said little, beyond acknowledging the basic tenets of their faith and enough illegal activities to land them in prison camps for life. Therefore, what the state "knew" about Witnesses, it learned largely from what other local residents told it. And these statements were carefully crafted to put villagers in the best possible light, avoid undue scrutiny, and shift blame for any local problems on to others.

In sum, Soviet officials initiated the investigation, but they allowed local residents to guide much of what followed. As was apparent with the farm, there were limits to how much the state was willing to accept. Generally speaking, however, villagers had considerable leeway in shaping the contours of the case and directing state attention toward the religious minority among them. The case file carefully records each accusation of an illegal religious service, each missed vote, and each publicly expressed belligerent attitude toward local authorities. Local residents did not need to conjure up a fictitious fifth column to explain why Soviet power had stumbled in the village. The Witnesses were readily available to be reimagined in that role.

A later investigation into Jehovah's Witnesses in Ukraine provides an important contrast. It also reminds us that while state crime prosecutions generally adhered to certain parameters, they could vary significantly. In 1952 state officials rounded up dozens of prominent Witnesses from several regions in Ukraine. After months of interrogation, the end result was identical to the Bila Tserkva case. The men and women were convicted of state crimes and sentenced to lengthy terms in prison camps. In many other respects, however, the cases were handled quite differently. Unlike the seven Bila Tserkva men, most of the defendants were accused of occupying positions of some authority in the underground religious community. They allegedly smuggled literature across borders, oversaw illegal printing presses, and communicated with the Watchtower Bible and Tract Society's representatives abroad. As such, the case hinged primarily on establishing individuals' positions in the organization and their connections to one another.[16]

Local communities and local informants figured only briefly in the investigation. Fewer interrogations addressed what the arrested individuals had done in their own villages and towns, or their interactions with neighbours. By this time just a few short years later, the state knew a great deal more about its borderlands, and about its religious minority communities. In turn, it needed local informants less. In this regard, the Bila Tserkva case marks a transitional period of Soviet power that already by the early 1950s was largely over. This centralization of control is also evident in the more limited role for regional officials. Rather than hold the accused men in the regional capital, the state shipped them to a secure prison in Kyiv. Interrogations dragged on for months, rather than weeks, and defendants were grouped together into several separate, but overlapping cases. When it came time to hold court hearings, the state chose to bypass the regional court system entirely. Instead, it used military tribunals run by the Ministry of Internal Affairs to handle the closed trials.

The later case also included some of the rhetoric absent in the Bila Tserkva investigation. In Bila Tserkva, local informants never imagined a conspiracy that reached much beyond the borders of their own village. By comparison, the 1952 investigation focused heavily on alleged international connections between Soviet Witnesses and their brethren abroad. Some of this may have been real, as Witnesses moved across the still porous borders of western and southern Ukraine in the years after the war's official end. Moreover, information conveyed from across these borders did sometimes reach the Witnesses' worldwide headquarters in Brooklyn. This reflects a coherent international religious community that maintained oversight over its individual congregations. For the Soviet state, however, this was evidence of a global conspiracy by its capitalist enemy, the United States, to undermine Soviet power. In one interrogation, conducted in Kyiv, the investigator repeatedly pressed one of the arrested men to admit his connections to American intelligence.

> Q: The confiscated literature from participants of the Jehovist anti-Soviet underground makes clear that the Jehovist underground is in the service of American imperialism. Provide the investigation with this information!

> A: I do not know the exact details, but I know that there is a Jehovist center in Brooklyn (USA) called the "Worldwide Jehovist Center." This Jehovist center and its leadership directs the actions of Jehovists in other countries. However, I do not know anything about the Jehovist underground being in the service of American imperialism.[17]

The interrogator dictated this broader context to the defendant, who was expected to agree with this damning summation. It is telling that this man's co-defendant (Vasily Dan) felt the need to state the following in an appeal of his conviction years later:

> While living in a Soviet country and fulfilling the will of Jehovah God (as it is written in the Bible), I was sentenced to 25 (twenty-five years) of imprisonment and five years' loss of civil rights. I was accused of having connections to the Americans at a time when I absolutely did not. I am a follower of Jehovah and not a follower of the Americans. I was accused of betraying the motherland and my own citizenship, and of having spread American propaganda and anti-Soviet literature at a time when my motherland is Jehovah, and not the Soviet motherland. I am not a Soviet citizen, but rather a Soviet resident.
>
> All of these facts [of the case] are false. Proclaiming God's good news is not American propaganda. I have never admitted to being an American agent. My reason and understanding were never directed at the liquidation of Soviet power and criminal actions.[18]

He understood that state officials in Kyiv continued to view his religion as an American front. He took pains in his appeal, therefore, to frame himself as merely a fervent religious believer, and one who continued to see himself as separate from Soviet society and its authority.

Even if the Bila Tserkva case did not include such accusations, village discussions of the trial and local gossip were less circumspect and included wilder accusations than the investigation's. Yury Marinchan's father was one of the defendants. He recalled that his father, Vasily, had been accused of being an American spy when he was arrested. The suggestion seemed preposterous to him. His father was a humble farmer and not exactly spy material. And, at least in the interrogation records, Vasily was never labelled as such. That said, what both he and his family understood about his case may have been rather limited by language barriers. Every interaction with state authorities, every interrogation, even the trial itself, was conducted in a foreign language he did not understand. Moreover, what Vasily told his son would have been conveyed years, perhaps even decades after the investigation ended. By that time, the state had acknowledged that it had falsely arrested many of its citizens on bogus charges, including American espionage. Vasily may have reasonably assumed that he also was arrested for this reason, especially since he did belong to a worldwide organization headquartered in the United States.

Even so, we should not dismiss Yury's recollection, which may tell us about how villagers spoke among themselves regarding the Witnesses among them. Given that the trial was closed to the public, rumours could easily spread in the absence of verifiable information. Moreover, the suggestion that the men were American spies had particular resonance. The heightened tensions of the Cold War created a climate in which many Soviet citizens suspected a new war might be on the horizon. Local newspapers fed into this atmosphere of fear and hatred. Readers were treated to a steady coverage of the alleged horrors of American life and foreign policy. Transcarpathian residents learned about "the power of the blood-soaked dollar" from their daily papers. On another morning, they might have read how Americans treated their pet dogs better than they did their poor fellow citizens.[19] Suspicions about their sectarian neighbours would only have increased once the state stepped in and arrested some of the men. Vasily may have been merely a dangerous troublemaker in the village, but residents could reasonably wonder if the state had found something even more sinister in its investigation. It is certainly possible that village gossip spoke about the men as "spies" even if the case file does not. After all, the men did not return after arrest. This created fertile ground for speculation about their neighbours' alleged crimes.

Of course, the men never returned home because they had been imprisoned in Uzhhorod. Once the charges had been filed and the investigation concluded, the only thing that remained was the trial itself. Six of the men awaited their day in court from a regional prison operated by the Ministry of Internal Affairs. Ivan Nan was held separately from the rest of the men. As the only one to volunteer evidence in the case, the state had isolated him from the others. This prevented him from interacting with his fellow defendants and made him more vulnerable to state pressure.

At least one of the wives appears to have made the long journey to the regional capital to visit their imprisoned husbands.[20] This would have been their last chance to see them. Once the men were convicted, they would be sent to labour camps too far away for the women to reach. Even the trip to Uzhhorod was long and expensive. The men's children did not get a chance to see their fathers at all. They had already said their goodbyes back in the village. It is unlikely that more than a few children understood the significance of this moment. Many were not old enough for school. Perhaps even the men did not comprehend the full implications of their arrest. Police arrests rarely allowed families more than a few moments, often spent in a rush to find warm clothes to take with them. In the weeks that followed, it may have taken the women some time before they realized that their husbands were no longer in the district at all, and then to track them down to a specific prison. If the state understood little about what happened in Bila Tserkva, the families were equally in the dark about events in Uzhhorod.

The families did not attend the trial itself. In the Soviet Union, the state sometimes held public trials of alleged traitors. These show trials were meant to showcase how the state dealt with dangerous criminals. This format was largely reserved for high-profile individuals.[21] The Bila Tserkva men did not fit this category. They, like most citizens accused of crimes against the state, received a hearing in a closed courtroom. The only individuals allowed to attend were those whom the prosecutor called as witnesses. Such trials were brief affairs. The prosecutor presented the basic facts of the case, as gathered from the investigation. The defendants had a chance to address the judge, but otherwise they were provided almost no resources to mount a serious defence. It is no wonder that most hearings lasted only a few hours, and sometimes far less than that. With only one side presenting evidence, and with the outcome a foregone conclusion, the court needed only enough time to go through the empty rituals of legality before announcing its decision.

At noon on 17 August 1949, the trial began. The court had prepared for the fact that none of the defendants spoke Ukrainian, the official language of the court. To resolve the issue, the men had the assistance of a Romanian translator. It was the same person who had translated for the state during their interrogations, which could not have inspired confidence in the translation. Still, it was their only option if they wanted to understand the proceedings at all. Through the translator, the court briefly confirmed the basic biographical details of each man.[22] Normally a formality, this portion of the trial raised an interesting question of perspective. The judge asked the men to clarify their nationality, which was listed as Romanian on the official forms. This was not mere curiosity. Soviet citizens were expected to have a nationality and identify themselves as such in all official interactions with the state. Nationality was something inherited, not consciously adopted, and it was presumed to exist and to matter for all citizens. Soviet forms always included a section for nationality. The "fifth point" on every Soviet passport listed the nationality of its owner. In the post-Stalin era, an individual whose parents had two different nationalities was allowed to choose between the two.[23] This decision came with consequences, as some nationalities were more advantageous than others. This was particularly true for Jewish citizens, who faced discrimination in higher education and career advancement due to their "nationality."[24]

For the defendants, the question of nationality was a tricky one. They had spent much of their adult lives as Czechoslovak citizens, followed by a brief period under Hungarian rule. At the same time, they spoke Romanian, as did nearly all their neighbours and the surrounding countryside. Mikhail Dan, a Witness from the neighbouring village of Serednie Vodiane, was arrested the previous year. He recalled how odd it was to hear himself accused of betraying his homeland by the judges in his trial. He noted, "I was born in Ukraine under the Czechoslovakian government and later lived under the rule of Hungary; now the Soviet Union has come into our territory, and I am Romanian by nationality. Which motherland did I betray?"[25] One scholar relays a strikingly similar anecdote from Transcarpathia, but one with a lighter tone:

> A visitor, encountering one of the oldest local inhabitants, asks about his life. The reply: 'I was born in Austria-Hungary. I went to school in Czechoslovakia. I did my army service in [Miklós] Horthy's Hungary, followed by a spell in prison in the USSR. Now I am ending my days in independent Ukraine.' The visitor expresses surprise at how much of the world the old man had seen. 'But no!,' he responds, 'I've never left this village!'[26]

On a practical note, the anecdote makes little sense because the man almost certainly left the village at least once when he was sent to prison. The seven men in this investigation were about to see the world for this same reason. Yet the fluidity of borders in this region made it difficult for local residents to understand the state's static notion of identity.

But, since the state demanded a concrete answer to the question, the defendants provided one. They told the judge that they were "Jehovah's Witnesses."[27] It is worth noting that Witnesses worldwide do not reject notions of citizenship or nationality. If asked, a Romanian Jehovah's Witness today would acknowledge both markers of identity. He would call himself a Romanian and a Jehovah's Witness. He might also indicate that national distinctions are not particularly important to him, and that his faith requires him to treat all nationalities as equal. It is a point of pride among Witnesses to cite instances where they have avoided involvement in worldwide conflicts along national, racial, or ethnic lines. For example, stories of Hutu Witnesses who sheltered their Tutsi neighbours during the 1994 Rwandan genocide have appeared in Society publications.[28]

This understanding of nationality was also true of Witnesses in the 1940s, which means that the men's identification as "Jehovah's Witnesses" was not merely reflective of their faith. Rather, it says something about how the men saw the newly created Soviet world around them. Simply put, they did not see themselves as "Soviet." Multiple states had required their loyalty, and a reasonable person might wonder if the Soviet system would not soon be replaced by yet another state that would make similar demands as well. Sovietization had not yet convinced them of the permanency of this new identity or the Soviet order. "Ukrainian" would have made even less sense to them. "Romanian" arguably offered a more stable identity, but then the Bila Tserkva villagers had never been part of a Romanian state. They were also relatively isolated from pan-Romanian sentiments that circulated in Romania proper and among communities in the Romanian diaspora. "Jehovah's Witness" might have seemed the most permanent identity available to them. By declaring themselves Witnesses, they also avoided linking themselves to a secular government that they considered doomed to destruction.

The men showed a similar lack of faith in Soviet institutions when informed of their legal rights by the judge. This included the right to have a court-appointed representative assist in their defence during the trial. The men informed the judge that they would prefer to place their trust in Jehovah rather than a state lawyer, but then refused to sign the official form documenting that they had waived their right to counsel. As a result, the court-appointed lawyer remained in place.[29] With these formalities out of the way, the judge addressed the men directly to explain the charges against them and ask them to enter their pleas. Each man responded with a plea of "not guilty." The prosecution and judge briefly conferred about how best to proceed in light of the fact that the men refused to admit responsibility for their actions. The prosecutor had sketched out a rather ambitious framework for the trial. Sixteen witnesses had been called to testify in court, and all had dutifully appeared on the designated trial date. Every one of them was an informant from the investigation. They had already been sworn in by the judge and informed of the penalties for perjury. If the men's decision to plead not guilty interfered with the prosecutor's plan of attack, he did not show it. All parties agreed that it made sense to begin the trial not with the slate of witnesses, but with the defendants themselves.[30] One by one, the defendants offered brief testimony. Vasily Bokoch spoke first:

> A: I became a Jehovah's Witness in 1943. I entered onto this path by reading the Bible. I do only what God tells me to do. Otherwise he will punish me.
> Q: With whom did you gather for prayers?
> A: I did not go anywhere. I only speak for myself. I am a Jehovah's Witness. I do not know about anyone else.
> Q: Did you obtain a passport and a draft card?
> A: I did not obtain either document. I live on Jehovah God's earth, but God does not teach us to defend it.
> Q: Do you recognize any authority?
> A: I recognize only the authority of Jehovah, who has transferred this authority to Jesus Christ.
> Q: Whom did you recruit into the Jehovists?
> A: I do not recall last names. When I became a Jehovah's Witness, I spoke about it with everyone so that they would also enter onto this path. Otherwise they would be destroyed. The Bible says that only Jehovah's Witnesses will survive and that everyone else will be destroyed.
> Q: Why did you not join the collective farm?
> A: God does not allow it. I may work at the farm, but I cannot sign up for the farm.[31]

Vasily also indicated that he had not signed up for state bonds and would not serve in the military. The court transcript provides less detail for the remaining six defendants. Rather than transcribe all the individual questions and answers, the court secretary noted that the men's answers were similar in content to those of Vasily. As a result, we only have fractured tidbits of information from the others.

Even from this incomplete testimony, it is clear that the men chose their words carefully to avoid endangering others. This becomes particularly evident when the prosecutor questioned each of the men to determine exactly when they became Jehovah's Witnesses and under what circumstances. As they had under interrogation, nearly all the men give the same explanation: they chose this faith as a result of reading the Bible. This was almost certainly not the whole truth, but it was a convenient truth. Dmitry Bokoch and Vasily Marinchan both provided nearly identical answers to this question. The men stated that they had joined the faith in 1942 (or possibly 1943). Dmitry testified that he became a Witness after "I received a Bible from a stranger who was a Jehovah's Witness." When it was Vasily Marinchan's turn to testify, he also became a Witness "having read the Bible that I received from an unknown man." A third defendant, Dmitry Marinchan, stated that he had gotten his Bible from his father. Guzo noted that he had purchased a Bible from a Jehovah's Witness but declined to give the man's name. Ivan Ona provided perhaps the murkiest summation: "I read the Bible myself, and I chose this path for myself."[32]

In fact, the congregation shared more than just Bibles; it also circulated illegal copies of the *Watchtower*, the Witnesses' bimonthly magazine. This literature was read at the illegal services held in private homes in the village. It is unlikely that the men had forgotten who had given them such a treasured item as a Bible, which would have been a valuable possession for these rural farmers. Dmitry Marinchan's daughter recalled that her father referred to new issues of the *Watchtower* as "white bread." One issue sometimes had to suffice for the entire village.[33] In short, the men's responses did not accurately reflect the community environment in which they entered into a new faith. At the same time, the unwillingness to name others in that community reflected the underlying strength of those bonds.

The testimony also reveals the importance the prosecution assigned to the question of baptism. Given that the state viewed the Witnesses as an illegal anti-Soviet organization, it was critical that it determine the "recruitment" mechanisms by which Soviet citizens were persuaded to betray their newly adopted homeland. Baptism was the initiation ceremony that marked individuals as agents in this subversive network. As with the previous question, the men obfuscated as much as possible. Vasily Marinchan admitted that he had been baptized by an individual from another village. He did not, however, name the man in question. It is possible that he did not actually know the man's name; introductions were sometimes skipped to protect those involved.[34] Regardless, Vasily told the prosecutor that it was not he who performed the baptism but Jehovah himself. Dmitry Marinchan echoed this sentiment in describing his own baptism. "Jehovah and Christ baptized me," he told the prosecutor.[35]

The men had enough sense to know that the state wanted the names of others, but they did not always make consistent decisions about when to withhold them. On a practical matter, the defendants differed over whether to admit that their family members were also Jehovah's Witnesses. When asked, Dmitry Marinchan told the court that his wife was in the faith. The state already had this information, making it rather pointless to deny an obvious fact. Yet Nutsu Guzo did precisely that in his own testimony. Questioned about his wife's faith, he responded, "Is my wife a Jehovah's Witness? I do not know. I only know about myself."[36]

The prosecutor likely anticipated that the most valuable testimony would come from Ivan Nan. After all, he was the only one of the defendants to offer information during the investigation, even if he quickly recanted it. Unfortunately for the state, Nan was not the star witness they had hoped for. The partial recording of his testimony is quite short and virtually identical to the answers from the other men:

> A: I became a Jehovah's Witness in 1943. I chose this path from the Bible, which I received from an unknown woman. I do not know any other Jehovists. I never attended a prayer service. Jehovah and Christ baptized me.
> Q: How many children do you have?
> A: Seven; the youngest is four and a half years old.[37]

Thus ended Nan's brief moment on the stand. Given that this represents only a brief summary of his remarks, it is reasonable to assume that the prosecutor asked Nan other questions. Perhaps he attempted to get Nan to affirm his earlier statements, but if so, he apparently did not do so. Nothing else he said was apparently noteworthy or useful enough to the state to warrant inclusion in the official record.

With the defendants' testimony concluded, the court adjourned for two minutes. The absurdly brief break, noted carefully in the transcript, reflects a court process that valued speed over depth. When court resumed, it turned to the state's witnesses. One after the other, the men's neighbours recounted the details they had already shared with investigators. The accused men did not carry passports or register for military service. They did not vote or buy state bonds. Mikhail Ona, who spoke first, began by declaring that the men did not recognize Soviet power. When the prosecution asked Ona to estimate how many Witnesses resided in Bila Tserkva, he responded that the village contained roughly four hundred "Jehovists." He also noted that this number had risen substantially in recent years. Ona may have disappointed the prosecutor, who prodded him to identify the locations of Witness prayer services. Ona could only reply that he knew the Witnesses continued to meet but did not know where at the moment.[38]

Bila Tserkva residents emphasized to the court how much time and effort they had spent in reaching out to wayward members of their community. Some of them had visited nearly every one of the defendants. Their words worked to absolve them of any responsibility. If the men had rejected Soviet power, it was not due to the lack of effort on the part of agitators. The village could not be blamed if a small minority joined a nefarious anti-Soviet organization that undermined Soviet institutions. On the contrary, their presence in court demonstrated that villagers and the state were united in their goal of rooting out such dangerous subversives.

The defendants watched most of this testimony with little involvement, making the few instances in which they did engage with their neighbours all the more illuminating. The first such moment came after Ivan Dan testified that he had seen the men gather together for a religious service. Then he qualified this statement a bit: he had only stood by the door, and so had not heard a word of what the men had said. Even so, he confidently described this illicit gathering as evidence of the men's involvement in illegal activities. Asked to confirm or deny this alleged event, the defendants declared Dan's testimony utterly false. Quite possibly it was on that occasion.[39]

Likewise, when the school principal, Alexander Pelladi, testified about the corrupting influence of the men on their children, Nan defended himself against this accusation. He noted that he sent his children to school but did not teach them anything, a broad statement that presumably only applied to religious indoctrination. In at least one instance, the defendants intervened to confirm an accusation. When Yury Fonduriak described how Guzo had refused to carry documents, Guzo agreed. He explained that it would have been an affront to God to do so.[40]

Anna Porchan was rather unique in her testimony. Unlike the largely male cast of informants, she had allegedly encountered the men as a potential "recruit" into the faith. The prosecution questioned her about the service she attended at the home of the Marinchan brothers. It had been attended by ten to fifteen Witnesses. The brothers encouraged her to join the faith or else she would perish; she demurred. The court transcript does not record any objections to this particular witness from the defendants.[41]

The last man to testify was Yury Kogut. As with his neighbours, Yury focused on what he knew about the men from his work as an agitator: "Defendants Dmitry and Vasily Marinchan did not want to accept Soviet documents. They refused to join the collective farm. They stated that it was not a godly organization. They said that they would not vote in the judicial elections because they had already voted for God and would never again cast a vote for anyone else."[42] From the perspective of Kogut and others, the defendants had stubbornly refused to listen to reason. Despite the earnest appeals of their more enlightened fellow citizens, the men clung to a worldview that rejected the basic tenets of Sovietization. This interpretation suggested that persuasion and education might never be enough to bring some minority communities into the Soviet fold. After all, if dozens of visits by agitators had failed to convince them of the superiority of Soviet power, it was unlikely that another dozen visits would do the trick. The only option then was to remove the men from society so that those who had embraced Soviet power could enjoy its full benefits.

After Kogut finished his statement, the prosecutor turned to Nan and asked him, "Do you recognize Soviet power?" Nan responded that he did not.[43] This answer affirmed what the neighbours had already told the state about the men. They would never join Soviet society, and their continued presence undermined everything the state wanted to accomplish in the village. The judge obviously felt that this was sufficient evidence to conclude the proceedings. The remaining three witnesses were dismissed.

The trial was near its end. Dmitry Marinchan alone is recorded as having spoken a few words in his own defence. He told the court, "I am not against Soviet power. I do only what God requires of me."[44] This statement may have been an attempt to mitigate the blunt rejection of Soviet power that had only just been voiced by Nan. Even so, Dmitry avoided a direct endorsement of Soviet power. Rather, he suggested that his actions flowed from his investment in a religious worldview rather than from a rejection of Soviet ideology. Still, his words left little doubt that when forced to choose between the two, he would side with Jehovah.

And with that, the court adjourned for one hour to prepare closing remarks. When it resumed, the prosecutor took to the floor to emphasize the "especially dangerous crimes" that warranted the full punishment allowed by the law. The court then gave the defendants the final word.

> Vasily Bokoch: This trial is wrong. I have done nothing. I ask to be released home as my wife is pregnant.
> Dmitry Bokoch: Jehovah will take me to him.
> Vasily Marinchan: Please do not punish me.
> Dmitry Marinchan: I am a Jehovah's Witness. God will punish those who condemn me.
> Nutsu Guzo: I am a Jehovah's Witness. I could not do anything against anyone.
> Ivan Ona: The court is wrong to condemn me.
> Ivan Nan: I do not ask the court for anything. I ask only that Jehovah hear me.[45]

The court adjourned for the judge to prepare the verdict. It did not take long to reach a decision. Just before six o'clock in the evening, the judge returned. The trial and deliberation had lasted less than one day. The court verdict reads as follows:

> As of 1942–43, the defendants have all been active participants and believers of the Jehovist sect, the most reactionary of all sects in Transcarpathia. Particularly in the village of Bila Tserkva, but also in the village of Serednie Vodiane, Rakhiv district, this has become the most widespread sect due to the actions of the defendants.
>
> During the course of the investigation and trial, each of the defendants has admitted their counter-revolutionary actions in failing to recognize Soviet power and in refusing to take part in

> the measures of the Communist Party and the organs of Soviet power. These actions, the defendants have explained, stem from the Jehovist slogan: "Those who do not believe in Jehovah God will be destroyed."
>
> As active participants in the sect, the defendants instilled these teachings in minors of both school and preschool age. This fact was confirmed by witnesses Pelladi and Porchan. Their testimony was not contradicted by the defendants, who explained that they did so because of their teachings, which are based on the theories of American reactionary Rutherford.
>
> All of the defendants stepped up their activities beginning in 1945 after the unification of Transcarpathia with Soviet Ukraine until the moment of their arrest, that is until 24 June 1949. All of the anti-Soviet activity by the defendants was intended to instill religious superstitions among the population. This is confirmed by the case material and the defendants' statements.[46]

The verdict is noticeable both for what it includes and for what it leaves out. It makes a direct link between the defendants' actions and Soviet power. Although it affirms that the men joined the faith before the end of World War II, it asserts that they became active sectarians in earnest only with the annexation of Transcarpathia. Moreover, it describes the Witnesses as not merely a counter-revolutionary organization but the most reactionary of all underground religious organizations in the entire region. At the same time, the verdict lists almost no specific actions in making this claim about counter-revolutionary activity. Beyond a general statement about boycotting party and state measures, it does not bother to affirm specific allegations made by the neighbours. Indeed, the verdict limits itself to one concrete crime: the recruitment of minors to the organization.

Last, the verdict vaguely refers to a shadowy individual, "Rutherford," described only as an "American reactionary." This is a reference to Joseph Franklin Rutherford, the interwar president of the Watch Tower Bible and Tract Society. He was neither the founder of the faith nor its current executive officer. More important, he had been dead for several years before the trial.[47] The phrasing suggests that the men themselves spoke about this man in their testimony, but neither the interrogation records nor the admittedly incomplete trial transcript confirm this fact. Why then refer to Rutherford at all? The answer almost certainly lies in the circulation of religious literature written by Rutherford among Transcarpathian Witnesses. A prolific author, Rutherford had penned numerous books and brochures about his faith, and the Watch Tower Bible and Tract Society had printed and distributed them in large numbers during the interwar period. Many of these publications had been translated into European languages.[48] At least one of the defendants owned a copy of one of them. A search of Vasily Bokoch's home on 24 June turned up a single Romanian-language brochure by Rutherford.[49]

Yet this does not fully explain the mention of Rutherford in the verdict. The interrogation records never mention any questions about this brochure. The judge also could not have reviewed this piece of evidence in writing the verdict. The case file indicates that the brochure was burned on 30 July just before the close of the investigation and a full two weeks before the trial. Thus, the only plausible explanation for this anomaly is that the judge had access to additional information about the Witnesses in crafting the decision. This information could have come from state-security files or from the regional religious council, both of which maintained information about Witnesses. Later Soviet publications and internal documents frequently referred to Witnesses as "Rutherfordists" and quoted passages from Rutherford's books.[50]

Undoubtedly, the inclusion of an alleged link between seven rural believers and an American reactionary was meant to strengthen the merits of the case and justify the harsh sentence. Even so, it is only a half-formed accusation in the verdict.

All the men faced the same fate. The court sentenced each to twenty-five years of imprisonment in a labour camp with loss of rights for an additional five years. The men also forfeited all their meagre property and were ordered to pay a fee to cover the legal services that they had attempted to waive at the start of the trial. The men duly refused to sign the form affirming that they understood the verdict.[51]

The appointed legal counsel promptly submitted an appeal on behalf of the men the following day. It was clearly not how the men would have articulated themselves. Given that the men had not asked for this lawyer's assistance, they likely had no role in preparing this document or agreeing to its submission to the court. Their signatures do not appear on it and the counsel makes no claim that it reflects their demands. That said, it did offer a sincere attempt to reframe the men's actions as the result of ignorance rather than counter-revolutionary sentiments:

> The defendants are all uneducated and have a rather low level of development. Their minds have been affected by a thousand years of slavery. They are inclined to mysticism, cultivated by the previous anti-people regimes whose goal was to extend their rule of darkness. These regimes drew the defendants to sectarianism during the Hungarian fascist occupation by preaching the rejection of government power.
>
> But sectarianism was first and foremost directed against the fascist occupiers (1942–44), and still has not been extinguished. This is primarily due to insufficient explanatory work. Thus, we cannot conclude that the defendants had direct counter-revolutionary intentions.[52]

The statement is both oddly vivid, with its references to mysticism and enslavement, and also fully in line with Soviet norms. While the men repeatedly cited theology and religious convictions in their defence, these justifications mattered little, if at all, to the Soviet state. Their self-appointed lawyer knew enough not to try this approach. Instead, he shifted the blame back on to two convenient targets: the agitators, who had failed at their task of re-educating their less enlightened neighbours, and the previous governments that had governed Transcarpathia before Soviet annexation. Both explanations absolved Soviet officials of any responsibility and suggested that further educational work in the village could resolve the problem entirely. In light of this interpretation, defence counsel requested that the sentence be reconsidered. Twenty-five years was too harsh; he asked that the court consider a "softer" punishment instead.

The Ukrainian Supreme Court disagreed with the well-intentioned, but ineffective lawyer; it upheld the decision. In its ruling a month later, it affirmed the conclusions of the original verdict, noting that the men had all admitted to their involvement in the "Jehovist sect," which, it repeated, was the most reactionary sect in the region.[53] The investigator stamped the file "secret" and sent it to the archive for storage.[54]

9

Release

The Soviet Union had condemned the seven men to near certain death. If they have survived the full twenty-five years, the men would all have been in their sixties by the time of release; the oldest among them would have been nearly seventy. After the verdict, the state dispatched the men to labour camps far from Transcarpathia. All of them ended up in camps within the Komi republic, an Arctic region rich with natural resources.[1] Most of the native inhabitants were reindeer herders. The remote location made it ideal for housing prisoners, who had no possibility of escape. The Gulag brought needed workers to the inhospitable region, providing free labour to exploit the massive coal seams discovered in the early 1930s.[2] To accommodate more and more prisoners, the region had undergone extensive development in the past two decades. Rail lines appeared, as did roads, and eventually towns, then cities. Nearly all this infrastructure was constructed for the service of the Gulag.[3]

Vasily Marinchan was sent to the Vorkuta camp. His brother, along with Dmitry Bokoch, Nutsu Guzo, and Ivan Ona were dispatched to the Mineral Camp in Inta, located in a more southerly area of Komi. Two men, Vasily Bokoch and Ivan Nan, were placed in the River Camp, a special camp near Vorkuta. The state had established these special camps within the Gulag a few years before for the control and isolation of political prisoners deemed especially dangerous to the Soviet order. Special camp prisoners had only minimal access to outside mail from their families, more restrictions on their movement within the camp, and longer workdays. They could only be assigned to "heavy physical labor under armed guard." In turn, guards were to refer to them not by their names, but by numbers sewn on their uniforms. The whole experience was meant to "dehumanize and punish" traitors to the state.[4] There is no indication why some of the men received this harsher treatment. Given that all the men received the same sentence, this placement is hard to explain. Dmitry Bokoch was the only identified "leader" in the indictment, and yet his brother was sent to this camp instead.

Some of the men worked long hours in underground coal mines.[5] The work was exhausting and dangerous, though those with underground shifts had greater protection from the Arctic winds. John Noble, an American who served time in Vorkuta in this period, described the harrowing experience of life and work in the camps in graphic detail:

> My life in Vorkuta was the closest thing possible to a living death. It was a grueling combination of slow but continuous starvation, exhausting work, killing cold, and abject monotony that destroyed many a healthier man than I …
>
> The first seven months of the winter 1950–1951, I had just enough stamina to make it back to the camp every night. After 'supper' in the *stolovaya*, our mess hall, I collapsed on my hard shelf in my filthy, snow-soaked work clothes. My face was deep red from the cold, and for two hours after coming indoors I felt as if a log fire were six inches from my nose. I could hardly lift my legs. My shoulder was blue from the slate car, and the palms of my hands had turned to elephant skin, each palm a large callous insensitive to cold, heat, or pain.

Noble weighed less than one hundred pounds, lost teeth due to lack of vitamins, and broke a rib after being pinned by a runaway coal car.[6] The year before the men arrived in Komi, an inspection of some of the Vorkuta camps found that only about a quarter of the prisoners had underwear and roughly half had warm boots.[7] Most of the prisoners survived these conditions in the postwar period, but meagre rations and excessive work norms took a major toll on their health.[8]

Back at home in Bila Tserkva, life for the men's families was difficult, to say the least. The convictions had granted the village soviet the authority to confiscate nearly everything that the families owned. Vasily Marinchan's family was allowed to keep their cow, but other families were not so lucky. The women had to figure out how to survive and raise their children without their husbands. Dmitry Marinchan's wife joined the farm to ensure food for the family. She travelled to nearby markets to find items that were not grown on the farm or on her own small plot of land. Even so, the family often came back from such shopping ventures empty-handed, unable to find sellers. Bread was a luxury the family struggled to obtain. The oldest daughter, not yet a teenager, sometimes took the family's remaining possessions to the local bazaar for bread money. All the young children ventured out into the woods for kindling.[9] The Nan family, with seven children at home, suffered enormously. When the state came to take away their cows, sheep, pigs, and other possessions, the family wept, powerless to prevent it. One of Nan's daughters, Maria, hid the family Bible under her dress, but the officials found even that and took it. Joining the collective farm gave the family enough food to survive, but only barely. Unable to afford soap, the children contracted scabies until a kindly neighbour helped the mother sooth the children's skin.[10]

Luckily for both the men and their families, it turned out that they did not need to wait twenty-five years to be reunited in Bila Tserkva. They simply had to outlive the dictator who oversaw this system of punishment. In 1953 Joseph Stalin died. While Soviet citizens publicly mourned his death, nearly 2.5 million inmates heard the news from behind barbed wire. They responded with mixed emotions. Some cheered; others wept.[11] The Soviet system had been so identified with its leader for nearly thirty years that it was hard to imagine life without him. Nor was there any certainty about what would follow and whether it would be better or worse than they had previously known.

For their part, Stalin's successors had inherited a volatile, overcrowded, and unprofitable prison complex, and it became apparent rather quickly that they were unwilling or unable to maintain it. Less than a month after the funeral, the state issued a public amnesty that was incredibly broad in its scope. It emptied the Gulag of nearly half its prison population by immediately releasing those whom it deemed to pose a relatively low risk to the public. This included "pregnant women, women with children under ten, juveniles, men over fifty-five, and women over fifty." It also sharply reduced the sentences of criminals who had been convicted for non-state crimes.[12] While these measures primarily affected non-political prisoners, i.e., those without Article 54/58 convictions, it still signalled a massive overhaul of the system. An additional amnesty in 1955 included some of those convicted of political crimes related to World War II.[13]

The state also initiated a formal review of old cases for state crimes and restored freedom and civil rights to some of those accused under Stalin's long tenure in power. This process of "rehabilitation" came too late for victims who had already died in the camps. The Bila Tserkva men, however, were still alive, and had nearly twenty years left on their sentences. They shared the hope of many inmates that this fate might be changed. Ona filed the first formal petition for review within months of Stalin's death. The men may have written other letters to party and state officials since their convictions; many prisoners did. That said, Ona's petition was the first time such requests were mentioned in the case file. A special review board in Uzhhorod requested the case file from the archives and combed through the original accusations and evidence. Although the request came only from Ona, the board evaluated the entirety of the case, including the validity of its charges against other individuals. Ultimately, however, the board reached the same conclusions as had the original court: "All of the convicted men conducted anti-Soviet activity to impede measures in the village."

The original appeal from Ona is not included in the case file. This makes it impossible to know exactly how Ona framed his request. Regardless, the review board was not impressed by its contents:

> The complaint submitted by convict I.Iu. Ona to the General Prosecutor's Office of the USSR provides no evidence to support his assertion that he allegedly was wrongly convicted and considers himself innocent.
>
> The complaint by convict Ivan Iurevich Ona is written in a Jehovist spirit. It is apparent that Ona remains hostile to the Soviet government, which he covertly refers to as a "satanic" government. Having reviewed the case materials, the board finds that convict Ona's complaint is without basis and does not merit approval.[14]

The board considered the case closed and returned the file to the archive in Uzhhorod.

Within a year, the matter was reopened for more thorough review by a regional commission. This second evaluation appears to have occurred at the behest of the state, rather than one of the men. The commission duly sorted through the original testimony by informants, citing them at length in their review. Whatever the shifting climate for political repression in the Soviet Union, informants' words still carried considerable weight with state officials. Neither review questioned the merits of these accusations or the possibility that they may have ascribed political motives to religious activities. The expert report concluded as follows:

> The sentence of twenty-five years, with five years loss of civil rights and confiscation of property, in the case of convicted men V.T. Bokoch, D.T. Bokoch, V.M. Marinchan, D.M. Marinchan, N.V. Guzo, I.Iu. Ona, and I.V. Nan, under articles 54-10, part 2, and 54-11 of the Criminal Code of USSR [Ukrainian Soviet Socialist Republic] is considered appropriate to the crime. The regional court decision should be upheld without alterations.[15]

Less than a week later, the man who prepared the report testified about his finding before the full commission, which upheld his recommendation. The post-Stalin rehabilitation process, intended to ferret out wrongful convictions of innocents, had less to offer individuals who had violated the absurdly broad statutes against counter-revolutionary activity. Reviews of the case quickly determined that the men had indeed belonged to an unsanctioned organization and did not recognize or support Soviet measures in the village. And with that, the case file was returned once again to the archives.[16]

Even so, the families of the men refused to abandon hope of a successful review. Two of the wives wrote directly to state officials to plead for mercy. In her petition to the state, Akseniia Nan carefully framed her husband as a victim of his own ignorance and unfamiliarity with the Soviet system. She noted that her family came from a "young region" that had only lived under Soviet power for a few short years, and that they had not had a chance to fully understand the new system. Her husband was uneducated and was not aware of the Soviet laws that now governed their village. Although the letter bore her initials, written in all capital letters next to her name, she had found someone to write it on her behalf, as she had not had the benefit of schooling. The letter also noted her own enormous suffering in the absence of her husband with seven young children at home.[17]

Maria Bokoch took a different approach. Her appeal letter emphasized that her husband, Vasily, no longer represented a threat to society:

> He was convicted in 1948 or 1949 for refusing to obtain a passport. They tried him in Uzhhorod. I am convinced that my husband has reformed himself over the past seven years. If released, I will personally vouch for the fact that he will live honestly and obey all Soviet laws.
>
> My husband left me with an eleven-year-old son. It has been very hard to live without him and to raise our son. I have worked on the collective farm for the past five years. I was never a member of the "Jehovist" sect, and I do not have, nor do I want to have any connections with them.
>
> I simply urge you to reconsider my husband's case and send him home.[18]

As with Akseniia, Maria probably did not write this letter herself. The document indicates that it was prepared in Rakhiv, the district seat, rather than in Bila Tserkva. Maria may have travelled to town to find someone sufficiently fluent in Russian and skilled in drafting formal letters, hoping this would improve the letter's reception by officials. The letter demonstrates how little the families knew about what had happened to their men. Unclear about even the date of his arrest, Maria seems unaware that her husband's problems with the state went beyond the lack of a passport. Given that her brother-in-law, Dmitry, had been arrested in 1948 for this specific crime, Maria and other family members of the arrested men may have assumed that the passport issue was the root of their troubles.

Both letters demonstrate that in the years since the men's convictions, the women had increasingly mastered the language of Soviet power. They knew how to frame their requests to make them understandable to the bureaucrats making the decisions. They also knew enough to seek outside assistance in making an effective appeal. As borderland residents, they came to this knowledge later than other Soviet citizens who had had decades of practice by then. They may not have necessarily believed in what they wrote, but they knew how to navigate the system to make it work for them as best they could.[19]

Within this Soviet framework, the letters took slightly different approaches to win over authorities. Akseniia did not mention faith at all in her letter. In this regard, her letter echoed the original appeal by the defence counsel to reframe the men's crimes as less serious and the result of ignorance rather than malice. In contrast, Maria directly reassured the state that her husband had learned his lesson and would no longer challenge Soviet power in the village. Her letter included a statement from the collective farm chair, who affirmed that Maria had joined the Malenkov farm in 1950 and was an "honest" worker.[20] This fact, and the trip to Rakhiv, suggests that Maria had invested more formal assistance than Akseniia in filing her appeal.

Ultimately, it took the intervention of the Prosecutor's Office in Kyiv to restore freedom to the men. The case file does not indicate what sparked the prosecutor's involvement in the case, though it is likely that copies of the wives' letters found their way to his office given that his appeal was filed shortly after their receipt. This would also have been in line with the standard procedure for rehabilitation in the post-Stalin era. Typically, it required the prisoner or a family member to make an appeal to a Soviet prosecutor, who would then review the original case file and reach a judgment. If the prosecutor found that the charges has not been warranted, he could then appeal to the USSR Supreme Court for the original conviction to be overturned or for the sentence to be reduced.[21]

Whatever initially motivated the prosecutor in Kyiv to read through the file, he concluded upon review that the original sentences had been overly harsh. Only Dmitry Bokoch, he noted, had been identified as a leader and preacher within the organization; the rest were rank-and-file members. To resolve the matter, the prosecutor filed a formal protest with the Supreme Soviet of Ukraine. The tone of this petition suggests that if the prosecutor did read the wives' letters, he found Akseniia's letter more persuasive. Much of his conclusion mimics her tone: "All of the convicted men come from working peasant families. Before arrest, they were engaged in socially useful labor. Only one of them, D.T. Bokoch, had a prior conviction. In terms of their level, they are all poorly educated and politically immature citizens. They are recent citizens of the Soviet Union and had not fully adjusted to the Soviet rule of law."[22] When the Supreme Court met to review the protest in fall 1955, it agreed with the prosecutor. Citing the same mitigating circumstances of poor education, lack of exposure to Soviet power, and mere rank-and-file involvement in an illegal organization, the court reduced the sentences of the men to time served.[23]

Even so, the prosecutor left no doubt that the men had committed the crimes for which they had been convicted. This fact put them at odds with many, even most, individuals convicted of state crimes from the Stalin era. The state could not declare the men innocent unless it intended to rewrite its criminal justice laws to allow ordinary citizens to form unsanctioned organizations, opt out of military service, and live in the border zones without identity papers. Likewise, Soviet laws would have to be modified to provide enough room for citizens to pick and choose when and how to participate in public life. None of these changes was forthcoming, even after the death of Stalin.

In short, the men remained criminals in the eyes of the state. The prosecutor's intervention did not rehabilitate them or restore their civil rights or property. The only difference was in how the state now viewed their illegal actions. Previously, the men had been underground leaders in a criminal network designed to destroy Soviet power in the village. Now, they were painted as peasant rubes who were duped into criminality by their own backwardness and ignorance. Neither interpretation sanctioned the right of Jehovah's Witnesses to practice a faith that lacked registration in the Soviet Union.

Six years after their conviction, the men began to return home.[24] They did not all arrive at the same time, as the men had been in different camps, and some had travel restrictions placed on them. Although released from the camps, Ivan Ona was kept in the city of Inta for several months under supervision.[25] While the records do not indicate that any of the other men were delayed in their homecoming, Yury Marinchan recalled that his father had to remain in Vorkuta for a year after his release. It is possible this was also the case for the other men.[26]

When the men finally came back to Bila Tserkva, it was the first time they had seen their families in several years. Although their wives and children had communicated with them in letters sent to the camps, mail was still a rare luxury, and none of the families had the resources to travel in person. When Ivan Nan arrived home, his wife met his train in the nearby town of Solotvyno. When he rode into the village on horseback, his children did not recognize the stranger in the black suit.[27] Some of their children were now adults. Some had been baptized in their absence and were now full members of the faith. Mistaken identity was not a problem for Vasily Marinchan, who had sent his wife and children a photograph.[28]

Not all the men were able to enjoy a full homecoming. When Dmitry Bokoch was arrested, his wife was already sick with tuberculosis. The family struggled in his absence to obtain medications. She died before his release, but the family decided not to tell him in their letters to him. He found out only when he came home. It was an upsetting homecoming.[29] Ivan Ona's wife was also deathly ill. Recall that during the investigation, he had justified the frequent Bible studies at his home by noting that his wife was confined to her bed and wanted visitors. She apparently willed herself to live long enough to see her husband again. When she died soon after his return, he married another Witness in the village.[30]

The community the men returned to was a study in contrasts. Sovietization had happened in Bila Tserkva. A new collective farm encompassed all the available farmland. Villagers sent their children to the local school and voted in elections. Their young men served in the Soviet Army. Even so, it remained a remote rural area. Electricity had not yet arrived for residents.[31] Central plumbing never happened at all, though officials continued to promise it, and larger nearby towns obtained it. Just as most villagers had gradually acquiesced to the reality of Soviet life, their Witness neighbours had also become a part of some of these institutions. Nearly all had joined the collective farm. The Watch Tower Bible and Tract Society had reassured the faithful that such a decision did not jeopardize their loyalty to Jehovah. With Shelever, the intransigent overseer of the congregation, no longer in his position, the Bila Tserkva Witnesses finally adopted this more moderate view. On a practical level, membership in the farm allowed the families to preserve a small private plot of land to grow crops. Even so, it was done only with reluctance. Yury Marinchan, one of Vasily's sons, recalls that the farm was seen as a "compromise" with the state that was to be avoided whenever possible.[32]

In the years since the arrest, some Witnesses had made their peace with this and other compromises. As one of the sons put it, "My father went into prison without a passport. He came out of prison with a passport."[33] Many of the alleged criminal actions of the 1949 investigation no longer framed interactions between Witnesses and local authorities. The men carried the necessary documents. They worked the farm (mostly). Their children attended school for at least the minimum number of years. They signed up for the military draft (but did not actually serve). Some may have voted, albeit with altered ballots, as was the practice of some Soviet Witnesses on election day.[34] And some men and women, and their children, may have drifted away from the faith entirely. There is nothing inherently unusual about this fact. All religions experience a diversity of choices and practices among believers, and all have adherents who no longer subscribe to its tenets and fade out of the community. The Witnesses are well known for their "theocratic" structure, which requires a greater level of obedience to certain norms than is typical in mainstream Christian denominations. This conformity was certainly present within Bila Tserkva. That said, expectations in the early postwar years were blurry as both local Witnesses and elders abroad struggled to figure out what it meant to be a Witness in a Soviet territory. Some of the major questions were resolved by the late 1950s when the men returned home. Even so, tensions and disagreements remained among Witnesses throughout the Soviet period.[35]

None of the men appears to have suffered further arrests or imprisonment, but the trauma of the event did not disappear as quickly. Widespread rehabilitation brought former prisoners back into Soviet society, and many citizens worried about the flood of criminals into their communities. A crime wave that accompanied the mass amnesties seemed to give credence to this view. Certainly some of the prisoners given early release were not political prisoners, but thieves, murderers, and robbers. Some returned to a life of crime, in part out of desperation and a lack of other options.[36] Even for those whom the state officially rehabilitated, declaring them innocent of any wrongdoing, their neighbours often remained suspicious and fearful. In Bila Tserkva, the village was not particularly happy to see the men's return. Dmitry Marinchan initially could not get registered in the village at all. There was a certain irony in this fact. He finally wanted a registration document, but now he could not get one from the very people who had demanded that he obtain one years prior. Faced with this difficult situation, he chose not to risk it and live without documentation, as he had before his arrest. Instead, he found temporary housing nearby in a neighbouring village where he worked. His family, who had not seen him at all for over six years, now only saw him on weekends when he could afford to make the trip.[37]

The men's children do not recall much discussion in the home about the time their fathers spent in prison and then in labour camps. This mirrors the experiences of many former Gulag prisoners, who kept silent about their experiences for decades. They continued to fear that the state could arrive at any moment to take them away again. Dissident scholar Roy Medvedev recalls that some prisoners "were afraid of doorbells because that's how their arrest and misfortune began." To spare themselves this daily trauma, they had their doorbells removed entirely.[38] Even if events after 1949 were rarely spoken about, their impact lingered in the families. When Dmitry

Marinchan did move back home, his children were so worried about another arrest that they warned him when they saw a stranger on the road. His son died at a young age of heart problems. The family noted how fearful he had been of the KGB, a factor they seemed to link to his untimely death.[39]

The men resumed a rather quiet and cautious existence in the village. Gruelling labour and inadequate food had left them in poor health. Dmitry Bokoch arrived home with stomach cancer. Until he succumbed to this illness, he scraped by with odd jobs as a carpenter and at a local paper mill.[40] Vasily Marinchan had lost so much weight from years of backbreaking work that he could barely walk.[41] He could no longer work, and only left his home to attend congregation meetings. Luckily, his sons were old enough to take over responsibilities for managing the home and garden.[42] Even so, he apparently remained active in the local congregation. A state list of all known "sectarian" groups and their leaders in 1957 listed his name along with the brother of Ivan Ona. The regional head of the Council for Religious Cult Affairs claimed to have spoken to both Vasily and his son to persuade the elder to vote and the younger to register for military service.[43]

Witnesses did not disappear, even if few of their neighbours joined them in their faith. Exactly how many citizens belonged to the Witnesses is nearly impossible to calculate with any certainty because state estimates range wildly.[44] While Soviet congregations did their best to keep track and smuggled out records to the international Society, these figures were not released to the public for fear of endangering individuals.[45] Yet it seems likely that no fewer than four thousand had undergone baptism and were active in Transcarpathia.[46] If we include children and youth, unbaptized members, and inactive members, the total is easily double this estimate. Even so, the state continued to reassure itself that this was a religious community in crisis, unable to adjust to the new conditions of life and irrelevant to the needs of Soviet citizens.[47]

The Witnesses did not abandon all the dangerous activities that led to the imprisonment of the seven men. They may have joined the farm, but they did not all become model Soviet citizens. At the most basic level, they continued to belong to an illegal religious community and to gather with one another to practice their faith. This happened even before the men returned home. Vasily Marinchan's wife took care of transporting religious literature in the congregation, a risky venture given that the couple had three young children.[48] Their son, Yury, recalled that the state briefly detained his mother as well but released her after several days. After this close call, surveillance of the Marinchan family gradually died down for a few years until the son came of age and became active in the religion in his own right.[49]

With the more senior men in the congregation behind bars, the community increasingly came to rely on the next generation. While women also took on more tasks to fill in the gap, the Witnesses' patriarchal structure shifted the burden heavily on to the young men. Yury Marinchan was only eleven when his father was arrested. Within a few years, he had earned a reputation as an active organizer in the village. Before Yury finished school at thirteen, the state had already identified him as a troublemaker. In one instance, officials pulled him out of his classroom for a lengthy interrogation. The men tried to persuade him to divulge information about the organization's activities. When he refused, the men pressured him to sign a statement they had already prepared. Pleading ignorance, Yury claimed not to know how to sign his name, despite being one of the top students in his year. This excuse did not convince officials, who tried to get him to sign a blank sheet of paper they had placed over the statement. Yury, sensing a trap, stood his ground and was ultimately sent home.[50] The anecdote also reveals how much had changed since his father's childhood. While Vasily had only two years of education, his son graduated from school along with his peers in the village. While he may not have gone on to the district high school, neither did almost any of his classmates.

For Yury and others, the post-Stalin state lowered the consequences for stepping out of line. Their parents' actions had nearly cost them their lives and permanently damaged their health. Within a few years of Stalin's death, the state phased out the use of Article 54/58 almost entirely. Citizens who engaged in unsanctioned religious activities were still criminals, but new legislation limited the criminal penalties to shorter sentences, usually less than ten years.[51] Prisoners could expect to serve out their sentences in harsh, far-flung prison camps, but they had the reasonable expectation of returning home to rejoin their families after serving their time. By the 1960s, even such shorter prison sentences became increasingly rare, as the state opted for "softer" punishments of fines, harassment, and child-custody revocations. It continued to send residents out as agitators, tasked with convincing their neighbours to abandon their faith and finally join Soviet society as loyal citizens.[52]

As a result, the children of the Bila Tserkva men were largely spared the fate of their fathers. Mikhail, the teenaged son of Dmitry Bokoch, may be the only immediate family member to suffer arrest. Already during the initial investigation, Mikhail narrowly avoided arrest along with his father. Village informants had identified him as a person of interest, and investigators were aware of his role in hosting youth gatherings for the congregation. What ultimately sealed his fate, however, was the issue of mandatory military service. His refusal to complete this requirement of Soviet citizenship earned him a five-year term in a labour camp, which he served in the northern region of Murmansk. Less than seven months into his sentence, he was released due to the amnesty declared in the wake of Stalin's death. This was a mixed blessing. He had won back his freedom but was still subject to military service requirements. In short, it was just a matter of time before the local draft board realized he had been released, summoned him back for duty, and convicted him again for the same crime that had sent him to a camp in the first place.[53] Within months, this second notice arrived at his home.

Faced with a certain return to a labour camp, this time as a repeat offender who would be subject to harsher sanctions, Mikhail chose to go underground instead, as had others in his village during the 1949 arrests. It was an opportune decision for the congregation, which needed a man who could run their newly established printing operation. In turn, Mikhail needed to lay low, out of sight of the local authorities. And so, though he knew little, if anything, about running a print shop, he agreed to the assignment. He repurposed a shed on his family's property as a carpentry workshop, and then constructed a hidden area within it to house the illegal equipment. Two other men laboured beside him. The printing operation allowed the congregation to duplicate religious literature for individual families rather than hand copy materials or share a single booklet among the entire population.[54]

Eventually the operation expanded and moved out of Mikhail's backyard. A more elaborate bunker was constructed in the mountains outside a nearby village. Incidentally, the circumstances of this move brought Mikhail back into contact with Ivan Ona, who had returned from the labour camp by this time and had resumed responsibilities in the congregation. Ivan helped the men settle into their new location. What Mikhail was doing was extremely dangerous, and only a handful of Witnesses were entrusted with this task due to the risks involved. In the early 1960s, a printer was shot and killed during a police raid on his bunker.[55] Only a year into Mikhail's career as a printer, the entire operation was put in jeopardy by the unexpected arrival of state-security officers in the village. The officers had come to arrest Yury, the brother of one of the printers. Yury had been smuggling religious literature across the border, which the men then duplicated on their printers. Somehow this activity had come to the attention of the state. Although other Witnesses tipped him off to the arrival of the officers, Yury made the difficult decision not to run. If he had, the officers would likely have conducted searches at nearby homes of other known Witnesses. That would have led them directly to Yury's brother and the printing operation. Instead, Yury allowed himself to be arrested. In the meantime, the printers quickly gathered up the rest of the equipment and moved it to the home of Ivan Ona. Until they were able to make the permanent move to the mountain location, Ivan's home served as their safe house.[56]

About three years into this job, Mikhail's luck ran out. The men were on the road when the police stopped them, having taken a truck to transport some of their newly printed literature to the neighbouring communities. The officers had clearly been tipped off in advance. Mikhail and one of the other printers were in the cab; the third man was in the truck bed. He jumped off when the truck came to a halt and made a break for it. Officers quickly caught up to him, foiling his escape attempt. Like his father, Mikhail found himself the subject of a lengthy interrogation in Uzhhorod. Already, however, twenty-five-year sentences were no longer the norm. Instead, he received an eight-year sentence. He served every day of it and returned home in 1966. It was an uncannily parallel experience to his father's homecoming a decade earlier. His father had returned home to find that his wife had died in his absence. When Mikhail returned home, he discovered that his father had succumbed to stomach cancer.

Although Mikhail was well into his thirties by this point, the military continued to hound him about his duty to serve. By this time, however, the men in Bila Tserkva had begun to register for conscription to avoid unnecessary entanglements with the authorities. Years of labour in the camps meant that when Mikhail reported to the local office to fill out forms, they exempted him for medical reasons.[57]

His return to Bila Tserkva appears to close the chapter on arrests of Witnesses in the village. Mikhail resumed his printing responsibilities but was never again caught or arrested. There do not appear to be any further trials for religious activity in the village, though the young men continued to face arrest for refusal of military service. Conflict with local authorities continued, however, even if it did not result in prison terms. Dmitry Bokoch's other son, Yury, was badly beaten by police on the road between Serednie Vodiane and Bila Tserkva. He had ventured out late one night to visit his soon-to-be wife. He was caught and ended up in the hospital from his injuries.[58] Vasily Marinchan's sons paid a fine for organizing the village's annual Memorial of Christ's Death, a religious holiday observed by all Witnesses worldwide each spring. The year the police raided the Marinchan home; the event was held late at night. The family kept the windows covered to avoid notice, but policemen, the village soviet chair, and local schoolteachers arrived nonetheless. When the congregation refused to let them into the home until they had finished the ceremony, the interlocutors forced their way in through an open window.[59]

Archival records and newspaper reports give us some further clues into Witness life in the village and surrounding area, and offer ample evidence that Witnesses remained active in this region. Both Transcarpathia and Bila Tserkva receive periodic mention as particular hotbeds of Witness activity. Newspapers from the region published accounts of Witnesses' alleged misdeeds and nefarious actions. One article noted how a resident of the neighbouring village of Serednie Vodiane had dodged agitators around election time and did not vote on election day.[60] Government records detail how local officials çontinued to uncover illegal community events. Officials raided a large gathering of Witnesses in 1970 in a wooded spot between Bila Tserkva and Serednie Vodiane; four men were assessed a heavy fine.[61] In surrounding villages, the state continued to bring criminal charges against Witnesses for crimes that amounted to little more than practising their faith. The district court convicted one Serednie Vodiane resident of illegal religious activities in 1984. The arrest stemmed from the man's speech at a funeral for a deceased Bila Tserkva resident and Witness elder. The verdict noted that over three hundred people allegedly listened to his oration, which included reference to the ongoing imprisonment of Witnesses for their faith. The man received four years in a labour camp and had his property confiscated.[62] Even without this paper trail, however, it would still be clear that Witnesses remained active in Bila Tserkva because they still live there today and have publicly spoken about their lives under Soviet power.[63]

Sweeping reforms of the Soviet system under the leadership of Mikhail Gorbachev in the late 1980s ushered in a more tolerant policy toward religious minorities. More importantly for the seven men, the Gorbachev period reopened the question of rehabilitation for those convicted of state crimes in the Stalin period.[64] While the Supreme Soviet, the unionwide parliament, dragged its feet on reform, individual union republics moved more quickly to put new measures in place. As a result, in April 1991 Ukraine passed legislation "on the rehabilitation of victims of political repression." Many of these republic-level laws, including in Ukraine, offered compensation to victims.[65]

It was in this environment, less than a month before the collapse of the Soviet Union in 1991, that the regional prosecutor's office gave the case one final review. This time, the state invested no effort in reviewing the evidence. After briefly acknowledging the men's actions, the original verdict, and the subsequent appeals, the state determined that "there is a lack of evidence to affirm the basis for this criminal conviction." In short, the men were found not to be criminals at all. Citing the decree on rehabilitation for "victims of political repression," the state overturned the convictions. The news came too late for nearly all the men. Only the Marinchan brothers lived long enough to learn that the state had declared them innocent. The rest had died before then; their next of kin in the village received rehabilitation certificates in the mail. The state was unable to track down Nutsu Guzo or his relations at all.[66]

A few weeks later, the Soviet system itself disappeared from Bila Tserkva. Ukraine became an independent country, and Transcarpathia changed hands once again. The villagers of Bila Tserkva had experienced life under Austro-Hungarian, Czechoslovak, Hungarian, and Soviet rule; now they adjusted to life under Ukrainian authority. This last transfer of power had an immediate impact on their livelihoods. The collective farm went out of business, its lands divided among the villagers. Many villagers received substantial allotments, far more than their families had enjoyed in the interwar period.[67] The land reform allowed farms to return to private ownership, but it did not spark a boom in commercial production. Rather, families continued to plant and harvest crops, most of them for personal consumption or local markets.[68]

The border between Romania remained, but villagers found it far easier to visit, particularly since they spoke the language. Trains began to run between Rakhiv district and the Romanian town of Sighet, and a bridge between Solotvyno and Sighet was eventually opened for both cars and pedestrians. Residents recalled seeing fewer border guards on patrol. While the river was largely off-limits along much of the border, this, too, became accessible in the post-Soviet period.[69] Some villagers managed to secure permanent work across the border, bringing much needed revenue into the region.

In this regard, the village's Romanian identity was enormously useful in the post-Soviet environment. The influx of Romanian wealth has been significant in recent years. Some residents have built impressive modern homes with their newfound resources. The local news media even posted videos to YouTube showing the "palaces" of the Romanian villages in Transcarpathia, Bila Tserkva included.[70] Still, the overall portrait of village life is more mixed than online McMansion photographs would suggest. Impressive estates sit alongside far more modest structures built in the postwar period. Not everyone had the skills and opportunity to take advantage of the border, particularly the elderly, who could hardly benefit from Romanian construction work. Overall, the region continued to struggle to provide sufficient industry and infrastructure for its residents well into the post-Soviet period. Many of the jobs in forestry and local factories disappeared in the difficult economic climate of the 1990s.[71] Car travel makes Bila Tserkva less isolated, however, than it had been in decades past. Buses also connect the village with other parts of the region, and trains run from nearby Solotvyno to Uzhhorod and other locations.

In contrast to Soviet institutions, Witness life in Bila Tserkva has never been stronger. In the chaotic decade that followed the Soviet collapse, Bila Tserkva built its first Kingdom Hall, an official house for worship. Mikhail Bokoch oversaw much of the construction. This allowed the congregation to worship and gather in public without fear of persecution or arrest. It took a year for Yury Marinchan to stop looking over his shoulder. He had been under scrutiny for so long that it was hard to comprehend what freedom meant. He could now walk around with nice clothes and a tie, religious literature in hand, and no one could stop him. In his mind, it was a "miracle."[72] Even the few elderly members who could recall the interwar period had never enjoyed this level of freedom. Now Witnesses could invite their neighbours to join them in public for services, and they were cautiously optimistic that this freedom might prove more lasting than the brief interludes of relative calm that had preceded earlier crackdowns on the community.

As of the 2010s, the village had six congregations and two Kingdom Halls.[73] With roughly one hundred individuals per congregation and only a few thousand residents total in the village, this is an extraordinarily high density of Jehovah's Witnesses. It is probably one of the highest concentrations anywhere in the world.[74] Anna Moish, the daughter of Vasily Marinchan, expressed how now "it is easy to serve God."[75] Mikhail Bokoch echoed this sentiment, remarking, "Thanks to Jehovah, now everything is good."[76] Young people in the congregations have grown up in this new reality. For them, the Soviet period is already history. Many families have joined since the collapse and do not share the same legacy of persecution. Already, a whole new generation in the village has no direct memory of Soviet power or its institutions. Some, including even some Witnesses, are not aware of what happened in their village. When Maria, the daughter of Ivan Nan, tells young people about it, they sometimes laugh and tell her that it is not possible.[77] Mikhail Bokoch recalled a similar dynamic. Young people have called his stories "nonsense." But those who have relatives who experienced it firsthand, he is careful to note, understand.[78]

Conclusion

The story of Bila Tserkva is part of the broader transformation of life in Transcarpathia. One historian has called the region a "genuine—perhaps even the quintessential" borderland.[1] Yet it has gotten less attention than the rest of postwar western Ukraine. This presents a problem for the historian because the history of one region cannot stand in for the other. Unlike other annexed territories along the western corridor, Transcarpathia had no pre-war history with the Soviet Union. Before 1944 the villagers of Bila Tserkva had no exposure to Soviet norms and expectations. The postwar experience was fundamentally new to them. Residents had been comparatively disengaged from the conflict, and accusations of betraying a homeland to which they did not yet belong played only a minor role in the investigation and trial.

This is not the case elsewhere in western Ukraine. In other regions, Soviet power arrived, retreated, and then returned. This series of events defined the postwar relationship of the state with its citizens. Simply put, the state obsessed over enemies in its midst long after the war was well and truly over, and it demanded loyalty even if it would have meant death at the hands of occupying authorities. As one historian writes, "Often simply surviving the occupation was tacitly marked as a sign of guilt." World War II defined the postwar Soviet Union and marked some citizens as irredeemable enemies.[2]

In general, security concerns loomed large over the entire borderland. The Cold War had begun, and citizens and state leaders alike worried about the prospect of war with the West. While state and citizens went about the business of reconstruction, the possibility that it could all be destroyed remained. Soviet citizens may have wanted some breathing room after years of violence, but what they experienced was a re-entrenchment of control. Bila Tserkva's location along the Soviet Union's western border made control over it all the more important to postwar Soviet officials. Bila Tserkva residents needed documents to not only make them citizens but also ensure the protection of the broader state from internal and external enemies. The state could not afford to have borderland residents with loyalties divided between the Soviet state and a religious community, much less one headquartered in the United States, the Soviet Union's Cold War enemy. Even if the case featured few, if any, direct accusations of collaboration or espionage, the men's arrest and lengthy sentences cannot be understood outside this broader political context.

In the aftermath of the war and reconstruction, Bila Tserkva became Soviet. It was the third time the territory had changed owners in the twentieth century. Vladislav Zubok argues, "Stalin's socialist empire used powerful ideology, nationalism, and social engineering to refashion society and elites. It introduced the uniformity of state industrialization and party systems. At the same time, it took away civil freedoms, wealth, cooperation, and human dignity and offered instead an illusion of social justice."[3] This transformation required years of sustained effort by central authorities and local activists alike. It necessitated the creation of new institutions, rituals, and markers of identity. Schools had to be built, collective farms created, elections held, and passports issued to the newly minted Soviet citizens. All this took work and involvement by local residents. At the same time, Sovietization required the destruction of the old. Soviet ideology did not allow space for alternative forms of meaning or patterns of life. All residents had to adapt themselves to their new environment, not just those who belonged to unregistered religious communities. If they did not, the state made their lives very difficult.

In Bila Tserkva, villagers chose a range of strategies to accommodate these new demands. At least a few actively embraced the task of building Soviet power. None was sufficiently earnest to join the Communist Party in the immediate postwar period, and only a handful signed up for the Komsomol. Nevertheless, some villagers became engaged enough to enlist as agitators and deputies in the village soviet. In their new but largely unpaid positions of authority, they extolled the virtues of the new system to their friends and neighbours. The effectiveness of their advocacy is difficult to measure. On the one hand, nearly all non-Witnesses voted in local elections. On the other hand, very few signed up for the collective farms until compelled to do so. These results suggest that even such activists, arguably the most committed to Sovietization in the village, had mixed feelings about the benefits of Soviet power. They might have shown up early in the morning to vote for their local deputies, but this enthusiasm did not necessarily translate when it came to enrolling their children in the dirty kindergarten or signing over their farmland to state control.

Arguably, the voices in Bila Tserkva most silenced from the available materials are the villagers who were neither Witnesses nor agitators. Only a small portion of residents played an active role in the investigation as informants, defendants, or family members. Even so, the case file hints at their presence in the village. Although informants blamed the setbacks in Sovietization by scapegoating one particular religious minority, this explanation ignores the muted support for Soviet institutions by everyone else in Bila Tserkva. Witnesses alone did not doom New Life farm; most villagers did not sign up during the initial collectivization. Likewise, Witnesses alone do not explain why villagers griped about the poor condition of the village club and library, and why few volunteered for mandatory labour brigades in the nearby forests.

Activists settled on the Witnesses because they offered a convenient means to displace responsibility, which in turn shielded other villagers from state scrutiny. Moreover, this scapegoating did not require any extraordinary imagination on the part of the state or local activists. Witnesses, by their own accounts at the time and decades later, were unwilling participants in Sovietization. Some of this recalcitrance can be understood through the Witnesses' unique theology, which interpreted secular institutions, including all worldly governments, as irreparably corrupt and doomed to destruction by God. Certainly this factor played the primary role in keeping Witnesses from voting in Soviet elections, serving in the military, or allowing their children to participate in extracurricular activities at the school. This stance conformed with the actions of Witnesses worldwide, including those in liberal-democratic countries.

At the same time, the nature of Soviet power itself is responsible for much of the Witnesses' abstention from Soviet life. On a practical level, heightened border control and tight limits on religious activities made it difficult for Bila Tserkva residents to gain access to information outside their village or district. From the state's perspective, this prevented anti-Soviet propaganda from infiltrating its society. Ironically, however, it also blocked moderating voices from being heard. In the case of Bila Tserkva and Rakhiv district as a whole, this isolation only made Witnesses more inclined to radical disengagement from Soviet power. In the post-Stalin era, Witnesses found ways to mitigate their involvement with the state by registering for military service (but not serving), obtaining passports, and joining the collective farm. This did not ultimately change their views about secular government, but it did reduce conflict with local authorities.

Last, Witnesses did not embrace Soviet institutions for some of the same reasons as their neighbours. Soviet power set lofty goals for building a better, happier life, but did not fully deliver on these promises in the first decade after annexation. It did not take the *Watchtower* magazine to tell villagers that life under Soviet rule left much to be desired. The 1949 investigation reflects a moment of transition for Transcarpathia. Annexation had happened, but it took years for the state to have full control of its territories and its citizens. The case rested on information gleaned from informants back in the village. Unlike subsequent trials of Witnesses, which often involved corroborating information produced by state bureaucrats and party members, the investigators had to rely almost entirely on what informants wanted to tell them. Moreover, these informants were themselves new to Soviet power and its expectations. Almost none were fluent in a language other than Romanian, few had more than a primary-school education, some had not joined the collective farm, and at least one had perhaps considered joining the Witnesses herself.

These men and women ultimately settled on a version of events that both shielded them from and aligned them with state goals. They reassured the state that only a religious minority stood between it and successful Sovietization. State and party measures were effective and could work in Bila Tserkva; they just needed the removal of a persistent religious minority. This allowed both the state and informants to envision a Soviet Bila Tserkva in the near future. It also limited the investigation to a marginal community, protecting everyone else in the village, at least for the moment. While the Witnesses did not create or ultimately buy into this politicized version of events, they did not wholly deny it either. Throughout the investigation, the men carefully constructed their answers to limit their own guilt and avoid exposing others to arrest. This strategy was not always successful or consistently maintained, but it is worth remembering that the men were at a significant disadvantage. They spoke only through a state-appointed interpreter, and they had only a limited sense of what the state knew, how it knew it, or what the penalties were for certain admissions.

That said, the men never denied the underlying actions that landed them in Uzhhorod, and then in labour camps in the Far North. They were Jehovah's Witnesses, and that identity carried a set of expectations, just as Soviet citizenship did for residents of Transcarpathia. Beyond limiting their interactions with the Soviet state, they also attended regular services, read religious literature, baptized others and were baptized themselves, and spoke about their faith to their neighbours. Witnesses saw these actions as necessary components of their faith in action, even if the state saw them as the activities of an anti-Soviet underground. In a certain sense, both were right. Witnesses were motivated by religious norms and theology, but in the context of Soviet power these actions were deeply political.

In her book about another Ukrainian borderland, Kate Brown offers a model for understanding how the Soviet Union created "uniform, homogenous, impersonal, and universal" spaces that could be effectively governed and controlled.[4] She explores the so-called *kresy*, a hard-to-define zone that now sits in central Ukraine due to wartime expansion of Ukraine's borders. She argues:

> Instead of a story of a strong state crushing, co-opting, or coercing its people into submission, we have one of a weak state threatened by people they were nominally ruling. The state was weak not by its own demerits alone, but for the same reason that the tsarist state was weak or undergoverned because people were unruly, which is another way of saying they had power, sometimes over each other, but more often over their own lives, to act and speak as they saw fit, as the customs and meanings of their particular daily lives dictated.[5]

Certainly we can take this conclusion too far. The state did crush, co-opt, and coerce people, even if it never fully achieved submission. It may have been weak in this early period, but it grew stronger over time as it learned more about the people and lands it now controlled. Over time, too, the people never stopped being unruly, but they spoke more often in the language of the state and learned to navigate its rules of behaviour so that they could continue to live their lives as they saw fit. While the *kresy* all but disappeared in the postwar era, and with it the unique culture that distinguished the borderland, the postwar history of Bila Tserkva is more mixed.

Ultimately, the Bila Tserkva investigation offers a snapshot of Soviet power that paradoxically faded quickly as the state established authority over the region. In 1949, as Sovietization of this borderland took place within a broader context of re-Stalinization throughout the USSR, it was still a weak state dependent on local residents both to implement Soviet power and enforce it. These informants had their own motivations for involvement in the Soviet project, but the state could not be all that selective about its allies in this critical period. As Sovietization transformed village life, state power became more embedded at the local level. Soviet institutions became permanent features in Bila Tserkva, and villagers accepted this reality, even if they did not necessarily embrace all aspects of it. The borderland never disappeared, and neither did Jehovah's Witnesses. This fact does not mean that Sovietization did not happen, just that the story of how it happened is messy and incomplete. Soviet power could not exist without the consent of at least some of the governed. The Bila Tserkva case demonstrates that it also survived for decades even without this consent from all its citizens.

Notes

INTRODUCTION

1 Shearer, "Stalinist Repression, Modernity, and the Social Engineering Argument," 105.
2 Shearer, *Policing Stalin's Socialism*, 405.
3 The case file of this investigation is listed under "Vasily Todorovich Bokoch et al." and is located in the State Security Service Archive of Transcarpathia in Uzhhorod, Ukraine (Arkhiv Upravlinnia Sluzhby Bezpeky Ukrainy v Zakarpats'kii oblasti (or AUSBUZO), fond (collection) 2558, opys (subgroup) 1, sprava (file) 819 (the original file number is 2411). Numbered pages of the file often contain both front and back text. The multi-volume file includes continuous page (arkush or ark.) numbers and thus volume (tom or t.) numbers have been omitted.
4 AUSBUZO, f. 2558, op. 1, spr. 819, ark. 209.
5 Like the Bokoch file, the case file of Alexander Bara et al. is held by AUSBUZO, f. 2558, op. 1, spr. 5523. The case file consists of multiple volumes, each paginated separately, and thus volume numbers are included in citations. The information about Vasily Dan's language skills and appeal appears in AUSBUZO, f. 2558, op. 1, spr. 5523, t. 2, ark. 33; t. 3, ark. 223, 231, 283–6.
6 Dumitru cautions that there is much we can never know about the nature of violence and its victims from these records alone. Dumitru, "Listening to Silence," 4–12.
7 Goldman, *Inventing the Enemy*, 20.
8 It is possible but unlikely that the interrogation times in the file are inaccurate. In other state investigations of Witnesses during this time period, long interrogation times were regularly recorded in the files, suggesting that the state did not typically obscure this aspect of its interrogation procedures in the official records. Prusin, "'Fascist Criminals to the Gallows!,'" 16.

9 State Archive of L'viv Oblast (Derzhavnyi arkhiv L'vivs'koi oblasti, or DALO), f. 3258, op. 1, spr. P-25018, t. 4, ark. 48. The organizational structure of local congregations changed over the history of the Society, as did the titles and responsibilities given to male members.

10 AUSBUZO, f. 2558, op. 1, spr. 5523, t. 2, ark. 212–13.

11 Yury and Makutsa Bokoch interview (with Ivan Bokoch) by author, 28 July 2013. Bila Tserkva, Ukraine. Yury is the son of Dmitry Bokoch; Ivan is Yury's son.

12 AUSBUZO, f. 2558, op. 1, spr. 819, ark. 23, 175.

13 Kuromiya, *Conscience on Trial*, 132.

14 This article has an excellent overview of the scholarship on postwar trials. Dumitru, "Listening to Silence," 4–12.

15 Penter, "Local Collaborators on Trial," 360–2.

16 McBride, "'A Sea of Blood and Tears,'" 25–7.

17 Tatiana Vagramenko has examined much of the archival record on these operations from the central SBU archive in Kyiv, Ukraine. Some of her initial research has been published in an edited volume. Vagramenko and Kapaló, eds, *Hidden Galleries*, 19, 30, 60.

18 Dan's name caused some confusion as his official documents listed him as Laslo Laslovich Dan. He clarified to investigators that the name was not common in Romanian (it is of Hungarian origin) and therefore everyone in the village referred to him as Vasily Vasilevich. AUSBUZO, f. 2558, op. 1, spr. 5523, t. 2. ark. 229–30.

19 Block, *Colonial Complexions*, 95–100.

20 Onaci, *Free the Land*, 81.

21 Kirsten Fermaglich explores the complicated reasons why Jewish immigrants and their children sometimes chose to alter their names after arrival in America. Fermaglich, *A Rosenberg by Any Other Name*.

22 The author of this book has an uncommon last name, "Baran." More accurately, it is uncommon for Americans but common for someone from Transcarpathia. She has met many people who assume that the name must be a shortened Slavic name, like Baranov or Baranovsky. Others have decided its spelling should be Baron or Barron, both of which are more common spellings than "Baran." In this instance, Baran is just Baran.

23 Cannato, *American Passage*, 401–3.

24 The investigator also listed two different birth years for several of the men. The file includes personal data forms that indicate when the state determined an official name and birth year for each man. AUSBUZO, f. 2558, op. 1, spr. 819, ark. 11, 34, 58, 131.

25 Regional archival records include the names of multiple Nutsus in the vil-

lage. The 2002 history of Ukrainian Witnesses produced by the Witnesses also includes reference to at least one local man named Nutsu. *2002 Yearbook of Jehovah's Witnesses*, 182.

26 Yury Marinchan interview by author, 27 July 2013. Bila Tserkva, Ukraine. Yury is the son of Vasily Marinchan.

CHAPTER ONE

1 Belousov et al., *Istoriia mist i sil Ukrains'koi RSR*, 524.

2 Hiroaki Kuromiya has described an investigation into Pentecostal life in the city of Bila Tserkva. Kuromiya, *Conscience on Trial*.

3 This region has many other names across historical periods and in various scholarly literatures, including Ruthenia, Carpathian Rus', Subcarpathian Rus', and Carpatho-Ukraine, among others. The region is known as Zakarpattia in present-day Ukraine. I use the English term "Transcarpathia" throughout this work.

4 The Tysa River is sometimes spelled Tisza.

5 On the "Rusyn question," see Batt, "Transcarpathia," 159–64.

6 Bila Tserkva declared Romanian a "regional language" in 2012, the first village to do so in Ukraine. Moser, *Language Policy and Discourse*, 392.

7 Liber, *Total Wars*, 29.

8 Olashyn, *Istoriia Zakarpattia*, 146.

9 Magocsi, "Carpathian Rus'," 452.

10 Plokhy, *The Gates of Europe*, 171.

11 The Vienna Awards in 1938 and 1940 provided German sanction for a dramatic expansion of Hungary's borders. The First Vienna Award did not extend to Rakhiv district or Bila Tserkva. Hungary only occupied the more easterly regions of Transcarpathia in March 1939. Ormos, *Hungary in the Age of the Two World Wars*, 297–8, 344–5, 58–9; Zeidler, *Ideas on Territorial Revision*, 260–71.

12 Plokhy, *The Gates of Europe*, 256–7.

13 AUSBUZO, f. 2558, op. 1, spr. 5523, t. 2, ark. 193, 241.

14 Braham and Miller, eds, *The Nazis' Last Victims*.

15 Braham, *The Politics of Genocide*, 84, 149–50, 208–11.

16 State Archive of Transcarpathia (Derzhavnyi arkhiv Zakarpats'koi oblasti, hereafter DAZO), f. R-130, op. 1, spr. 9, ark. 122.

17 Kathryn David details how Soviet officials often treated Galicia (formerly Polish territory) and Transcarpathia as fundamentally the same, and applied policies developed for Galicia to the other region, ignoring important distinctions between the two. This argument appears in chapter 6 of her dissertation. David, "One Ukraine, under God."

18 Eaton, "Exclave," 173, 225.
19 Yekelchyk, *Stalin's Empire of Memory*, 48–52.
20 Khruschchev, *Khrushchev Remembers*, 147.
21 Yekelchyk, *Stalin's Empire of Memory*, 48–9.
22 Shandor, *Carpatho-Ukraine in the Twentieth Century*, 261–7.
23 Dovhanych, Sheketa, and Delehan, eds, *Vozz'iednannia*, 17–18.
24 Bucur, *Heroes and Victims*, 241–2. Wiesel, *Night*.
25 Coopersmith, *The Electrification of Russia*, 175.
26 Ivanych, "Kolkhoznye elektrostantsii," 1.
27 DAZO, f. R-130, op. 1, spr. 2, ark. 161.
28 Ibid.
29 "Radiofikatsiia sela Belaia Tserkov'," *Sovetskoe Zakarpat'e*, 27 August 1949, 1.
30 DAZO, f. R-130, op. 1, spr. 9, ark. 234.
31 A recent history of Jewish communities in Transcarpathia cites an interview with a Jewish resident of Bila Tserkva who moved to the village from neighbouring Solotvyno in 1955. She recalls that five Jewish families lived in the village at that time. Quilitzsch, "Everyday Judaism on the Soviet Periphery," 239.
32 The *Watchtower* has had slight variations in its title over the years. I will refer to the magazine as the *Watchtower* for simplicity's sake but include the full title in the endnotes.
33 The best survey of the Jehovah's Witnesses' history and theology is George D. Chryssides, *Jehovah's Witnesses*. M. James Penton also offers an overview in his now-dated work, *Apocalypse Delayed*. For the Witnesses' own version of their history, see *Jehovah's Witnesses: Proclaimers of God's Kingdom*.
34 *1927 Year Book of the International Bible Students Association*, 86.
35 *1930 Year Book of the International Bible Students Association*, 93.
36 *1935 Year Book of Jehovah's Witnesses*, 104–5.
37 "Memorial Reports," 248.
38 *2002 Yearbook of Jehovah's Witnesses*, 129–30.
39 Tylniak was interviewed about the event in the early 2000s. His name is listed as Mikhailo Tilniak in this publication. He recalls that his arrest in 1949 had been at the behest of a local Baptist leader. Likely he had reason to suspect that this individual had informed on him. *2002 Yearbook of Jehovah's Witnesses*, 129, 165.
40 AUSBUZO, f. 2558, op. 1, spr. 5523, t. 3, ark. 332 (attached envelope of documents). The last name is sometimes spelled as Tilniak in other portions of the case file, but the official verdict on his trial lists him as Tylniak. His arrest is also mentioned in a Society publication: *2002 Yearbook of Jehovah's Witnesses*, 165.

41 Ibid., 133.
42 Ibid., 129–30.
43 The Society produces its own Bible translation, known as the New World Translation, which it has gradually translated into many of the world's languages, including Russian, Ukrainian, and Romanian. All quotes from the Bible in this book will use this translation. The name "Jehovah's Witnesses" was introduced in 1931. Chryssides, *Jehovah's Witnesses*, 93.
44 Penton, *Apocalypse Delayed*, 64–8. Readers may be surprised not to see the issue of blood transfusions mentioned in this book given that Witnesses worldwide have abstained from them since the 1940s. Blood transfusions were still a relatively new medical procedure in the late 1940s and would not have reached rural Ukraine; they do not appear in the case file or any other supporting documentation about Bila Tserkva Witnesses in this time period. Chryssides, *Jehovah's Witnesses*, 191–2.
45 Ionete, "Majority, Minorities and Religious Pluralism in Romania."
46 Pleszar, "The Truth Shall Make You Free," 224.
47 Dan was also arrested in 1948 and received a ten-year sentence. His name is listed as Mykhailo Dan in the 2002 *Yearbook of Jehovah's Witnesses*, 144.
48 Dan wrote this biography as part of an appeal. He was convicted of state crimes in 1953 and penned this letter shortly thereafter. AUSBUZO, f. 2558, op. 1, spr. 5523, t. 3, ark. 278–86.
49 A 1946 chart of the village population inaccurately lists the entire village as Greek Catholic. DAZO, f. R-130, op. 1, spr. 9, ark. 234.
50 2002 *Yearbook of Jehovah's Witnesses*, 154.
51 The Jehovah's Witnesses do not have a minimum age for baptism. For children raised in the faith, it can be at a relatively young age. Dmitry Marinchan's daughter recalled that she was baptized at eight years old. Maria Popsha (née Marinchan) interview by author, 28 July 2013. Bila Tserkva, Ukraine. This last name is spelled as both Popshe and Popsha in the records.
52 The Watch Tower Bible and Tract Society counts only active, baptized individuals in its membership statistics. As a result, official estimates tend to undercount the total number of practitioners of the faith. By comparison, a 1946 Soviet report estimated the membership at two hundred adults. DAZO, f. R-1490, op. 1, spr. 8, ark. 6-7. For scholarly discussion of Witness membership totals, see Sturgis, "Institutional versus Contextual Explanations," 293–4.
53 AUSBUZO, f. 2558, op. 1, spr. 5523, t. 2, ark. 243.
54 Other cases against Jehovah's Witnesses in this time period do sometimes contain photographs as part of the initial intake record. The case file gives no indication as to why photographs were not taken for this particular investigation.

55 The Society abandoned the practice of asking for donations to cover the costs of literature in the 1990s, largely for legal reasons regarding sales tax collection in the United States. Chryssides, *Jehovah's Witnesses*, 123–4.
56 "Memorial Reports," 248–9.
57 Mikhail Bokoch interview by author, 27 July 2013. Bila Tserkva, Ukraine.
58 AUSBUZO, f. 2558, op. 1, spr. 819, ark. 399; Yury Marinchan interview by author, 27 July 2013. Bila Tserkva, Ukraine.
59 Eby, *Hungary at War*, 20–1.
60 Maria Popsha (née Marinchan) interview by author, 28 July 2013. Bila Tserkva, Ukraine.
61 Society literature circulated widely among Witnesses in Ukraine, but the influx of new publications declined in the immediate postwar period in response to tighter border controls that resulted in arrests and made the importation of new literature difficult and dangerous. Lists of confiscated Society publications appear in many case files of state investigations in Ukraine during this period. Mikhail Bokoch recalls that starting in the 1950s when he was directly involved in underground printing work, it was primarily the *Watchtower* that was reprinted. The other bimonthly magazine at the time, *Awake!*, was reprinted much less frequently because it was so difficult to obtain regular copies of it. Mikhail Bokoch interview by author, 27 July 2013. Bila Tserkva, Ukraine. Mikhail is the son of Dmitry Bokoch.
62 The man appealed his arrest, and his case ultimately became the basis for the 1942 Supreme Court decision, *Chaplinsky v. New Hampshire*, which established the "fighting words" doctrine. Greenawalt, *Fighting Words*, 50–1.
63 Garbe, *Between Resistance and Martyrdom*, 484.
64 The Witnesses released a film to document this history along with teacher resources for the classroom. *Jehovah's Witnesses Stand Firm Against Nazi Assault*.
65 AUSBUZO, f. 2558, op. 1, spr. 5523, t. 3, ark. 332 (attached envelope of documents).
66 A list of several co-conspirators was included in the case file; the investigator noted that police were unable to find the men to arrest them. This included Vasily Ona and Ivan Bokoch, among others. AUSBUZO, f. 2558, op. 1, spr. 819, ark. 372.
67 Dmitry Marinchan's daughter recalled that her father was a local overseer, a position of some responsibility within the faith community. Maria Popsha (née Marinchan) interview by author, 28 July 2013. Bila Tserkva, Ukraine.
68 Chryssides, *Jehovah's Witnesses*, 127–8.
69 State-security files from Ukraine confirm that women, and not just men, were arrested and tried in the immediate postwar period. Most notably, the

state convicted several men and women at a 1953 military tribunal that followed several months of interrogations in Kyiv. Both the men and women were accused of holding leadership positions among Jehovah's Witnesses across several regions of Ukraine. AUSBUZO, f. 2558, op. 1, spr. 5523, t. 3, ark. 332 (attached envelope of documents).

70 One study of arrests during the "Great Terror" in the Soviet Union found that roughly 95 per cent of those sentenced were men. This same study found that "religious personnel" were overrepresented among arrested women, suggesting that women who engaged in organized religious activity were particular targets of state repression. Ilič, "The Forgotten Five per Cent," 131–3.

71 Anna Moish (née Marinchan) interview by author, 27 July 2013, Bila Tserkva, Ukraine. Anna is the daughter of Vasily Marinchan.

72 Maria Popsha (née Marinchan) interview by author, 28 July 2013. Bila Tserkva, Ukraine.

73 Yury Marinchan interview by author, 27 July 2013. Bila Tserkva, Ukraine.

74 She recalled how she and the other children followed him to the village soviet and were hushed by the officers to stop crying. Maria Borody (née Nan) interview by author, 28 July 2013. Bila Tserkva, Ukraine.

CHAPTER TWO

1 Mikhail Bokoch interview by author, 27 July 2013. Bila Tserkva, Ukraine.

2 AUSBUZO, f. 2558, op. 1, spr. 5523, t. 1, ark. 219.

3 The state provided separate passports to the lucky few permitted to travel internationally. The Soviet passport system began in 1932. Garcelon, "Colonizing the Subject." See also Kessler, "The Passport System," 477–504.

4 Baiburin, "Rituals of Identity," 96.

5 State Archive of the Russian Federation (Gosudarstvennyi arkhiv Rossiiskoi Federatsii, hereafter GARF), f. 9401, op. 12, delo (file) 138, list (page) 18, cited in Werth, *Cannibal Island*, 15.

6 Shearer, *Policing Stalin's Socialism*, 246–7.

7 Ibid., 249.

8 GARF, f. 6991, op. 6, dd. 880–90.

9 Collective farm workers were finally issued internal passports in 1979. Garcelon, "Colonizing the Subject," 97.

10 Ibid.

11 DAZO, f. R-130, op. 1, spr. 9, ark. 76.

12 DAZO, f. R-130, op. 1, spr. 2, ark. 49–50.

13 Donald Filtzer charts the difficulties in conscripting labour after the war and in keeping labourers in factory jobs, even with the heavy use of repression. Filtzer, *Soviet Workers and Late Stalinism*, 246–7.
14 DAZO, f. R-130, op. 1, spr. 62, ark. 262–63.
15 DAZO, f. R-130, op. 1, spr. 76, ark. 229–30.
16 DAZO, f. R-130, op. 1, spr. 5, ark. 8–9.
17 DAZO, f. R-130, op. 1, spr. 46, ark. 78–80.
18 Mikhail Bokoch recalled that most Witnesses in the village were opposed to Soviet passports during the early postwar period. Mikhail Bokoch interview by author, 27 July 2013. Bila Tserkva, Ukraine.
19 AUSBUZO, f. 2558, op. 1, spr. 819, ark. 368–69.
20 Ibid., 369.
21 Ibid., 48, 95, 119.
22 Ibid., 69–70.
23 This informant testified about the family of Nutsu Dan, who was not arrested as part of the investigation but was frequently mentioned by informants as an active member of the faith community. AUSBUZO, f. 2558, op. 1, spr. 819, ark. 205.
24 AUSBUZO, f. 2558, op. 1, spr. 819, ark. 380.
25 Yekelchyk, *Stalin's Citizens*, 147.
26 Jones, *Everyday Life*, 229–30.
27 AUSBUZO, f. 2558, op. 1, spr. 819, ark. 182.
28 Ibid., 185. Policeman Zin issued fines to several men (ark. 231).
29 Ibid., 234.
30 Ibid., 187.
31 Ibid., 201.
32 Ibid., 203.
33 Both Yury Bokoch (son of Dmitry) and his son, Ivan, noted the confusion about passports. Yury and Makutsa Bokoch (with Ivan Bokoch), interview by author, 28 July 2013. Bila Tserkva, Ukraine.
34 GARF f. 6991, op. 3, d. 1114, ll. 61–62.
35 Central State Archive of Supreme Bodies of Power and Government of Ukraine (Tsentral'nyi derzhavnyi arkhiv vyshchykh orhaniv vlady ta upravlinnia Ukrainy, hereafter TSDAVOVU), f. 4648, op. 2, spr. 196, ark. 30.
36 AUSBUZO, f. 2558, op. 1, spr. 819, ark. 450–62.
37 The Society estimates the total number of exiled Witnesses in the 1951 operation at 9,500. State sources confirm the accuracy of this estimate. Information on the 1949 exile is more limited, but the exile order lists 345 sectarian families. Thus, it is reasonable to assume a total of at least ten thousand exiled Witnesses between the two operations. 2002 *Yearbook of*

Jehovah's Witnesses, 169; Odintsov, *Sovet ministrov SSSR postanovliaet*, 44–45; and Pasat, *Trudnye stranitsy istorii Moldovy*, 455–6.

38 Viola, *The Unknown Gulag*. See also Pobol' and Polian, eds, *Stalinskie Deportatsii*; Polian, *Against Their Will*.

39 Corley, *Religion in the Soviet Union*, 255–7.

40 Baran, *Dissent on the Margins*, 110–11.

CHAPTER THREE

1 Liber, *Total Wars*, 252.

2 Dale, "'Being a Real Man,'" 116.

3 Liber, *Total Wars*, 252.

4 Alexander Statiev includes in his figure "the total number of people engaged in its [resistance] activities between 1944 and 1950, including supply, training, intelligence collection, propaganda, and medical service." Statiev, *The Soviet Counterinsurgency*, 106.

5 Timothy Johnston argues that war gossip was also a way for ordinary citizens to express their discontent with the Soviet system. He writes that it "functioned as a language of dissent for the disaffected in the post-war period." Johnston, "Subversive Tales?," 98.

6 Reese, *The Soviet Military Experience*, 149.

7 "Moguchaia armiia sovetskoi derzhavy," *Sovetskoe Zakarpat'e*, 23 February 1949, 1.

8 Reese, *The Soviet Military Experience*, 50–1.

9 For an overview of conscription and military service, see Eaton, *Daily Life in the Soviet Union*, 88–93.

10 Mikhail Bokoch interview by author, 27 July 2013. Bila Tserkva, Ukraine.

11 Penton, *Apocalypse Delayed*, 55–6.

12 "Neutrality," *The Watchtower Announcing Jehovah's Kingdom*, 1 November 1939, 333.

13 Ibid., 323–3.

14 2002 *Yearbook of Jehovah's Witnesses*, 144, 152–3.

15 DAZO, f. R-130, op. 1, spr. 17, ark. 25–27.

16 Mikhail Bokoch interview by author, 27 July 2013. Bila Tserkva, Ukraine.

17 AUSBUZO, f. 2558, op. 1, spr. 819, ark. 6, 19–20.

18 Both served in the Czechoslovak Army (1926–28). Ibid., ark. 112, 139.

19 Anna Moish (née Marinchan) interview by author, 27 July 2013. Bila Tserkva, Ukraine, and Yury Marinchan interview by author, 27 July 2013. Bila Tserkva, Ukraine. See also AUSBUZO, f. 2558, op. 1, spr. 819, ark. 66, 68, 399.

20 Ibid., ark. 164.

21 Ibid., 87.
22 Ibid., 78, 88, 91–3.
23 Ibid., 88–9.
24 Ibid., 92–3.
25 Ibid., 383.
26 Ibid., 13–14.
27 Ibid., 229.
28 Ibid., 181.
29 Ibid., 219.
30 AUSBUZO, f. 2558, op. 1, spr. 5523, t. 3, ark. 61.
31 Mikhail Bokoch interview by author, 27 July 2013. Bila Tserkva, Ukraine.
32 For conscientious objection by Witnesses in other Soviet bloc countries, see Ramet, *Social Currents in Eastern Europe*, 167.
33 "Konstitutsionnoe pravo na al'ternativnuiu sluzhbu otbiraiut u molodykh liudei posle resheniia verkhovnogo suda o likvidatsii organizatsii Svidetelei Iegovy," *Svideteli Iegovy v Rossii*, 11 May 2017, https://www.jw-russia.org/news/17051113-160.html (accessed 5 January 2021).
34 Sang-Hun, "South Korean Jehovah's Witnesses."

CHAPTER FOUR

1 Heinzen, *Inventing a Soviet Countryside*, 159.
2 Gross, *Revolution from Abroad*, 113.
3 Yekelchyk, *Stalin's Citizens*, 192.
4 Plamper, *The Stalin Cult*.
5 Brooks, *Thank You, Comrade Stalin!*, 195.
6 "Nevidkladni zavdannia sil's'kykh rad," *Sotsialistychna pratsia*, 8 January 1948, 1.
7 "Den' vyborov," *Sovetskoe Zakarpat'e*, 30 January 1949, 1.
8 DAZO, f. R-130, op. 1, spr. 60, ark. 62.
9 "Za Stalina, za rodinu, za mir!," *Sovetskoe Zakarpat'e*, 19 December 1950, 1.
10 Zubkova, *Russia after the War*, 75–6.
11 The council did not monitor the Russian Orthodox Church's legal activities. A separate body, the Council for Russian Orthodox Church Affairs, was responsible for this task.
12 Kashirin, "Protestant Minorities in the Soviet Ukraine," 32–3.
13 This particular example, from TSDAVOVU, f. 4648, op. 2, spr. 45, ark. 28–30, is cited, along with several others, in Kashirin, "Protestant Minorities in the Soviet Ukraine," 39–43.

14 TSDAVOVU, f. 4648, op. 4, spr. 22, ark. 127.
15 The document itself is not dated, but the file folder indicates it was likely prepared between mid-November and mid-December 1946. A title, "Report on Evangelical Christian-Baptists," was written on top in pen, perhaps much after the document was originally prepared since its contents do not match this designation. DAZO, f. R-1490, op. 1, spr. 8, ark. 6–7.
16 TSDAVOVU, f. 4648, op. 4, spr. 22, ark. 127.
17 Chryssides, *Jehovah's Witnesses*, 54, 80.
18 The Society has documented a small number of individuals who belonged to the faith or corresponded with its offices in the pre-war period. Baran, *Dissent on the Margins*, 16–19.
19 For a brief earlier history of this religion, see Himka, *Religion and Nationality in Western Ukraine*, 5–8.
20 Semeniuk, *Hodi!*, 4–5. For a detailed overview of Greek Catholic relations with the postwar Soviet state in Ukraine, see Bociurkiw, *The Ukrainian Greek Catholic Church*. For a broader view of Orthodoxy in this period, see Denysenko, *The Orthodox Church in Ukraine*.
21 For reasons for the wartime thaw in church-state relations, see Chumachenko, *Church and State in Soviet Russia*, 6–9; Miner, *Stalin's Holy War*.
22 Kotkin, *Stalin: Waiting for Hitler*, 569–72.
23 DAZO, f. R-1490, op. 1, spr. 13, ark. 15–20.
24 DAZO, f. R-1430, op. 1, spr. 41, ark. 55.
25 Friedgut, *Political Participation in the USSR*, 114.
26 AUSBUZO, f. 2558, op. 1, spr. 819, ark. 177.
27 Ibid., 192.
28 Ibid., 179.
29 Ibid., 213, 215.
30 The parable and the reference to "two masters," sometimes translated as "God and Mammon," appears in both Matthew 6:24 and Luke 16:13.
31 Dori, "Jehovah Never Abandoned Us," 26.
32 AUSBUZO, f. 2558, op. 1, spr. 819, ark. 231–3.
33 Maria Popsha (née Marinchan) interview by author, 28 July 2013. Bila Tserkva, Ukraine.
34 Witness membership statistics are based on "active publishers," the technical term for individuals who regularly engage in evangelism. The door-to-door ministry became a "trademark" of the Witnesses in the early twentieth century under the leadership of the Society's second president. Knox, *Jehovah's Witnesses and the Secular World*, 109.
35 Engardio and Shepard, *Knocking*.

36 AUSBUZO, f. 2558, op. 1, spr. 819, ark. 200–1.

37 "Povidomlennia tsentral'noi vyborchoi komisii po vyborakh do verkhovnoi rady SRSR pro rezul'taty vyboriv," *Sotsialistychna pratsia*, 16 March 1950, 1.

38 DAZO, f. R-1490, op. 1, spr. 63, ark. 6–7.

39 Wittner, *The Struggle Against the Bomb*, 182–3.

40 Peladii, "V im'ia mohutnisti ridnoi bat'kivshchyny," 3.

41 "Pod Stokgol'mskim vozzvaniem podpisalos' 96.360.866 sovetskikh grazhdan," *Sovetskoe Zakarpat'e*, 13 July 1950, 1.

42 "Moguchii golos sovetskogo naroda," *Sovetskoe Zakarpat'e*, 18 October 1950, 1.

43 Additional information on Witness refusals comes from a later 1955 peace campaign, as officials from several regions reported repeated issues with getting signatures for this effort from local Witnesses. Russian State Archive of Contemporary History (Rossiiskii gosudarstvennyi arkhiv noveishei istorii, hereafter RGANI), f. 5, op. 16, d. 709, ll. 129–32; d. 711, ll. 102–8.

44 The Bara case file contains a commissioned report from a Kyiv literature office about confiscated newsletters from the Witnesses. It notes that the Society advised its members against signing the Stockholm petition. AUSBUZO, f. 2558, op. 1, spr. 5523, t. 3, ark. 168.

45 Tsiboulski, "A Promise I Am Determined to Keep," 21.

46 AUSBUZO, f. 2558, op. 1, spr. 5523, t. 3, ark. 63.

CHAPTER FIVE

1 The Soviet Union issued its first state bonds in 1928. The state repeatedly manipulated its policies to avoid timely payments to bonds holders. Ioffe, *Soviet Law and Soviet Reality*, 213–14.

2 For suggestions on giving bonds as gifts, see the US Treasury information page on purchasing bonds, https://www.treasurydirect.gov/indiv/planning/plan_gifts.htm (accessed 12 December 2018).

3 "O vypuske chetvertogo gosudarstvennogo zaima vosstanovleniia i razvitiia narodnogo khoziaistva SSSR," *Sovetskoe Zakarpat'e*, 4 May 1949, 1; Zverev, "S ogromnym voodushevleniem trudiashchiesia Zakarpat'ia podpisyvaiutsia na novyi zaem," 2.

4 For a detailed history of Soviet bond campaigns, including the story of beekeeper Ferapont Golovatyi, see Ironside, "Rubles for Victory," 799–828.

5 Kashirin, "Protestant Minorities in the Soviet Ukraine," 238.

6 "Kolkhoznoe krest'ianstvo Zakarpat'ia druzhno podpisyvaetsia na zaem," *Sovetskoe Zakarpat'e*, 7 May 1949, 1.

7 Les'o, "Gosudarstvennye zaimy," 2.
8 Yekelchyk, *Stalin's Citizens*, 113.
9 Zubkova, *Russia after the War*, 70.
10 AUSBUZO, f. 2558, op. 1, spr. 819, ark. 183.
11 Ibid.
12 Ibid., 229.
13 Ibid., 232.
14 Ibid., 186–7.
15 Ibid., 219.
16 Ibid., 228.
17 A roundup of prominent Witnesses in the underground community led to a lengthy investigation and military tribunal in Kyiv in 1953. Among the defendants were several individuals from Stanislav region. The Ten Points memo is included in the Bara case file: AUSBUZO, f. 2558, op. 1, spr. 5523, t. 3, ark. 332 (attached envelope of documents). A copy of the Ten Points memo also appears in the Bokoch case file: AUSBUZO, f. 2558, op. 1, spr. 819, ark. 390 (attached envelope of documents). Both versions are nearly identical, and likely come from the same original source.
18 2002 *Yearbook of Jehovah's Witnesses*, 164–5, 196–7; 2008 *Yearbook of Jehovah's Witnesses*, 94–5, 134–5.
19 On "theocratic" governance, see Piersma, "True to Their Faith," 1:138.
20 "Fear Them Not," *The Watchtower and Herald of Christ's Presence*, 1 November 1933, 330.
21 For divisions in postwar Romania, see 2006 *Yearbook of Jehovah's Witnesses*, 116. For Ukraine, see 2002 *Yearbook of Jehovah's Witnesses*, 192–6. For Czechoslovakia, see 2000 *Yearbook of Jehovah's Witnesses*, 186–9.
22 Mikhail Bokoch interview by author, 28 July 2013. Bila Tserkva, Ukraine.
23 A circuit overseer is responsible for overseeing several congregations. Shelever's biography can be pieced together from multiple sources, including mentions in both the Bokoch and Bara case files, and from Mikhail Bokoch interview by author, 28 July 2013, Bila Tserkva, Ukraine.
24 Under arrest in 1952, another Transcarpathian elder Alexander Bara confirmed that Shelever had opposed the Ten Points instruction. AUSBUZO, f. 2558, op. 1, spr. 5523, t. 1, ark. 62–63.
25 AUSBUZO, f. 2558, op. 1, spr. 819, ark. 197.
26 Ibid., 94–5.
27 Nan recanted this portion of his statement in a subsequent interrogation. Ibid., 170–5.
28 Ibid., 390.

CHAPTER SIX

1 "Prazdnik shkol'nikov," *Sovetskoe Zakarpat'e*, 1 September 1949, 3.
2 Tarusova, "Obuchenie pervoklassnikov," 3.
3 Kuchmenko, "Vospitanie sovetskogo patriotizma na urokakh literatury," 3.
4 This document is quoted in Brandenberger, *National Bolshevism*, 197–201.
5 Kirschenbaum, *Small Comrades*, 49.
6 Kelly, *Children's World*, 104–8.
7 Kelly, "A Joyful Soviet Childhood," 9.
8 "Persha sesiia Zakarpats'koi oblasnoi rady deputativ trudiashchykh," *Zakarpats'ka pravda*, 16 January 1948, 1.
9 DAZO, f. R-130, op.1, spr. 30, ark. 15.
10 "Persha sesiia Zakarpats'koi oblasnoi rady deputativ trudiashchykh," 1; "Oblasna narada v pytanni likvidatsii nepys'mennosti i malopys'mennosti," *Zakarpats'ka pravda*, 7 March 1948, 3.
11 DAZO, f. R-130, op. 1, spr. 30, ark. 15.
12 Shul'ha, ed., *Sotsialistychni peretvorennia na Zakarpatti za 25 rokiv radians'koi vlady*, 2.
13 Panachin, Kolmakovaia, and Ravkin, eds, *Ocherki istorii shkoly i pedagogicheskoi mysli narodov SSSR*, 132.
14 "Po okruzi," *Sotsialistychna pratsia*, 11 July 1948, 2.
15 DAZO, f. R-130, op. 1, spr. 30, ark. 15.
16 The spelling of Alexander Pelladi's last name varies between the case file and the newspaper columns penned by him in this period. It is also spelled differently in the 1952 investigation of other Jehovah's Witnesses, in which Pelladi again served as an informant.
17 AUSBUZO, f. 2558, op. 1, spr. 5523, t. 3, ark. 59.
18 DAZO, f. R-130, op. 1, spr. 63, ark. 176–81.
19 Sliusarchuk, *Sotsialistychna pratsia*, 2.
20 DAZO, f. R-130, op. 1, spr. 76, ark. 93.
21 "Oblasna narada v pytanni likvidatsii nepys'mennosti i malopys'mennosti," 3.
22 DAZO, f. R-130, op. 1, spr. 76, ark. 93.
23 Iurchenko, "Ozdorovyty robotu klubu," 4.
24 "Polipshyty kerivnytstvo kul'tosvitnimy zakladamy," *Soltsialistychna pratsia*, 11 November 1948, 1.
25 Chernenko and Kostiuchenko, "Moish 'rozporiadyvsia,'" 2.
26 Porchan, "Budut i u nas sportivnye ploshchadki," 3.
27 AUSBUZO, f. 2558, op. 1, spr. 819, ark., 226–7.
28 William Gobitis to "Our School Directors," 5 November 1935, William Gobitis Papers, Manuscript Division, Library of Congress, quoted in Peters, *Judging Jehovah's Witnesses*, 37.

29 Smith, "The Persecution of West Virginia Jehovah's Witnesses," 180.

30 Witnesses do not run their own educational institutions for children, nor encourage parents to keep children out of public-school systems. While Witnesses are generally cautious, if not skeptical about higher education, this issue did not arise in Bila Tserkva since rural residents had no expectation that their children would continue schooling past the primary level. Knox, *Jehovah's Witnesses and the Secular World*, 49; Chryssides, *Jehovah's Witnesses*, 176.

31 AUSBUZO, f. 2558, op. 1, spr. 819, ark. 226.

32 Maria Popsha (née Marinchan) interview by author, 28 July 2013. Bila Tserkva, Ukraine.

33 Cheng, *Creating the "New Man,"* 28–31.

34 Yurchak, *Everything Was Forever*, 80–1.

35 Blinnikov, *A Geography of Russia and Its Neighbors*, 221.

36 Raleigh, *Soviet Baby Boomers*, 85–6.

37 AUSBUZO, f. 2558, op. 1, spr. 819, ark. 227.

38 Ibid., 236–7.

39 Ibid., 236.

40 Zajda, *Education in the USSR*, 9–10.

41 Ramet, ed., *Religious Policy in the Soviet Union*, 13–14.

42 The "Catholic" churches in this document almost certainly refer to Greek Catholic churches given their presence in this district. DAZO, f. R-130, op. 1, spr. 40, ark. 74.

43 DAZO, f. R-1430, op. 1, spr. 41, ark. 55.

44 GARF, f. 6991, op. 3, d. 1117, ll. 20–1.

45 Russian State Archive of Socio-Political History (Rossiiskii gosudarstvennyi arkhiv sotsial'no-politicheskoi istorii), f. 17, op. 125, d. 506, l. 184.

46 TSDAVOVU, f. 4648, op. 2, spr. 181, ark. 90–96.

47 "Half a Century under Totalitarian Tyranny," *Awake!*, 22 February 1999, 12.

48 "Communist Leaders Fear Bible Truth," *The Watchtower Announcing Jehovah's Kingdom*, 1 April 1956, 217.

49 2002 *Yearbook of Jehovah's Witnesses*, 233.

50 When Hungary occupied Transcarpathia, it shut down the local Kingdom Halls. *Ibid.*, 130, 142.

51 AUSBUZO, f. 2558, op. 1, spr. 5523, t. 3, ark. 242, 248.

52 Mikhail recalls that this period of relative freedom had ended by 1946 or 1947. Mikhail Bokoch interview by author, 27 July 2013. Bila Tserkva, Ukraine.

53 AUSBUZO, f. 2558, op. 1, spr. 5523, t. 3, ark. 66–7.

54 Ibid., t. 2, ark. 243, 244.

55 AUSBUZO, f. 2558, op. 1, spr. 819, ark. 206–9.

56 Ibid., ark. 197.

57 Ibid., 389.
58 Ibid., 237.
59 Ibid., 144–5.
60 Ibid., 269.
61 Ibid., 166–7.
62 Ibid., 170.
63 Ibid., 170–3.
64 Ibid., 174–5.
65 Sawatsky, *Soviet Evangelicals since World War II*, 298.
66 AUSBUZO, f. 2558, op. 1, spr. 819, ark. 197–8; Mikhail Bokoch interview by author, 27 July 2013. Bila Tserkva, Ukraine.
67 Yury Marinchan recalled Mikhail leading such gatherings at this time. Yury Marinchan interview by author, 27 July 2013. Bila Tserkva, Ukraine.
68 Solomon, *Soviet Criminal Justice under Stalin*, 209–11.
69 AUSBUZO, f. 2558, op. 1, spr. 819, ark. 236–7.
70 Mikhail Bokoch interview by author, 27 July 2013. Bila Tserkva, Ukraine. In the 1952 investigation, Pelladi mentions hearing a rumor in 1948 that a Witness (not Bokoch) in the village had gathered around thirty school-age children to listen to readings from the Bible. He does not place himself at the event, but this information suggests that Pelladi was keeping a close eye on instances in which local Witnesses instructed children in the faith. AUSBUZO, f. 2558, op. 1, spr. 5523, t. 3, ark. 60.
71 AUSBUZO, f. 2558, op. 1, spr. 819, ark. 48.
72 Ibid., 338–9.
73 Ibid., 400.

CHAPTER SEVEN

1 The interwar Czechoslovak government had superficially addressed this problem through land reform legislation and redistribution. Jordan and Klemenčič, eds, *Transcarpathia: Bridgehead or Periphery?*, 102–5.
2 Mikhail Bokoch interview by author, 27 July 2013. Bila Tserkva, Ukraine.
3 "Pro zaprovadzhennia platnoi trudhuzhpovynnosti na lisozahotivliakh v sezon 1948–1949 rokiv," *Sotsialistychna pratsia*, 4 November 1948, 2.
4 Mikhail Bokoch interview by author, 28 July 2013. Bila Tserkva, Ukraine.
5 DAZO, f. R-130, op. 1, spr. 47, ark. 201.
6 DAZO, f. R-130, op. 1, spr. 46, ark. 230–38.
7 AUSBUZO, f. 2558, op. 1, spr. 819, ark. 219, 231.
8 Chryssides, *Jehovah's Witnesses*, 176–7.
9 The deported population reached as many as 1.8 million. Viola, *The Unknown Gulag*, 6–7.

10 The editors of a documentary volume on collectivization note that deportation "quickly became a purely political exercise, aimed less at specific economic categories of peasants than at village leaders, rural elites, and anyone who dared oppose regime policies in the countryside." Viola et al., *The War against the Peasantry*, 215.
11 Marples, *Stalinism in Ukraine in the 1940s*, 26–41.
12 Allina-Pisano, "'Opting Out' under Stalin and Khrushchev," 61.
13 Jordan and Klemenčić, *Transcarpathia: Bridgehead or Periphery?*, 107–8.
14 Vehesh and Fedinec, eds, *Zakarpattia 1919–2009 rokiv: istoriia, polityka, kul'tura*, 318; Olashyn, *Istoriia Zakarpattia*, 214–22.
15 Olashyn, *Istoriia Zakarpattia*, 224.
16 "Po voprosam kolkhoznogo stroitel'stva," *Sovetskoe Zakarpat'e*, 26 March 1949, 4.
17 "Po voprosam kolkhoznogo stroitel'stva." *Sovetskoe Zakarpat'e*, 17 May 1949, 3.
18 Jordan and Klemenčić, *Transcarpathia: Bridgehead or Periphery?*, 108.
19 In his study of postwar agriculture in the region, Zhulkanych notes the weak presence of the party at the village level, a situation that significantly impeded collectivization. Of the few communists who existed in the villages, many did not want to join the collective farms. Zhulkanych, *Ahrarno-vyrobnychi ta sotsial'no-ekonomichni vidnosyny na Zakarpatti*, 40–1.
20 Baberowski, *Scorched Earth*, 150.
21 "Shyroko i povsiakdenno propahuvaty kolhospnyi lad!," *Zakarpats'ka pravda*, 12 June 1948, 1.
22 "Shyrshe propahuvaty perevahy kolhospnoho ladu," *Zakarpats'ka pravda*, 15 January 1948, 1.
23 "Vony pishly kolhospnym shliakhom," *Zakarpats'ka pravda*, 6 July 1948, 1.
24 "Shyrshe propahuvaty perevahy kolhospnoho ladu," 1.
25 "Kollektivizatsiia – zakon sotsialisticheskogo razvitiia," *Sovetskoe Zakarpat'e*, 17 December 1948, 1.
26 "Po shliakhu do sutsil'noi kolektyvizatsii," *Sotsialistychna pratsia*, 15 July 1948, 1.
27 DAZO, f. R-130, op. 1, spr. 30, ark. 66–67.
28 For example, the 1 December issue of *Sovetskoe Zakarpat'e* in 1948 featured an editorial on the inevitable triumph of collective farms throughout the region and a full page of testimonials about the superiority of the farms.
29 DAZO, f. R-130, op. 1, spr. 33, ark. 170–4.
30 "K novym pobedam kolkhoznogo stroia," *Sovetskoe Zakarpat'e*, 1 December 1948, 1.
31 DAZO, f. R-130, op. 1, spr. 47, ark. 184–5.
32 DAZO, f. R-130, op. 1, spr. 30, ark. 66–7.

33 DAZO, f. R-130, op. 1, spr. 44, ark. 1–15.
34 L. Alim, "Na IV plenum okruzhnomu KP(b)U," *Sotsialistychna pratsia*, 29 May 1949, 2.
35 "V plenum Zakarpatskogo obkoma KP(b)U," *Sovetskoe Zakarpat'e*, 9 September 1949, 1.
36 "VI plenum Zakarpatskogo obkoma KP(b)U," *Sovetskoe Zakarpat'e*, 27 December 1949, 3.
37 DAZO, f. R-1662, op. 1, spr. 1, ark. 1–3.
38 DAZO, f. R-130, op. 1, spr. 32, ark. 200; f. R-1334, op. 1, spr. 9, ark. 13–15.
39 DAZO, f. R-130, op. 1, spr. 47, pp. 200–3.
40 Tarasov, "Novyi kolhosp," 1.
41 For a chart of Bila Tserkva households in 1946, see DAZO, f. R-130, op. 1, spr. 9, ark. 234.
42 Peladii, "Boiovu zustrich vesni v kolhospi 'Nove Zhittia,'" 1.
43 DAZO, f. R-130, op. 1, spr. 48, ark. 180–1.
44 AUSBUZO, f. 2558, op. 1, spr. 819, ark. 193.
45 DAZO, f. R-130, op. 1, spr. 54, ark. 108–9.
46 DAZO, f. R-1662, op. 1, spr. 1, ark. 12–24.
47 DAZO, f. R-130, op. 1, spr. 54, ark. 108–9.
48 Ellipses appear after the shortened word "kolkh" but seem only to indicate in both instances that the word has been shortened, rather than that certain words have been left out of the document. AUSBUZO, f. 2558, op. 1, spr. 819, ark. 390 (attached envelope of documents).
49 Yury and Makutsa Bokoch (with Ivan Bokoch) interview by author, 28 July 2013. Bila Tserkva, Ukraine.
50 DAZO, f. R-1662, op, 1, spr. 1, ark. 28–29.
51 AUSBUZO, f. 2558, op. 1, spr. 819, ark. 193–4.
52 Ibid., 178, 182.
53 Ibid., 184–8.
54 Ibid., 199.
55 Jehovah's Witnesses use the phrase "system of things," a reference to Matthew 13:49, to signify what they view as the current, corrupted world order that precedes the establishment of a millennial kingdom on earth. For Ona's comments, see AUSBUZO, f. 2558, op. 1, spr. 819, ark. 196, 199.
56 Ibid., 199.
57 Ibid., 304.
58 Ibid., 200.
59 Ibid., 201.
60 Ibid., 206.
61 Ibid., 201.

62 Ibid., 201–2.
63 Ibid., 244, 257.
64 DAZO, f. R-1662, op. 1, spr. 1, ark. 25.
65 Ganson, *The Soviet Famine*, xv.
66 AUSBUZO, f. 2558, op. 1, spr. 819, ark. 182–3.
67 Ibid., ark. 231.
68 DAZO, f. R-1334, op. 1, spr. 23, ark. 1.
69 Fitzpatrick, *Stalin's Peasants*, 4.
70 Sheila Fitzpatrick notes that the kulak label was sometimes applied by the dominant local religious community onto a less powerful religious community. Fitzpatrick, *Everyday Stalinism*, 123.
71 Iholkin, "Nanesty rishuchyi udar po kurkuliah i ikh posibnykakh," 2.
72 Tsiupko, "Rishuchu vidcich kurkuliam, zabezpechyty pratsiu kolhospnykiv," 2; Baryshaev, "Kogda ne vedut bor'bu s kulakami," 2.
73 Zdorovets, "Mozhno li prinimat' v kolkhoz kulakov?," 2.
74 "Who Resist Communism?," *Awake!*, 8 January 1950, 1.
75 DAZO, f. R-130, op. 1, spr. 44, ark. 8–12.
76 Some of the men on the kulak rolls were identified as hostile to Soviet power, but without reference to their religious affiliation. They may also have been Witnesses. DAZO, f. R-130, op. 1, spr. 27, ark. 97–101.
77 DAZO, f. R-130, op. 1, spr. 27, ark. 97–101.
78 AUSBUZO, f. 2558, op. 1, spr. 819, ark. 355–61.
79 The village drafted numerous kulak rolls, and both names and information vary, making it difficult to determine the exact land holdings and status of villagers. For two lists from 1949, see DAZO, f. R-130, op. 1, spr. 48, ark. 188–89; spr. 57, ark. 12–85.
80 AUSBUZO, f. 2558, op. 1, spr. 819, ark, 355–61.
81 Ibid., 177, 179, 185, 190, 214, 225.
82 Ibid. For Vasily Bokoch, ark. 3–19; for Dmitry Bokoch, ark. 25–41; for Marinchan brothers, ark. 50–87; for Guzo, ark. 107–112, 141; for Nan, ark. 146–65.
83 AUSBUZO, f. 2558, op. 1, spr. 819, ark. 190.
84 Ibid., pp. 381–8.
85 Ibid., 397–407.
86 DAZO, f. R-1334, op. 1, spr. 25.
87 Mikhail Bokoch interview by author, July 27, 2013. Bila Tserkva, Ukraine.
88 AUSBUZO, f. 2558, op. 1, spr. 819, ark. 10.
89 Ibid., 56.
90 Ibid., 32, 77, 106, 129, 153.
91 Maria Borody (née Nan) interview by author, July 28, 2013. Bila Tserkva, Ukraine.

92 DAZO, f. R-130, op. 1, spr. 14, ark. 4–5.
93 Uzhans'kyi, "Na kolhospomu toku," 1.
94 Moish, "Hotuiemos' do sviata," 1.
95 Semenenko, "Rik po shliakhu novoho zhyttia," 2.
96 DAZO, f. R-1662, op. 1, spr. 1, ark. 40.
97 DAZO, f. R-130, op. 1, spr. 47, ark. 194.
98 DAZO, f. 1662, op. 1, spr. 1, ark. 44–5.
99 Pichkur, "Vykonaiemo vkazivki tovarysha Stalina zrobyty kolhospy bil'shovyts'kymy, a kolhospnykiv zamozhnymy," 2.
100 "Za dal'she pidnesennia sil'skoho hospodarstva," *Sotsialistychna pratsia*, 26 January 1950, 2; DAZO, f. R-130, op. 1, spr. 60, ark. 6–9.
101 DAZO, f. R-130, op. 1, spr. 83, ark. 20.
102 DAZO, f. R-130, op. 1, spr. 60, ark. 9–10.
103 DAZO, f. R-130, op. 1, spr. 59, ark. 27. This was part of a broader consolidation of small farms during this period. Lytvyn, *Ukraina u pershomu povoiennomu desiatylitti (1946–1955)*, 132.
104 AUSBUZO, f. 2558, op. 1, spr. 819, ark. 435.
105 Maria Borody (née Nan) interview by author, 28 July 2013. Bila Tserkva, Ukraine.
106 Anna Moish (née Marinchan) interview by author, 27 July 2013, Bila Tserkva, Ukraine.
107 In a valuable microstudy of postwar Solontsy on the Czechoslovak border, Jessica Allina-Pisano argues that while villagers there joined the local farm with minimal resistance, they did not invest in the new system, participating only when necessary and "opting out" when not. Allina-Pisano, "'Opting Out' under Stalin and Khrushchev," 58–66.
108 Marples, *Stalinism in Ukraine in the 1940s*, 114–15.

CHAPTER EIGHT

1 AUSBUZO, f. 2558, op. 1, spr. 819, ark. 372.
2 Ibid., ark. 194.
3 Ibid., 364.
4 Ibid., 380.
5 Ibid., 381.
6 Ibid., 383.
7 Ibid., ark, pp. 381–2.
8 Ibid., 382.
9 Gross, *Revolution from Abroad*, 165.
10 Khlevniuk, *The History of the Gulag*, 165–6, 366–7; Barnes, *Death and Redemption*, 84-6.

11 Dobson, *Khrushchev's Cold Summer*, 47.
12 Krushinskii, "Apostoly porokhovoi bochki," 6.
13 A 1986 publication, for example, described the Witnesses as a "channel for the penetration of bourgeois ideology and clerical-extremist views into our country." Vrublevskaia et al., *Organizatsiia i metodika ateisticheskogo vospitaniia*, 230.
14 Johnston, *Being Soviet*, 167–90.
15 The head of the Jewish Anti-Fascist Committee, the actor Solomon Mikhoels, was murdered by state officials, who disguised the death as a car accident. Zubok, *A Failed Empire*, 56–60.
16 AUSBUZO, f. 2558, op. 1, spr. 5523.
17 Ibid., t. 1, ark. 269–70.
18 Ibid., t. 3, ark. 285–6.
19 "Pod vlast'iu krovavogo dollara," *Sovetskoe Zakarpat'e*, 2 November 1950, 3.
20 Anna Moish (née Marinchan) interview by author, July 27, 2013. Bila Tserkva, Ukraine.
21 Sharlet, "Stalinism and Soviet Legal Culture," 166.
22 AUSBUZO, f. 2558, op. 1, spr. 819, ark. 397.
23 Simonsen, "Inheriting the Soviet Policy Toolbox," 1070–1.
24 Slezkine, *The Jewish Century*, 337.
25 2002 *Yearbook of Jehovah's Witnesses*, 163.
26 Batt, "Transcarpathia: Peripheral Region at the 'Centre of Europe,'" 155.
27 AUSBUZO, f. 2558, op. 1, spr. 819, ark. 398.
28 2012 *Yearbook of Jehovah's Witnesses*, 198–222.
29 AUSBUZO, f. 2558, op. 1, spr. 819, ark. 398.
30 Ibid.
31 The court secretary recorded the exchange in an awkward mixture of first and third person. For the sake of clarity, I have transcribed it entirely in first person. Ibid., 398–9.
32 Ibid., 399.
33 Maria Popsha (née Marinchan) interview by author, July 28, 2013. Bila Tserkva, Ukraine.
34 Yury Marinchan, baptized at a location in Serednie Vodiane at ten years old, recalled that he was not given the name of the man who baptized him. This was done to protect the man should Yury be asked to denounce him. Yury Marinchan interview by author, July 27, 2013. Bila Tserkva, Ukraine. Anna Moish recalled a similar situation when she was baptised, and for the same reason. She was baptized at eighteen years old. Anna Moish (née Marinchan) interview by author, July 27, 2013. Bila Tserkva, Ukraine.
35 AUSBUZO, f. 2558, op. 1, spr. 819, ark. 399.

36 Ibid.
37 Ibid.
38 Ibid., 400.
39 Ibid.
40 Ibid, 400–1.
41 Ibid., 400.
42 Ibid., 401.
43 Ibid.
44 Ibid., 402.
45 As with the previous testimony, the court secretary recorded these remarks in both first and third person; I have adhered to first person for the sake of consistency. Ibid., 402.
46 Ibid., 404–5.
47 Rutherford was the legal counsel for the Society's founder, Charles Taze Russell, and became president of the Society in 1917; he maintained this position until his death in 1942. Chryssides, *Jehovah's Witnesses*, 77–8.
48 Baran, *Dissent on the Margins*, 21.
49 AUSBUZO, f. 2558, op. 1, spr. 819, ark. 8.
50 For example, a 1955 report from the Council for Religious Cult Affairs in Ukraine noted that "Jehovists" are also called "Rutherfordists." Central State Archive of Civic Organizations of Ukraine (Tsentral'nyi derzhavnyi arkhiv hromads'kykh ob'iednan' Ukrainy, or TSDAHO), f. 1, op. 24, spr. 4038, ark. 109–10.
51 AUSBUZO, f. 2558, op. 1, spr. 819, ark. 405, 408.
52 Ibid., ark. 409–10.
53 Ibid., 411–2.
54 Ibid., ark. 414.

CHAPTER NINE

1 AUSBUZO, f. 2558, op. 1, spr. 819, ark. 420–5, 445–6.
2 Barenberg, *Gulag Town, Company Town*, 15–18.
3 Applebaum, *Gulag: A History*, 82–4.
4 Barenberg, *Gulag Town, Company Town*, 97–8.
5 Anna Moish (née Marinchan) interview by author, 27 July 2013. Bila Tserkva, Ukraine; Yury Marinchan interview by author, 27 July 2013. Bila Tserkva, Ukraine.
6 Noble, *I Was a Slave in Russia*, 94, 100, 104–5.
7 GARF, f. 9401, op. 37, d. 4547, cited in Applebaum, *Gulag: A History*, 225.
8 The death rate in Vorkuta declined dramatically from a high of 147 per 1,000 in 1943 to 7.5 per 1,000 in 1953. Barenberg, *Gulag Town, Company Town*, 92.

9 Maria Popsha (née Marinchan) interview by author, 28 July 2013. Bila Tserkva, Ukraine.
10 Maria Borody (née Nan) interview by author, 28 July 2013. Bila Tserkva, Ukraine.
11 For prisoner statistics, see Hardy, *Gulag after Stalin*, 12. For prisoner reactions to Stalin's death, see Barnes, *Death and Redemption*, 204.
12 Hardy, *Gulag after Stalin*, 23.
13 Ibid., 38.
14 AUSBUZO, f. 2558, op. 1, spr. 819, ark. 419.
15 Ibid., 431.
16 Ibid., 432–3.
17 Ibid., 434.
18 Ibid., 435.
19 Stephen Kotkin's masterful study of Stalinism uses the term "speaking Bolshevik" to talk about how Soviet citizens mastered the language of the state. Kotkin, *Magnetic Mountain*, 220–2.
20 AUSBUZO, f. 2558, op. 1, spr. 819, ark. 436.
21 Satter, *It Was a Long Time Ago*, 119.
22 AUSBUZO, f. 2558, op. 1, spr. 819, ark. 437–8.
23 Ibid., 439–44.
24 The prosecutor's office and Supreme Court decisions reduced Dmitry Bokoch's sentence to ten years, and Vasily Bokoch's, Nutsu Guzo's, and Ivan Ona's to seven years; and the remaining men's sentences to time served. Despite this fact, all of the men were released from the camps within a few months of one another in the final months of 1955.
25 Ibid., ark. 465.
26 Yury Marinchan interview by author, 27 July 2013. Bila Tserkva, Ukraine.
27 Maria Borody (née Nan) interview by author, 28 July 2013. Bila Tserkva, Ukraine.
28 Anna Moish (née Marinchan) interview by author, 27 July 2013, Bila Tserkva, Ukraine.
29 Mikhail Bokoch interview by author, 27 July 2013. Bila Tserkva, Ukraine. Yury and Makutsa Bokoch (with Ivan Bokoch), interview by author, 28 July 2013. Bila Tserkva, Ukraine.
30 Mikhail Bokoch interview by author, 28 July 2013. Bila Tserkva, Ukraine.
31 Mikhail Bokoch interview by author, 27 July 2013. Bila Tserkva, Ukraine.
32 Yury Marinchan interview by author, 27 July 2013. Bila Tserkva, Ukraine.
33 Yury and Makutsa Bokoch (with Ivan Bokoch), interview by author, 28 July 2013. Bila Tserkva, Ukraine.
34 Some Witnesses preferred to cast ballots but would mark them to indicate

that they were voting for Jehovah God and not for any of the listed candidates. This was in keeping with guidance from the Society in their publications. Baran, *Dissent on the Margins*, 121.

35 There is some indication from archival records that such divisions were present in Bila Tserkva. A 1983 report from the Council for Religious Affairs claimed that the Bila Tserkva Witnesses were split between two factions and disagreed over whether to seek registration with the state. It is worth noting that the report counted over three hundred Witnesses in the village. TSDAHO, f. 4648, op. 7, spr. 241, ark. 63–4. Beyond the village itself, Soviet secret police regularly exploited disagreements among Witnesses to sow mistrust and confusion within the community and to isolate prominent elders by sowing doubt about their loyalty to the faith. Baran, *Dissent on the Margins*, 91–7.

36 Dobson, *Khrushchev's Cold Summer*, 39.

37 Maria Popsha (née Marinchan) interview by author, 28 July 2013. Bila Tserkva, Ukraine.

38 Satter, *It Was a Long Time Ago*, 120.

39 Maria Popsha (née Marinchan) interview by author, 28 July 2013. Bila Tserkva, Ukraine.

40 Mikhail Bokoch interview by author, 27 July 2013. Bila Tserkva, Ukraine.

41 Anna Moish (née Marinchan) interview by author, 27 July 2013, Bila Tserkva, Ukraine.

42 Yury Marinchan interview by author, 27 July 2013. Bila Tserkva, Ukraine.

43 The report from the council wrongly identifies the men's names in part, but almost certainly refers to the same Vasily Marinchan as in the case file. The son's birth date is the same, the patronymic matches that of the father, and the report notes that the father had been sentenced to twenty-five years. TSDAVOVU, f. 4648, op. 4, spr. 214, ark. 37–9, 125.

44 GARF, f. 6991, op. 3, d. 1113, l. 189. A lengthy report from this council in 1956 estimates that there had been perhaps eight thousand Witnesses in Transcarpathia in earlier years, but that the number had dwindled to roughly three thousand. GARF, f. 6991, op. 3, d. 1117, l. 100. Another report from 1954 estimates the number as having been at 2,300 in recent years, but down to 1,800 in the region at present. GARF 6991, op. 3, d. 1116, l. 27. Another council report from 1974 gives the exact figure of 3,796 Witnesses. DAZO, f. 1., op. 7, spr. 98, ark. 48. In short, there is no consistency across reports even from the same government institution.

45 Baran, *Dissent on the Margins*, 86–7, 112.

46 Four thousand represents the low end of state estimates of Witnesses in the late 1970s and early 1980s. KGB estimates for this period are as high as nine thousand. DAZO, f. 1, op. 9, spr. 59, ark. 62, 69.

47 A 1977 KGB memo noted that 190 people had left the Witnesses in the past year, and that another 672 had joined. Yet it cited these figures as proof that the religion no longer attracted much interest. DAZO, f. 1, op. 9, spr. 59, ark. 62.
48 Anna Moish (née Marinchan) interview by author, 27 July 2013. Bila Tserkva, Ukraine.
49 Yury Marinchan interview by author, 27 July 2013. Bila Tserkva, Ukraine.
50 Ibid.
51 Taylor, "Sectarians in Soviet Courts," 277–88; Furov, "Stanovlenie zakonodatel'stva o kul'takh," 15–17.
52 Baran, *Dissent on the Margins*, 155–63.
53 Soviet law allowed draft dodgers to be convicted multiple times, and serve multiple sentences, for the same crime. GARF f. 428, op. 3, d. 457, ll. 27–9.
54 Maria Popsha recalled that in the early postwar period, the entire village had shared a single copy of the Witnesses' magazine, *The Watchtower*. Maria Popsha (née Marinchan) interview by author, 28 July 2013. Bila Tserkva, Ukraine.
55 2002 *Yearbook of Jehovah's Witnesses*, 216-17.
56 Mikhail Bokoch interview by author, 28 July 2013. Bila Tserkva, Ukraine.
57 Ibid.
58 Yury and Makutsa Bokoch (with Ivan Bokoch), interview by author, 28 July 2013. Bila Tserkva, Ukraine.
59 Yury Marinchan interview by author, 27 July 2013. Bila Tserkva, Ukraine.
60 Shmyg, "Teni v novom dome," 3.
61 RGANI, f. 5, op. 63, d. 89, l. 275.
62 TSDAVOVU, f. 4648, op. 4, spr. 322, ark. 207–9.
63 This includes interviews with residents of Transcarpathia (and Bila Tserkva) in the official history of Witnesses in Ukraine published by the Society as part of its 2002 *Yearbook of Jehovah's Witnesses*.
64 Smith, *Remembering Stalin's Victims*, 142–5.
65 AUSBUZO, f. 2558, op. 1, spr. 819, ark. 470–1; Smith, *Remembering Stalin's Victims*, 144–5.
66 AUSBUZO, f. 2558, op. 1, spr. 819, ark. 470–94.
67 Mikhail Bokoch interview by author, 27 July 2013. Bila Tserkva, Ukraine.
68 Kalantaridis, "Globalization and Entrepreneurial Response," 285–99.
69 Jóźwiak, "Negotiating the Territory in a Transcarpathian Urban-Type Settlement," 221–5.
70 "Palatsy Biloi Tserkvy ta Nyzhn'i Apshi vrazhaiut' Ukraintsiv," *Rakhiv News*, http://www.rakhivnews.in.ua/novini/rakhivschina/405-palaci-bloyi-cerkvi-ta-nizhnyi-apsh-vrazhayut-ukrayincv.html (accessed 8 May 2017).

71 For scholarship on the deconstruction of collective farms in post-Soviet Transcarpathia, see Dickinson, "Gender, Work and Economic Restructuring in a Transcarpathian (Ukraine) Village," 387–401; Allina-Pisano, *The Post-Soviet Potemkin Village*.

72 Yury Marinchan interview by author, 27 July 2013. Bila Tserkva, Ukraine.

73 Ivan Bokoch, in Anna Moish (née Marinchan) interview by author, 27 July 2013. Bila Tserkva, Ukraine.

74 Interestingly, a 2018 *Watchtower* article highlighted this concentration of Witnesses in three other nearby villages (including Serednie Vodiane) but did not mention Bila Tserkva itself. "An Abundant Harvest!," *The Watchtower Announcing Jehovah's Kingdom*, May 2018, 32.

75 Anna Moish (née Marinchan) interview by author, 27 July 2013. Bila Tserkva, Ukraine.

76 Mikhail Bokoch interview by author, 27 July 2013. Bila Tserkva, Ukraine.

77 Maria Borody (née Nan) interview by author, 28 July 2013. Bila Tserkva, Ukraine.

78 Mikhail Bokoch interview by author, 27 July 2013. Bila Tserkva, Ukraine.

CONCLUSION

1 Dabrowski, "Borderland Encounters," 193.

2 The definitions of wartime crimes were hopelessly broad, leaving nearly everyone vulnerable to repression for insufficient dedication to the Soviet cause. Weiner, *Making Sense of War*, 111.

3 Zubok, *A Failed Empire*, 61.

4 Brown, *A Biography of No Place*, 230.

5 Ibid., 13.

Bibliography

ARCHIVES

Arkhiv Upravlinnia Sluzhby Bezpeky Ukrainy v Zakarpats'kii oblasti (State Security Service Archive of Transcarpathia, or AUSBUZO)

Derzhavnyi arkhiv L'viv'skoi oblasti (State Archive of Lviv Oblast, or DALO)

Derzhavnyi arkhiv Zakarpats'koi oblasti (State Archive of Transcarpathia, or DAZO)

Gosudarstvennyi arkhiv Rossiiskoi Federatsii (State Archive of the Russian Federation, or GARF)

Rossiiskii gosudarstvennyi arkhiv noveishei istorii (Russian State Archive of Contemporary History, or RGANI)

Rossiiskii gosudarstvennyi arkhiv sotsial'no-politicheskoi istorii (Russian State Archive of Socio-Political History)

Tsentral'nyi derzhavnyi arkhiv hromads'kykh ob'iednan' Ukrainy (Central State Archive of Civic Organizations of Ukraine, or TSDAHO)

Tsentral'nyi derzhavnyi arkhiv vyshchykh orhaniv vlady ta upravlinnia Ukrainy (Central State Archive of Supreme Bodies of Power and Government of Ukraine, or TSDAVOVU)

NEWSPAPERS

Sotsialistychna pratsia (Socialist Work)

Sovetskoe Zakarpat'e/Radians'ka Zakarpattia (Soviet Transcarpathia)

Zakarpatskaia pravda/Zakarpats'ka pravda (Transcarpathian Truth)

PUBLISHED SOURCES

1927 Year Book of the International Bible Students Association. Brooklyn: International Bible Students Association, 1927.

1930 Year Book of the International Bible Students Association. Brooklyn: Watch Tower Bible and Tract Society, Peoples Pulpit Association, and International Bible Student Association, 1929.

1935 Year Book of Jehovah's Witnesses. Brooklyn: Watch Tower Bible and Tract Society, Peoples Pulpit Association, and International Bible Student Association, 1934.

2000 Yearbook of Jehovah's Witnesses. Brooklyn: Watchtower Bible and Tract Society of New York, 2000.

2002 Yearbook of Jehovah's Witnesses. Brooklyn: Watch Tower Bible and Tract Society of New York, and International Bible Students Association, 2002.

2006 Yearbook of Jehovah's Witnesses. Brooklyn: Watchtower Bible and Tract Society of New York, 2006.

2008 Yearbook of Jehovah's Witnesses. Brooklyn: Watchtower Bible and Tract Society of New York, 2008.

2012 Yearbook of Jehovah's Witnesses. Brooklyn: Watch Tower Bible and Tract Society of New York, 2012.

"An Abundant Harvest!" *The Watchtower Announcing Jehovah's Kingdom*, May 2018, 32.

Alim, L. "Na IV plenum okruzhnomu KP(b)U." *Sotsialistychna pratsia*, 29 May 1949, 2.

Allina-Pisano, Jessica. "'Opting out' under Stalin and Khrushchev: Postwar Sovietization in a Borderland Magyar Village." *Problems of Post-Communism* 58, no. 1 (2011): 58–66.

– *The Post-Soviet Potemkin Village: Politics and Property Rights in the Black Earth.* Cambridge: Cambridge University Press, 2008.

Applebaum, Anne. *Gulag: A History.* New York: Doubleday, 2003.

Baberowski, Jörg. *Scorched Earth: Stalin's Reign of Terror.* Translated by Stephen Gilbert, Ivo Komljen, and Samantha Jeanne Taber. New Haven, CT: Yale University Press, 2016.

Baiburin, Albert. "Rituals of Identity: The Soviet Passport." In *Soviet and Post-Soviet Identities*, edited by Catriona Kelly and Mark Bassin, 91–109. Cambridge: Cambridge University Press, 2012.

Baran, Emily B. *Dissent on the Margins: How Soviet Jehovah's Witnesses Defied Communism and Lived to Preach about It.* New York: Oxford University Press, 2014.

Barenberg, Alan. *Gulag Town, Company Town: Forced Labor and Its Legacy in Vorkuta.* New Haven, CT: Yale University Press, 2014.

Barnes, Steven A. *Death and Redemption: The Gulag and the Shaping of Soviet Society.* Princeton, NJ: Princeton University Press, 2011.

Baryshaev, I. "Kogda ne vedut bor'bu s kulakami." *Sovetskoe Zakarpat'e*, 1 August 1948, 2.

Batt, Judy. "Transcarpathia: Peripheral Region at the 'Centre of Europe.'" In *Region, State and Identity in Central and Eastern Europe*, edited by Judy Batt and Kataryna Wolczuk, 155–77. New York: Routledge, 2013. Repr., originally published in London by Frank Cass in 2002.

Belousov, V. I., ed. *Istoriia mist i sil Ukrains'koi RSR. Zakarpats'ka oblast'.* Kyiv: Holovna redaktsiia Ukrains'koi radians'koi entsyklopedii Akademii Nauk URSR, 1969.

Blinnikov, Mikhail S. *A Geography of Russia and Its Neighbors.* New York: Guilford Press, 2011.

Block, Sharon. *Colonial Complexions: Race and Bodies in Eighteenth-Century America.* Philadelphia: University of Pennsylvania Press, 2018.

Bociurkiw, Bohdan R. *The Ukrainian Greek Catholic Church and the Soviet State (1939–1950).* Edmonton: Canadian Institute of Ukrainian Studies Press, 1996.

Braham, Randolph L. *The Politics of Genocide: The Holocaust in Hungary*. Rev. and enl. ed. Vol. 1. New York: Columbia University Press, 1993.

Braham, Randolph L., and Scott Miller, eds. *The Nazis' Last Victims: The Holocaust in Hungary*. Detroit: Wayne State University Press, 2002.

Brandenberger, David. *National Bolshevism: Stalinist Mass Culture and the Formation of Modern Russian National Identity, 1931–1956.* Cambridge, MA: Harvard University Press, 2002.

Brooks, Jeffrey. *Thank You, Comrade Stalin! Soviet Public Culture from Revolution to Cold War.* Princeton, NJ: Princeton University Press, 2000.

Brown, Kate. *A Biography of No Place: From Ethnic Borderland to Soviet Heartland.* Cambridge, MA: Harvard University Press, 2003.

Bucur, Maria. *Heroes and Victims: Remembering War in Twentieth-Century Romania*. Bloomington: Indiana University Press, 2009.

Cannato, Vincent J. *American Passage: The History of Ellis Island*. New York: Harper Perennial, 2010.

Cheng, Yinghong. *Creating the "New Man": From Enlightenment Ideals to Socialist Realities*. Honolulu: University of Hawai'i Press, 2009.

Chernenko, V., and P. Kostiuchenko. "Moish 'rozporiadyvsia.'" *Sotsialistichnya pratsia*, 5 September 1950, 2.

Chryssides, George D. *Jehovah's Witnesses: Continuity and Change*. Farnham, UK: Ashgate, 2016.

Chumachenko, Tatiana A. *Church and State in Soviet Russia: Russian Orthodoxy from World War II to the Khrushchev Years.* Edited and translated by Edward E. Roslof. Armonk, NY: M.E. Sharpe, 2002.

"Communist Leaders Fear Bible Truth." *The Watchtower Announcing Jehovah's Kingdom*, 1 April 1956, 209–18.

Coopersmith, Jonathan. *The Electrification of Russia, 1880–1926*. Ithaca, NY: Cornell University Press, 1992.

Corley, Felix. *Religion in the Soviet Union: An Archival Reader.* New York: New York University Press, 1996.

Dabrowski, Patrice M. "Borderland Encounters in the Carpathian Mountains and Their Impact on Identity Formation." In *Shatterzone of Empires: Coexistence and Violence in the German, Habsburg, Russian, and Ottoman Borderlands*, edited by Omer Bartov and Eric D. Weitz, 193–208. Bloomington: Indiana University Press, 2013.

Dale, Robert. "'Being a Real Man': Masculinities in Soviet Russia during and after the Great Patriotic War." In *Gender and the Second World War: Lessons of War*, edited by Corinna Peniston-Bird and Emma Vickers, 116–34. London: Palgrave Macmillan, 2017.

David, Kathryn. "One Ukraine, under God: Church, State, and the Making of the Postwar USSR." PhD diss., New York University, 2020.

"Den' vyborov." *Sovetskoe Zakarpat'e*, 30 January 1949, 1.

Denysenko, Nicholas E. *The Orthodox Church in Ukraine: A Century of Separation*. DeKalb, IL: Northern Illinois University Press, 2018.

Dickinson, J.A. "Gender, Work and Economic Restructuring in a Transcarpathian (Ukraine) Village." *Nationalities Papers* 33, no. 3 (2005): 387–401.

Dobson, Miriam. *Khrushchev's Cold Summer: Gulag Returnees, Crime, and the Fate of Reform after Stalin.* Ithaca, NY: Cornell University Press, 2009.

Dori, Nasho. "Jehovah Never Abandoned Us." *The Watchtower Announcing Jehovah's Kingdom*, 1 January 1996, 24–8.

Dovhanych, O.D., A.M. Sheketa, and M.V. Delehan, eds. *Vozz'idnannia: zbirnyk arkhivnykh documentiv i materialiv (traven' 1944–sichen' 1946 rr.) pro vozz'idnannia Zakarpats'koi Ukrainy z radians'koiu Ukrainoiu*. Uzhhorod: Zakarpattia, 2000.

Dumitru, Diana. "Listening to Silence: What Postwar Trial Materials Resist Revealing About the Holocaust." *S:I.M.O.N.* 7, no. 1 (2020): 4–12.

Eaton, Katherine B. *Daily Life in the Soviet Union*. Westport, CT: Greenwood Press, 2004.

Eaton, Nicole. "Exclave: Politics, Ideology, and Everyday Life in Königsberg-

Kaliningrad, 1928–1948." PhD diss., University of California–Berkeley, 2013.

Eby, Cecil D. *Hungary at War: Civilians and Soldiers in World War II.* University Park: Pennsylvania State University Press, 2010.

Engardio, Joel P., and Tom Shepard, dir. *Knocking.* USA: Open Door Productions, 2006.

"Fear Them Not." *The Watchtower and Herald of Christ's Presence*, 1 November 1933, 323–31.

Fermaglich, Kirsten. *A Rosenberg by Any Other Name: A History of Jewish Name Changing in America*. New York: New York University Press, 2018.

Filtzer, Donald. *Soviet Workers and Late Stalinism: Labour and the Restoration of the Stalinist System after World War II*. Cambridge: Cambridge University Press, 2002.

Fitzpatrick, Sheila. *Everyday Stalinism: Ordinary Life in Extraordinary Times.* New York: Oxford University Press, 1999.

– *Stalin's Peasants: Resistance and Survival in the Russian Village after Collectivization.* New York: Oxford University Press, 1994.

Friedgut, Theodore H. *Political Participation in the USSR*. Princeton, NJ: Princeton University Press, 2014.

Furov, V. "Stanovlenie zakonodatel'stva o kul'takh." *Nauka i religiia*, no. 10 (1979): 15–17.

Ganson, Nicholas. *The Soviet Famine of 1946–47 in Global and Historical Perspective*. New York: Palgrave Macmillan, 2009.

Garbe, Detlef. *Between Resistance and Martyrdom: Jehovah's Witnesses in the Third Reich.* Translated by Dagmar G. Grimm. Madison: University of Wisconsin Press, 2008.

Garcelon, Marc. "Colonizing the Subject: The Genealogy and Legacy of the Soviet Internal Passport." In *Documenting Individual Identity: The Development of State Practices in the Modern World*, edited by Jane Caplan and John Torpey, 83–100. Princeton, NJ: Princeton University Press, 2001.

Goldman, Wendy Z. *Inventing the Enemy: Denunciation and Terror in Stalin's Russia*. Cambridge: Cambridge University Press, 2011.

Greenawalt, Kent. *Fighting Words: Individuals, Communities, and Liberties of Speech*. Princeton, NJ: Princeton University Press, 1995.

Gross, Jan. *Revolution from Abroad: The Soviet Conquest of Poland's Western Ukraine and Western Belorussia*. Enl. ed. Princeton, NJ: Princeton University Press, 2002.

"Half a Century under Totalitarian Tyranny." *Awake!*, 22 February 1999, 10–16.

Hardy, Jeffrey S. *The Gulag after Stalin: Redefining Punishment in Khrushchev's Soviet Union, 1953–1964*. Ithaca, NY: Cornell University Press, 2016.

Heinzen, James W. *Inventing a Soviet Countryside: State Power and the Transformation of Rural Russia, 1917–1929*. Pittsburgh: University of Pittsburgh Press, 2004.

Himka, John-Paul. *Religion and Nationality in Western Ukraine: The Greek Catholic Church and the Ruthenian National Movement in Galicia, 1867–1900*. Montreal: McGill-Queen's University Press, 1999.

Iholkin, M. "Nanesty rishuchyi udar po kurkuliah i ikh posibnykakh." *Sotsialistychna pratsia*, 20 March 1949, 2.

Ilič, Melanie. "The Forgotten Five per Cent: Women, Political Repression and the Purges." In *Stalin's Terror Revisited*, edited by Melanie Ilič, 116–39. New York: Palgrave Macmillan, 2006.

Ioffe, Olimpiad S. *Soviet Law and Soviet Reality*. Leiden, Netherlands: Martinus Nijhoff, 1985.

Ionete, Catalin. "Majority, Minorities and Religious Pluralism in Romania." In *Religion, Politics and Nation-Building in Post-Communist Countries*, edited by Greg Simons and David Westerlund, 179–98. New York: Routledge, 2016.

Ironside, Kristy. "Rubles for Victory: The Social Dynamics of State Fundraising on the Soviet Home Front." *Kritika* 15, no. 4 (2014): 799–828.

Iurchenko, I. "Ozdorovyty robotu klubu." *Sotsialistychna pratsia*, 8 June 1950, 4.

Ivanych, M. "Kolkhoznye elektrostantsii." *Sovetskoe Zakarpat'e*, 7 September 1949, 1.

Jehovah's Witnesses Stand Firm Against Nazi Assault. Brooklyn: Watchtower Bible and Tract Society of New York, and the International Bible Students Association, 1996.

Jehovah's Witnesses: Proclaimers of God's Kingdom. Brooklyn: Watchtower Bible and Tract Society of New York, and the International Bible Students Association, 1993.

Johnston, Timothy. *Being Soviet: Identity, Rumour, and Everyday Life under Stalin 1939–1953*. New York: Oxford University Press, 2011.

– "Subversive Tales? War Rumours in the Soviet Union, 1945–1947." In *Late Stalinist Russia: Society between Reconstruction and Reinvention*, edited by Juliane Fürst, 94–122. New York: Routledge, 2006.

Jones, Jeffrey W. *Everyday Life and the "Reconstruction" of Soviet Russia during and after the Great Patriotic War, 1943–1948*. Bloomington, IN: Slavica Publishers, 2008.

Jordan, Peter, and Mladen Klemenčić, eds. *Transcarpathia: Bridgehead or*

Periphery? Geopolitical and Economic Aspects and Perspectives of a Ukrainian Region. Frankfurt: Peter Lang, 2004.

Jóźwiak, Ignacy. "Negotiating the Territory in a Transcarpathian Urban-Type Settlement." In *Trangressing Boundaries: Humanities in Flux*, edited by Marija Wakounig and Markus Peter Beham, 215–28. Münster, Germany: LIT Verlag, 2013.

"K novym pobedam kolkhoznogo stroia." *Sovetskoe Zakarpat'e*, 1 December 1948, 1.

Kalantaridis, Christos. "Globalization and Entrepreneurial Response in Post-Socialist Transformation: A Case Study from Transcarpathia, Ukraine." *European Planning Studies* 8, no. 3 (2000): 285–99.

Kashirin, Alexander. "Protestant Minorities in the Soviet Ukraine, 1945–1991." PhD diss., University of Oregon, 2010.

Kelly, Catriona. *Children's World: Growing Up in Russia, 1890–1991*. New Haven, CT: Yale University Press, 2007.

– "A Joyful Soviet Childhood: Licensed Happiness for Little Ones." In *Petrified Utopia: Happiness Soviet Style*, edited by Marina Balina and Evgeny Dobrenko, 3–18. New York: Anthem Press, 2009.

Kessler, Gijs. "The Passport System and State Control over Population Flows in the Soviet Union, 1932–1940." *Cahiers du Monde russe* 42, no. 2/4 (2001): 477–504.

Khlevniuk, Oleg V. *The History of the Gulag: From Collectivization to the Great Terror.* Translated by Vadim A. Staklo. New Haven, CT: Yale University Press, 2004.

Khruschchev, N. S. *Khrushchev Remembers.* Edited and translated by Strobe Talbott. Commentary and notes by Edward Crankshaw. Boston: Little, Brown, 1970.

Kirschenbaum, Lisa A. *Small Comrades: Revolutionizing Childhood in Soviet Russia, 1917–1932*. New York: RoutledgeFalmer, 2000.

Knox, Zoe. *Jehovah's Witnesses and the Secular World: From the 1870s to the Present*. London: Palgrave Macmillan, 2018.

"Kolkhoznoe krest'ianstvo Zakarpat'ia druzhno podpisyvaetsia na zaem." *Sovetskoe Zakarpat'e*, 7 May 1949, 1.

"Kollektivizatsiia – zakon sotsialisticheskogo razvitiia." *Sovetskoe Zakarpat'e*, 17 December 1948, 1.

"Konstitutsionnoe pravo na al'ternativnuiu sluzhbu otbiraiut u molodykh liudei posle resheniia verkhovnogo suda o likvidatsii organizatsii Svidetelei Iegovy," *Svideteli Iegovy v Rossii*, 11 May 2017, https://www.jw-russia.org/news/17051113-160.html (accessed 5 January 2021).

Kotkin, Stephen. *Magnetic Mountain: Stalinism as a Civilization*. Berkeley: University of California Press, 1995.

– *Stalin: Waiting for Hitler, 1929–1941*. New York: Penguin, 2017.

Krushinskii, S. "Apostoly porokhovoi bochki." *Pravda*, 18 March 1959, 6.

Kuchmenko, Z. "Vospitanie sovetskogo patriotizma na urokakh literatury." *Sovetskoe Zakarpat'e*, 1 September 1949, 3.

Kuromiya, Hiroaki. *Conscience on Trial: The Fate of Fourteen Pacifists in Stalin's Ukraine*. Toronto: University of Toronto Press, 2012.

Les'o, P. "Gosudarstvennye zaimy." *Sovetskoe Zakarpat'e*, 29 April 1950, 2.

Liber, George O. *Total Wars and the Making of Modern Ukraine, 1914–1954*. Toronto: University of Toronto Press, 2016.

Lytvyn, V.M. *Ukraina u pershomu povoiennomu desiatylitti (1946–1955)*. Kyiv: Li-Terra, 2004.

Magocsi, Paul Robert. "Carpathian Rus': Interethnic Coexistence without Violence." In *Shatterzone of Empires: Coexistence and Violence in the German, Habsburg, Russian, and Ottoman Borderlands*, edited by Omer Bartov and Eric D. Weitz, 449–62. Bloomington: Indiana University Press, 2013.

Marples, David R. *Stalinism in Ukraine in the 1940s*. New York: St. Martin's Press, 1992.

McBride, Jared G. "'A Sea of Blood and Tears': Ethnic Diversity and Mass Violence in Nazi-Occupied Volhynia, Ukraine, 1941–1944." PhD diss., University of California, Los Angeles, 2014.

"Memorial Reports." *The Watch Tower and Herald of Christ's Presence*, 15 August 1925, 248–9.

Miner, Steven Merritt. *Stalin's Holy War: Religion, Nationalism, and Alliance Politics, 1941–1945*. Chapel Hill: University of North Carolina Press, 2003.

"Moguchaia armiia sovetskoi derzhavy." *Sovetskoe Zakarpat'e*, 23 February 1949, 1.

"Moguchii golos sovetskogo naroda." *Sovetskoe Zakarpat'e*, 18 October 1950, 1.

Moish, Iu. "Hotuiemos' do sviata." *Sotsialistychna pratsia*, 22 September 1949, 1.

Moser, Michael. *Language Policy and Discourse on Languages in Ukraine under President Viktor Yanukovych (25 February 2010–28 October 2012)*. Stuttgart, Germany: ibidem-Verlag, 2013.

"Neutrality." *The Watchtower Announcing Jehovah's Kingdom*, 1 November 1939, 323–33.

"Nevidkladni zavdannia sil's'kykh rad." *Sotsialistychna pratsia*, 8 January 1948, 1.

Noble, John. *I Was a Slave in Russia: An American Tells His Story*. New York: Devin-Adair, 1958.

"Oblasna narada v pytanni likvidatsii nepys'mennosti i malopys'mennosti." *Zakarpats'ka pravda*, 7 March 1948, 3.

Odintsov, M. I. *Sovet ministrov SSSR postanovliaet: "Vyselit' navechno!"* Moscow: Art-Biznes-Tsentr, 2002.

Olashyn, A.V. *Istoriia Zakarpattia*. Mukachevo: Karpats'ka vezha, 2009.

Onaci, Edward. *Free the Land: The Republic of New Afrika and the Pursuit of a Black Nation-State*. Chapel Hill: University of North Carolina Press, 2020.

Ormos, Mária. *Hungary in the Age of the Two World Wars, 1914–1945*. Translated by Brian McLean. Highland Lakes, NJ: Atlantic Research and Publications; Boulder, CO: Social Science Monographs, 2007.

"O vypuske chetvertogo gosudarstvennogo zaima vosstanovleniia i razvitiia narodnogo khoziaistva SSSR." *Sovetskoe Zakarpat'e*, 4 May 1949, 1.

Panachin, F.G., M.N. Kolmakovaia, and Z.I. Ravkin, eds. *Ocherki istorii shkoly i pedagogicheskoi mysli narodov SSSR (1941–1961)*. Moscow: Pedagogika, 1988.

Pasat, V. I. *Trudnye stranitsy istorii Moldovy*. Moscow: Terra, 1994.

Peladii, O. "Boiovu zustrich vesni v kolhospi 'Nove Zhittia.'" *Sotsialistychna pratsia*, 27 March 1949, 1.

– "V im'ia mohutnisti ridnoi bat'kivshchyny." *Sotsialistychna pratsia*, 16 July 1950, 3.

Penter, Tanja. "Local Collaborators on Trial: Soviet War Crimes Trials under Stalin (1943–1953)." *Cahiers du Monde russe* 49, no. 2/3 (2008): 341–64.

Penton, M. James. *Apocalypse Delayed: The Story of Jehovah's Witnesses*. Toronto: University of Toronto Press, 1985.

"Persha sesiia Zakarpats'koi oblasnoi rady deputativ trudiashchykh." *Zakarpats'ka pravda*, 16 January 1948, 1.

Peters, Shawn Francis. *Judging Jehovah's Witnesses: Religious Persecution and the Dawn of the Rights Revolution*. Lawrence: University Press of Kansas, 2000.

Pichkur, V. "Vykonaiemo vkazivki tovarysha Stalina zrobyty kolhospy Bil'shovyts'kymy, a kolhospnykiv Zamozhnymy." *Sotsialistychna pratsia*, 19 March 1950, 2.

Piersma, Tineke. "True to Their Faith: The Persecution of Jehovah's Witnesses in the Netherlands during World War II." In *Jehovah's Witnesses in Europe: Past and Present*, 2 vols, edited by Gerhard Besier and Katarzyna Stokłosa, 1:135–219. Newcastle upon Tyne, UK: Cambridge Scholars Publishing, 2016.

Plamper, Jan. *The Stalin Cult: A Study in the Alchemy of Power*. New Haven, CT: Yale University Press, 2012.

Pleszar, Antoni. "The Truth Shall Make You Free." *The Watch Tower and Herald of Christ's Presence*, 15 July 1938, 224.

Plokhy, Serhii. *The Gates of Europe: A History of Ukraine*. New York: Basic Books, 2015.

"Po okruzi." *Sotsialistychna pratsia*, 11 July 1948, 2.

"Po shliakhu do sutsil'noi kolektyvizatsii." *Sotsialistychna pratsia*, 15 July 1948, 1.

"Po voprosam kolkhoznogo stroitel'stva." *Sovetskoe Zakarpat'e*, 17 May 1949, 3.

"Po voprosam kolkhoznogo stroitel'stva." *Sovetskoe Zakarpat'e*, 26 March 1949, 4.

Pobol', N.L., and P.M. Polian, eds. *Stalinskie Deportatsii, 1928–1953*. Moscow: Materik, 2005.

"Pod Stokgol'mskim vozzvaniem podpisalos' 96.360.866 sovetskikh grazhdan." *Sovetskoe Zakarpat'e*, 13 July 1950, 1.

Polian, Pavel. *Against Their Will: The History and Geography of Forced Migrations in the USSR*. Budapest: Central European University Press, 2004.

"Polipshyty kerivnytstvo kul'tosvitnimy zakladamy." *Soltsialistychna pratsia*, 11 November 1948, 1.

Porchan, Petr. "Budut i u nas sportivnye ploshchadki," *Sovetskoe Zakarpat'e*, 6 July 1950, 3.

"Povidomlennia tsentral'noi vyborchoi komisii po vyborakh do verkhovnoi rady *SRSR* pro rezul'taty vyboriv." *Sotsialistychna pratsia*, 16 March 1950, 1.

"Prazdnik shkol'nikov." *Sovetskoe Zakarpat'e*, 1 September 1949, 3.

"Pro zaprovadzhennia platnoi trudhuzhpovynnosti na lisozahotivliakh v sezon 1948–1949 rokiv." *Sotsialistychna pratsia*, 4 November 1948, 2.

Prusin, Alexander Victor. "'Fascist Criminals to the Gallows!': The Holocaust and Soviet War Crimes Trials, December 1945–February 1946." *Holocaust and Genocide Studies* 17, no. 1 (2003): 1–30.

Quilitzsch, Anya. "Everyday Judaism on the Soviet Periphery: Life and Identity of Transcarpathian Jewry after World War II." PhD diss., Indiana University, 2016.

"Radiofikatsiia sela Belaia Tserkov'." *Sovetskoe Zakarpat'e*, 27 August 1949, 1.

Raleigh, Donald J. *Soviet Baby Boomers: An Oral History of Russia's Cold War Generation*. New York: Oxford University Press, 2012.

Ramet, Sabrina Petra, ed. *Religious Policy in the Soviet Union*. Cambridge: Cambridge University Press, 1993.

– *Social Currents in Eastern Europe: The Sources and Consequences of the Great Transformation*. 2nd ed. Durham, NC: Duke University Press, 1995.

Reese, Roger R. *The Soviet Military Experience: A History of the Soviet Army, 1917–1991*. New York: Routledge, 2000.

Sang-Hun, Choe. "South Korean Jehovah's Witnesses Fight Stigma of Not Serving in Army." *New York Times*, 4 October 2015, A8.

Satter, David. *It Was a Long Time Ago, and It Never Happened Anyway: Russia and the Communist Past.* New Haven, CT: Yale University Press, 2012.

Sawatsky, Walter. *Soviet Evangelicals since World War II*. Scottdale, PA: Herald Press, 1981.

Semenenko, I. "Rik po shliakhu novoho zhyttia." *Sotsialistychna pratsia*, 1 September 1949, 2.

Semeniuk, Ihor. *Hodi!* Kyiv: Derzhpolitvydav URSR, 1950.

Shandor, Vincent. *Carpatho-Ukraine in the Twentieth Century: A Political and Legal History.* Cambridge, MA: Distributed by Harvard University Press for the Ukrainian Resarch Institute, 1997.

Sharlet, Robert. "Stalinism and Soviet Legal Culture." In *Stalinism: Essays in Historical Interpretation*, edited by Robert C. Tucker, 155–79. New York: Norton, 1977.

Shearer, David. "Stalinist Repression, Modernity, and the Social Engineering Argument." In *The Anatomy of Terror: Political Violence under Stalin*, edited by James Harris, 105–22. New York: Oxford University Press, 2013.

Shearer, David R. *Policing Stalin's Socialism: Repression and Social Order in the Soviet Union, 1924–1953*. New Haven, CT: Yale University Press, 2009.

Shmyg, A. "Teni v novom dome." *Zakarpatskaia pravda*, 28 August 1975, 1.

Shul'ha, I.H., ed. *Sotsialistychni peretvorennia na Zakarpatti za 25 rokiv radians'koi vlady.* Uzhhorod: Uzhhorods'kyi derzhavnyi universytet, Akademiia Nauk URSR, 1970.

"Shyroko i povsiakdenno propahuvaty kolhospnyi lad!" *Zakarpats'ka pravda*, 12 June 1948, 1.

"Shyrshe propahuvaty perevahy kolhospnoho ladu." *Zakarpats'ka pravda*, 15 January 1948, 1.

Simonsen, Sven Gunnar. "Inheriting the Soviet Policy Toolbox: Russia's Dilemma over Ascriptive Nationality." *Europe-Asia Studies* 51, no. 6 (1999): 1069–87.

Slezkine, Yuri. *The Jewish Century*. Princeton, NJ: Princeton University Press, 2004.

Sliusarchuk, H. *Sotsialistychna pratsia*, 30 July 1950, 2.

Smith, Chuck. "The Persecution of West Virginia Jehovah's Witnesses and the Expansion of Legal Protection for Religious Liberty." In *New Religious Movements and Religious Liberty in America*, edited by Derek H. Davis and Barry Hankins, 155–82. Waco, TX: Baylor University Press, 2003.

Smith, Kathleen E. *Remembering Stalin's Victims: Popular Memory and the End of the USSR*. Ithaca, NY: Cornell University Press, 1996.

Solomon, Peter H. *Soviet Criminal Justice under Stalin.* Cambridge: Cambridge University Press, 1996.

Statiev, Alexander. *The Soviet Counterinsurgency in the Western Borderlands*. Cambridge: Cambridge University Press, 2010.

Sturgis, Paul W. "Institutional versus Contextual Explanations for the Growth of Jehovah's Witnesses in the United States, 1945–2002." *Review of Religious Research* 49, no. 3 (2008): 290–300.

Tarasov, M. "Novyi kolhosp." *Sotsialistychna pratsia*, 11 November 1948, 1.

Tarusova, I. "Obuchenie pervoklassnikov." *Sovetskoe Zakarpat'e*, 1 September 1949, 3.

Taylor, Pauline B. "Sectarians in Soviet Courts." *Russian Review* 24, no. 3 (1965): 278–88.

Tsiboulski, Marian. "A Promise I Am Determined to Keep." *Awake!*, 22 June 1998, 20–4.

Tsiupko. "Rishuchu vidcich kurkuliam, zabezpechyty pratsiu kolhospnykiv." *Sotsialistychna pratsia*, 12 February 1948, 2.

Uzhans'kyi, I. "Na kolhospomu toku." *Sotsialistychna pratsia*, 7 August 1949, 1.

"V plenum Zakarpatskogo obkoma KP(b)U." *Sovetskoe Zakarpat'e*, 9 September 1949, 1.

Vagramenko, Tatiana, and James Kapaló, eds. *Hidden Galleries: Material Religion in the Secret Police Archives in Central and Eastern Europe*. Zurich: LIT Verlag, 2020.

Vehesh, Mykola, and Csilla Fedinec, eds. *Zakarpattia 1919–2009 rokiv: istoriia, polityka, kul'tura*. Uzhhorod: Lira, 2010.

"VI plenum Zakarpatskogo obkoma KP(b)U." *Sovetskoe Zakarpat'e*, 27 December 1949, 3.

Viola, Lynne. *The Unknown Gulag: The Lost World of Stalin's Special Settlements*. New York: Oxford University Press, 2007.

Viola, Lynne, V.P. Danilov, N.A. Ivnitskii, and Denis Kozlov, eds. *The War against the Peasantry, 1927–1930: The Tragedy of the Soviet Countryside*. Translated by Steven Shabad. New Haven, CT: Yale University Press, 2005.

"Vony pishly kolhospnym shliakhom." *Zakarpats'ka pravda*, 6 July 1948, 2.

Vrublevskaia, V.V., V.I. Garadzha, and R.P. Zolotareva. *Organizatsiia i metodika ateisticheskogo vospitaniia*. Moscow: Politizdat, 1986.

Weiner, Amir. *Making Sense of War: The Second World War and the Fate of the Bolshevik Revolution*. Princeton, NJ: Princeton University Press, 2001.

Werth, Nicolas. *Cannibal Island: Death in a Siberian Gulag*. Translated by Steven Rendall. Princeton, NJ: Princeton University Press, 2007.

"Who Resist Communism?" *Awake!*, 8 January 1950, 16–19.

Wiesel, Elie. *Night*. Translated by Marion Wiesel. New York: Hill & Wang, 2006.

Wittner, Lawrence S. *The Struggle against the Bomb*. Vol. 1, *One World or None: A History of the World Nuclear Disarmament Movement through 1953*. Stanford, CA: Stanford University Press, 1993.

Yekelchyk, Serhy. *Stalin's Citizens: Everyday Politics in the Wake of Total War*. New York: Oxford University Press, 2014.

– *Stalin's Empire of Memory: Russian-Ukrainian Relations in the Soviet Historical Imagination*. Toronto: University of Toronto Press, 2004.

Yurchak, Alexei. *Everything Was Forever, Until It Was No More: The Last Soviet Generation*. Princeton, NJ: Princeton University Press, 2006.

"Za dal'she pidnesennia sil'skoho hospodarstva." *Sotsialistychna pratsia*, 26 January 1950, 2.

"Za Stalina, za rodinu, za mir!" *Sovetskoe Zakarpat'e*, 19 December 1950, 1.

Zajda, Joseph I. *Education in the USSR*. New York: Pergamon Press, 1980.

Zdorovets, I. "Mozhno li prinimat' v kolkhoz kulakov?" *Sovetskoe Zakarpat'e*, 24 August 1948, 2.

Zeidler, Miklós. *Ideas on Territorial Revision in Hungary, 1920–1945*. Translated by Thomas J. and Helen DeKornfeld. Boulder, CO: Social Science Monographs; Wayne, NJ: Center for Hungarian Studies and Publications, 2007.

Zhulkanych, N.M. *Ahrarno-vyrobnychi ta sotsial'no-ekonomichni vidnosyny na Zakarpatti (1945–1990 roky)*. Uzhhorod: Uzhhorods'kyi natsional'nyi universytet, 2002.

Zubkova, Elena. *Russia after the War: Hopes, Illusions, and Disappointments, 1945–1957*. Edited and translated by Hugh Ragsdale. Armonk, NY: M.E. Sharpe, 1998.

Zubok, Vladislav M. *A Failed Empire: The Soviet Union in the Cold War from Stalin to Gorbachev*. Chapel Hill: University of North Carolina Press, 2007.

Zverev, A. "*S ogromnym voodushevleniem trudiashchiesia Zakarpat'ia podpisyvaiutsia na novyi zaem.*" *Sovetskoe Zakarpat'e*, 4 May 1949, 2.

Index

www.ingramcontent.com/pod-product-compliance
Lightning Source LLC
LaVergne TN
LVHW040600130826
845408LV00028B/293
* 9 7 8 0 2 2 8 0 1 0 5 5 5 *